Irish Pubs in America
HISTORY, LORE AND RECIPES

Irish Pubs in America

HISTORY, LORE AND RECIPES

by Robert Meyers *with* Ron Wallace

Deeds Publishing | Atlanta

Copyright © 2014 – Robert Meyers and Ron Wallace, doing business as Pub Book Publishing LLC

ALL RIGHTS RESERVED – No part of this book may be reproduced in any form or by any electronic or mechanical means, including information storage and retrieval systems, without permission in writing by the authors, except by a reviewer who may quote brief passages in a review.

This book is as factual as personal experience, extensive research, and interviews will allow. Any errors are unintended, and the authors apologize for any omissions or errors.

Printed in the United States of America

All text and photographs, except where otherwise noted, are by Robert Meyers.
Published by Deeds Publishing LLC, Marietta, GA
www.deedspublishing.com

Cover photograph used by permission—McSorley's Old Ale House—Detroit Institute of Arts/Bridgeman Art Library

Layout and Design by Mark Babcock. Photo editing by Matt King.

Library of Congress Cataloging-in-Publications Data is available on request.

ISBN 978-1-937565-75-6

Books are available in quantity for promotional or premium use. For information, write Deeds Publishing, PO Box 682212, Marietta, GA 30068 or info@deedspublishing.com.

10 9 8 7 6 5 4 3 2 1

To Linda, a fair Irish lass, editor way beyond excellent, CFO and my constant inspiration. She kept me on track throughout the writing process. She is the love of my life who just happens to be my wife.

- Bob Meyers

For my wife Kate who has been my partner and best friend through thick and thin, up and down—fortunately mostly up. I can't thank her enough for arranging all those trips across the country to visit more pubs than we can count and the endless hours she devoted to the recipe section of this book.

- Ron Wallace

Table of Contents

A Terrible Beauty, Seattle, WA	12	*McGillin's Olde Ale House,* Philadelphia, PA	152
The Black Rose, Boston, MA	18	*McGuire's Irish Pub,* Pensacola, FL	156
The Black Sheep, Philadelphia, PA	24	*McGurk's Irish Pub & Garden,* St. Louis, MO	166
Butch McGuire's, Chicago, IL	30	*McSorley's Old Ale House,* New York, NY	172
Casey's, Los Angeles, CA	36	*Meehan's Public House,* Atlanta, GA	182
Coleman's Authentic Irish Pub, Syracuse, NY	40	*Molly's Shebeen,* New York, NY	188
The Druid, Cambridge, MA	46	*Murphy's Bar & Grill,* Honolulu, HI	192
The Dubliner, Washington, DC	50	*Murphy's Grand Irish Pub,* Alexandria, VA	198
Durty Nelly's, San Francisco, CA	56	*Nallen's Irish Pub,* Denver, CO	204
Emmit's Irish Pub, Chicago, IL	60	*Nine Fine Irishmen,* Las Vegas, NV	208
Fadó Irish Pub, Chicago, IL	64	*Olde Blind Dog,* Milton & Brookhaven, GA	212
The Field, Dania Beach, FL	70	*O'Reilly's,* San Francisco, CA	222
Finn McCool's Irish Pub, New Orleans, LA	76	*O'Rourke's,* South Bend, IN	228
Four Green Fields, Tampa, FL	84	*O'Toole's Irish Pub,* Honolulu, HI	238
The Green Dragon Tavern, Boston, MA	88	*Owl 'N Thistle,* Seattle, WA	242
The Irish Bank, San Francisco, CA	94	*Paddy Reilly's Music Bar,* New York, NY	246
The Irish Inn, Glen Echo, MD	98	*Patrick McGovern's Pub,* St. Paul, MN	250
Johnny Foley's Irish House, San Francisco, CA	104	*The Perfect Pint Public House,* New York, NY	256
Kell's Irish Restaurant and Pub, Portland, OR	108	*Raglan Road,* Lake Buena Vista, FL	262
Kelly's Wesport Inn, Kansas City, MO	114	*Rí Rá,* Atlanta, GA	268
The Kerry Irish Pub, New Orleans, LA	118	*Scruffy Murphy's,* Denver, CO	274
Kevin Barry's Irish Pub, Savannah, GA	122	*Tír na nÓg,* New York, NY	278
The Local & Kieran's, Minneapolis, MN	128	*Tom Bergin's Old Horseshoe Tavern,* Los Angeles, CA	282
The Little Shamrock, San Francisco, CA	136	*Waxy O'Connor's,* Fort Lauderdale, FL	286
Mac McGees, Decatur, GA	140	*Wolfe Tone's Pub,* Upperville, VA	292
Maguires Hill 16, Fort Lauderdale, FL	146	*Recipes*	298

Introduction
With a Wee Bit o' History

There are only two kinds of people in the world, The Irish, and those who wish they were.
                                              - Anonymous

THERE IS JUST SOMETHING ABOUT an Irish pub that draws a person in. Time seems to stop when you are having a pint with friends, or celebrating one of life's great moments in the comforting warmth of your favorite pub. If you enumerate the things you consider most Irish: castles, freckles and red hair, luminous green landscapes, literature, U2, shamrocks and the Book Of Kells, pubs would unquestionably be close to the top. Whether in Ireland or some faraway country, an Irish pub (which stands for public house), is an exuberant refuge where you see people of all stations in life enjoying camaraderie, drinking ales or whiskey, debating and having a good time. Throughout history, Irish pubs have provided a lot more than just friendship and ales, however. Some offered meals, groceries, even hardware and encouraged local musicians to show off their talents. It is said that in the United States, if a pub converts to an Irish theme, sales may triple.

In Dublin, and in small towns and villages throughout the Emerald Isle, the pub has traditionally represented the nucleus of social life and *craic,* that hard to define Irish capacity for cheerful conversation and good times. Traditions and local customs are preserved and important issues are sliced and diced in many directions by enthusiastic, often verbose, sometimes slightly sotted, protagonists.

Historically, the passion for craic came with a price, however. During the challenging times that prevailed throughout much of Irish history, the public drinking house provided respite from the terrible living and working conditions endured by poor farmers and tenement dwellers. By the mid-1600s when the population of Dublin was some 20,000, there were more than 1000 alehouses, and Dublin had garnered a reputation for uncontained drunkenness.

In modern day Ireland, the situation is quite different. Changing lifestyles, regulatory reforms and the weak economy have altered the Irish pub business and many pubs have closed their doors. The good news is that Irish pubs are sprouting up all over the world. The Irish Pub is still alive and well, adapting to a changing world and continuing to offer its patrons a sense of community, fellowship and craic. Nowhere is this trend truer than in the United States.

The title "oldest pub in Ireland" has been hotly debated over the years. It appears that the oldest pubs date back to the 10th century. While age is not required to make a pub a desirable gathering place, there is some comfort sharing a pint in the same room where famous authors or revolutionaries downed theirs. Obviously, Irish pubs in the United States do not have the same centuries-old tradition, but they do admirably capture the charm and enduring essence of the Irish pub mystique.

Preface

THIS BOOK IS MORE THAN a survey of Irish pubs. It is a tribute to Irish culture and the contributions the Irish have made to the United States. Originally drawn to the US by poor economic conditions in their homeland, Irish immigrants have contributed mightily to the US economy, culture and politics. Indeed, all Americans owe a great debt of gratitude to our Irish compatriots.

The book represents the personal selection of what we consider to be outstanding examples of Irish pubs in the United States. It is not intended to be a guide book nor an exhaustive inventory of pubs. Selection was based on personal knowledge, recommendations by well-informed people and extensive research. We sought a variety of pubs from quite small and intimate to large establishments capable of serving hundreds of people at a time. As in Ireland, some pubs are independently owned; others are part of groups of pubs with corporate ownership. We realize that many wonderful pubs are not included.

We sought to identify truly distinctive establishments. With so many pubs profiled, it was important to search for the uniqueness of each pub, lest the reader quickly lose interest. We spent many hours with pub owners, managers, employees and patrons digging out the secrets that made these pubs unique. We hope that this book will provide a worthy introduction to the Irish pub phenomenon in our country.

At some point in our travels it became evident that we should include a selection of Irish recipes provided by pubs, either signature dishes from their menus, or more often from family recipe collections.

To write our book, we traveled all across our great land, marveled at its richness and beauty, secure in the knowledge that at the end of each perfect day, a tall pint of Guinness awaited. It was hard work, but as the trite old saying goes, someone had to do it, and we did it with gusto. Some have enviously referred to our efforts as the longest pub crawl in history.

We are indebted to many people who helped and supported us throughout our journey, but especially to our wives, Linda Meyers, and Kate Wallace, each of whom patiently assisted every step of the way.

Bob Meyers' career was in the US Foreign Service and in the private sector. He is the author of the award-winning coffee table book *Bygone Treasures and Timeless Beauties: Barns of Old Milton County.* Ron Wallace was formerly President of UPS International. His book *The Power of the Campaign Pyramid* was published in 2012 and *What Brown Did For Me* in 2013.

-Bob Meyers and Ron Wallace

A Terrible Beauty

SEATTLE, WASHINGTON

A Poem Comes To Life

*And now in time to be,
Wherever green is worn,
Are changed, changed utterly,
A terrible beauty is born.*
William Butler Yeats
Easter, 1916

JENNA SHANNON-GARVEY ALWAYS WANTED TO own a pub on the water. Finally, in 2013 her dream became a reality with the opening of A Terrible Beauty on the upscale south shore of Lake Union. One has to be on the alert to find the pub for it is easily overlooked from the land. Not so from the water where the circular patch of Irish green lawn beside the pub is easily spotted from the magnificent yachts that sail the lake.

A Terrible Beauty is adjacent to an exclusive private yacht club with its impressive collection of pleasure craft berthed a stone's throw from the entrance to the pub. The prime location provides attractive business opportunities. In the spring and summer the pub will serve hungry boaters from a small fish and chips take-out shop next to the dock. What could be better than a Guinness and some Irish snacks on the water or at outdoor tables after a run up the lake?

Lake Union is a 580-acre-lake fresh water lake carved out by a glacier 12,000 years ago. Situated entirely within the city limits of Seattle, appropriately nicknamed The Emerald City. The lake is connected to Puget Sound by the Lake Washington Ship Canal. Completed in 1934 by the U.S. Army Corps of Engineers, the canal is listed on the National Register of Historic Places.

Jenna began modestly three years ago when she opened her first pub in Renton with six employees. Now she owns three pubs and has 150 employees. With six children and a chaotic schedule, she believes the business has reached a comfortable and perfect size.

The new two-story pub is small and charming, modern and sleek, yet somehow very Irish. Jenna's love of beautiful things is evident throughout. She designed the pub and selected every item, old and new, giving the pub its particular appeal. She and their son Mick carried out much of the installation and refinishing work themselves.

The main floor is well lit. The ceiling is made of stained glass and rounds, logs split lengthwise, from an old lumber mill. The second story is dimly lit to preserve the night view of the city. Its floor is antique fir rescued from a warehouse in Seattle. Hand-made tiles from an old farmhouse form the roof of the fish and chips shop which is visible from the second floor. The tiles were dug from old mud and lovingly cleaned one by one. The energetic Jenna refinished all the vintage tables herself. At night, gazing through the large second floor windows, while catching a glimpse of Seattle's landmark Space Needle lit up against the dark sky, one almost feels an urge to take a giant step onto the stern of one of the nearby yachts.

RIGHT: Richly polished wood and a beautiful stained glass ceiling invite patrons to relax in style in the main bar area. On stage in the background is Seattle vocalist/guitarist Erin McNamee.

A Terrible Beauty

William Butler Yeats (1865-1939) was one of Ireland's most celebrated poets and recipient of the 1923 Nobel Prize in Literature. He was born in Dublin and later moved to London in 1867 where his father sought to advance his career as a painter. When William was 15, his family returned to Dublin where he attended school. He published his first poetry five years later.

His early works were strongly influenced by his interest in Irish mythology and the occult. Although raised as a Protestant, Yeats became a supporter of the emerging largely Catholic working-class nationalist movement that sought independence from Great Britain.

In his poem "Easter, 1916" Yeats uses the phrase "a terrible beauty" to great poetic effect. The poem describes the Easter Rising in April 1916 when a group of Irish nationalists attempted to foment a popular uprising against British rule. A small band of fighters seized the Dublin post office and other strategic buildings in the city. After a week of fighting, the rebels surrendered. Fifteen leaders were arrested, executed and made martyrs. Although the Rising failed militarily, it generated strong antipathy toward Britain among the general public and contributed to the unrest and violence that plagued Ireland for so many years.

The poem consists of 80 lines of at times challenging text that eulogizes the fallen revolutionaries and laments the futility of their deaths. The words "a terrible beauty" appear at the end of each of the poem's three stanzas. The contradictory words are used for special effect, terrible because many people died unnecessarily; beauty because it awakened the public.

A Terrible Beauty was also the name of a 1958 novel by Arthur Roth set in Northern Ireland during World War II. The novel was the basis for the 1960 film by the same name starring Robert Mitchum and Richard Harris.

To understand the origin of the pub's name we must go back to Jenna's early years. She was born in Belfast and at age 10 moved with her family to Washington where her father took a job with Boeing Company. In 1980 her father gave her a book so she would never forget her origin, *Ireland: A Terrible Beauty* by the noted author Leon Uris and his wife Jill. The book changed Jenna's life. First published in 1975 at the height of the Troubles, the book of Jill's photographs and Leon's text provides an exceptional snapshot of a moment in time. It is a tribute to the Irish "unconquerable spirit [that] endures through a tragic history." Copies of the book are placed strategically throughout the pub, inviting patrons to reflect upon Ireland's tumultuous past.

For Jenna, the new pub represents much more than beautiful things. It is an acknowledgement of the indomitable Irish spirit. It is about personal ambition and confidence, the hard times and the good times. It is about where she wanted to go and the unwavering dedication and hard work that made it all possible. A fairy tale come true.

ABOVE: Behind the bar

OPPOSITE: Sailboat invasion on a sunny afternoon

The Black Rose

BOSTON, MASSACHUSETTS

Nothing but the Best

If you refuse to accept anything but the best, you often get it.   -W. Somerset Maugham

IF YOU ASK PEOPLE IN Boston to name the best-known Irish pub in town, The Black Rose will usually get the nod. A local institution since 1976, this is a musical pub with live entertainment every day of the year, save Christmas. John Denver's last public appearance occurred here when he gladly sang a few songs after enjoying an evening chatting with patrons at the bar, a week before his untimely death.

When visitors walk in they are struck by the sheer size of the premises. The first floor consists of a single large room with a long bar at one end and some two dozen tables. The smaller upstairs, often used for special events, features an island bar and an inviting fireplace area. With a capacity of 420, The Black Rose is the largest distributor of Guinness beer in the Northeast.

The name originates from a 16th or 17th century poem Róisín Dubh, meaning little black rose, and is one of Ireland's most famous political songs. It supposedly originated in the encampments of Red Hugh O'Donnell, a chieftain who led a rebellion against the English government in Ireland in the late 16th century. The title is an allegorical name for Ireland, and the song was always sung in

The Heady History of Beer

Beer brewing originated with the ancient Sumarians some 6000 years ago in Mesopotamia in what is modern-day Iraq. Beer figured in their religious practices as well as in everyday life. The more rigid Babylonians, who subsequently ruled the region, regulated every aspect of beer production, distribution and consumption. About 1600 B.C. the Babylonians were overthrown and a succession of warring rulers controlled the land for several centuries. Once Egypt asserted the dominant role in the region, beer assumed great importance. Bread and beer made up the daily meal in ancient Egypt. Beer also treated various maladies and was used to pay the wages of workers and slaves.

After the Egyptians came the Greeks, followed three hundred years later by the Romans. The Romans preferred wine, but Egyptians did not give up their precious brew. Egypt remained under Roman influence until about 640 A.D. when the Arab conquest integrated Egypt into the Moslem world, and Egyptian brewing succumbed to Islamic abstinence. Henceforth, brewing would take place in northern portions of the Roman Empire.

As the Roman Empire expanded its territory across northern Europe, an elaborate road network was established. To quench the thirst of the Roman Legions, inns called *tabernae* were built along the network. At the same time, Christian monks, with their knowledge of agriculture, became adept at brewing. They built breweries inside monasteries and constructed their own network of inns to support pilgrims en route to holy sites.

Throughout Europe, ale was the most common table beverage, often brewed by women at home. Over time, some home brewers offered ale and whiskey to tired workers and travelers.

Out of those murky beginnings, the Irish public house evolved and became the great social institution that it is today.

The modern brewing industry is an enormous business characterized by a few global giants offering numerous brands alongside many smaller national breweries and even smaller craft beer producers. Beer lovers never before had it so good.

Irish so the English would not understand it. Many Irish musicians have recorded the haunting melody including Sinead O'Connor, Caitlín Maude, The Flying Column, Matt Cunningham and numerous others.

Large numbers of tourists are drawn here and enjoy having their photos taken by the bright red front door. Paul Wilson, who hails from Dublin, is an executive with Glynn Hospitality Group, which owns the pub. He reports that The Black Rose is one of a very few Irish pubs in the United States that are widely known in Ireland. He believes that people keep coming back because of the staff. "We hire personality – we can teach everything else." The entertainment factor is important too. "People can only carry on conversation for so long." Recently a couple came into the pub and carefully unfolded a faded paper placemat that they had treasured since their visit many years before. They wanted the staff to sign it, just as the staff had done long ago because their first experience had been so unforgettable.

ABOVE: About 100 kegs of beer are delivered each week. Each keg weighs 160.5 pounds, the beer accounting for 130.8 pounds of the total. Deliveries are made three times a week.

OPPOSITE: A black and white tile floor separates the bar from the restaurant.

ABOVE: Pub mascot Gary the Gargoyle. One day Gary turned up missing. The staff was distraught until a clerk at the Hilton Hotel called to report that a guest had left the statue on his bed with a note: "Please return me to my home at The Black Rose." Fortunately, the guest remembered where he had been the night before. That was a happy day at the pub!

LEFT: Main floor of The Black Rose with the main bar running along the rear wall. Pub walls are lined with flags of most of Ireland's 32 counties. The largest county in area is County Cork; the smallest is County Louth, often called the Wee County.

The Black Sheep occupies the right half of one of Philadelphia's architectural gems.

The Black Sheep

PHILADELPHIA, PENNSYLVANIA
Historic Haven

I feel sorry for people who don't drink. When they wake up in the morning, that's as good as they're going to feel all day.   -Frank Sinatra

THE THREE STORY RED/ORANGE BRICK townhouse that is home to The Black Sheep was purchased by publican James Stephens in 1999. This dimly lit retreat is one of Philadelphia's architectural gems. Designed by famed Philadelphia architect Frank Miles Day and built in 1890 for local business leader Edward R. Wood, the building reflects various European influences that Day observed and sketched during his travels abroad. Located in the historic and affluent Rittenhouse District, the structure is really two houses designed to look like one. The Black Sheep occupies one of the two houses. It is believed that Wood's family occupied both houses until they sold the building in the 1940s.

In the mid-1940s the building was converted into apartments. One of the two conjoined houses may have been used at one time as an orphanage and later as a firehouse.

In 1997 the building was the subject of a heated controversy pitting historic preservationists against property rights defenders. The owner of one of the two townhouses sought to convert the ground floor

ABOVE: The main bar
RIGHT: The Black Sheep's entrance is on the right.

into a garage for his cars. After much intense debate he received a favorable split-vote nod from the Historical Commission to cut a large opening in the building's facade, and the garage was built.

James' business partner Gene Lefevre, an architect by training with a deep interest in historical preservation, used his skills to help restore the historic building which had experienced so many alterations over the decades. For example, he did extensive research on the wall coverings and applied mock-leather with intricate Art Nouveau designs just as they appeared in the building's heyday. They named their pub The Black Sheep, "because I am kind of the black sheep of the family," says James.

James' background is colorful, to say the least. He was raised in Belfast where his feisty great grandfather lost his eye sight in a bar fight. His grandfather started in the milk delivery business and became quite successful. He bought a large house which later became the well-known Drumkeen Hotel. The popular thirty room hotel was finally demolished in the mid-1990s after multiple bombings severely damaged it during the Troubles. Today the site is occupied by the large Forestside shopping mall in a much changed and very cosmopolitan Belfast. James' father was a merchant, the first Protestant head of the Northern Ireland Vintners Association, and responsible for bringing Sunday store openings to Belfast and the rest of Northern Ireland.

James attended the world-famous Ballymaloe Cookery School which sits in the middle of a 100-acre organic farm in Shanagarry in County Cork, near Middleton, long known as a center of the Irish whiskey distilling industry. Following a short spell in the hotel business, and after satisfying his wanderlust with a stint in Australia, he immigrated to the United States where he worked as a bartender in Philadelphia for six

years before acquiring his own pub.

In less than 15 years, The Black Sheep has become a local institution. It consistently receives high ratings on local Top Ten lists, reflecting James' view that "having a good time starts at the front door." "Cozy" and "warm" are terms frequently used to describe the small pub—capacity 180—with its partially raised main floor and fireplace and smaller gathering areas in the basement and upstairs. The pub hosts eight or nine parties each week: engagements, weddings, christenings, and office parties. The walls are plain; James doesn't believe in artifact overkill, the bar and banquettes are dark, the wainscoting is oak and the front door is bright red. Perfection!

ABOVE: Heavily sculpted Art Nouveau mock-leather wall coverings recall the early days of this historic building.

RIGHT: The upstairs bar.

Butch McGuire's

CHICAGO, ILLINOIS

Living a Full Life

You can't make both ends meet if you are sitting on one. -Butch McGuire

THE 200 YARD TUNNEL THAT ran under the alley from the speakeasy to the Hotel Ambassador is no longer accessible, and few can remember how the well-to-do and the well-connected could sneak off for a tryst without fear of discovery. During Prohibition the building that today houses Butch McGuire's saloon was home to Kelly's Pleasure Palace, one of many illicit speakeasies in Chicago's Gold Coast. In the 1950s, the space was taken up by Bobby Farrell's Duchess Show Lounge, a quite sleazy strip joint, mobster run according to some. It was described in one newspaper report as, "full of hookers, pimps and gamblers."

When Robert "Butch" McGuire took a chance and opened his pub in 1961, he breathed new life into the building and by extension into the neighborhood. Butch was one of those legendary saloon keepers who lived life to the fullest and who continues to evoke fond memories long after his death. In 2006 thousands of people gathered under tents outside his pub to honor him at a post funeral celebration of his life—and an amazing life it was. It seems that everyone who knew him has a yarn to spin.

RIGHT: It is easy to spot Butch McGuire's with its green facade and extra wide awning. The pub is a Chicago icon. Above the building's terracotta ceramic clad facade, lion head scuppers at the base of the roof top parapet let rainwater drain off instead of pooling on the roof. Pineapples have long been a popular design element. They symbolize friendship and hospitality.

To establish his eponymous pub, Butch borrowed $560 from his mother to convert Bobby Farrell's strip joint into a bar that did much more than serve drinks. Butch used his pub to make the world a better place while at the same time furthering his business interests. Many artists, college students and flight attendants for United and American Airlines lived in nearby Old Town. Butch intuitively catered to that audience.

He was an early champion of women's rights, and in the process established one of the first singles bars in the nation. He made it acceptable for women to enter a bar unescorted. Butch figured that by catering to women, the men would show up. Women were treated with utmost respect at Butch McGuire's. Until the 1980s when the pub was full, if a man did not offer his seat to a lady, he was unceremoniously thrown out. Pub staff would escort single women from their apartments to the pub and escort them back home. Several thousand marriages had their origins in the pub.

As recently as the 1960s Chicago's Barmaids Ordinance prohibited women unrelated to the owner from tending bar. Butch defied the rule and hired women to work behind the bar. In 1974 the US District Court ruled that laws restricting the conduct of women in bars are "discriminatory on their face, overboard and vague." A plaque celebrating the ruling is affixed to the building.

The business continues to be family owned after more than half a century. Son Bobby McGuire is a chip off the old block: gregarious, committed and always present. He carries on the traditions that made the bar such a success, such as the annual Butch McGuire's Christmas celebration. What began with a few balloons and ornaments has become an eye-popping display of lights, garlands and four holiday trains that run throughout the pub on overhead tracks. Bobby says, "Butch taught me a great deal about this business and I often remember his words of advice. He also gave me the confidence to find my own way and that is the most valuable lesson of them all."

The three-story building has a terracotta facade and ornate roof typical of Victorian architecture popular in

The long bar runs the length of the eastern wall. Built in the 1940s it came from Bobby Farrell's Duchess Show Lounge. Dancing girls would perform on a stage behind the bartenders.

the United States in the late 1800s and early 1900s. The site was originally owned by William Bush, who planned to erect a "large, high grade apartment hotel," which was never built. Using the foundation prepared for the erstwhile hotel, noted Chicago architect Samuel Marx designed a "combination building" including a banquet hall, billiard hall, restaurant, stores, lodge hall and "high class bachelors' hotel" in 1914.

The extra-long green awning of today's Butch McGuire's can't be missed. The handsome interior consists of three rooms: the main bar, the Antique Room reflecting Butch's penchant for collecting anything old and the Chicago Room, a back room filled with Chicago memorabilia. The ceiling is cluttered with all manner of odds and ends that Butch collected over the years

Butch McGuire was a people person. He enjoyed a full life and lives on through the many lives he touched and the stories people like to tell about him.

ABOVE: Butch was a collector of antiques and art. Struggling local artists often traded paintings for alcohol. LeRoy Neiman (1921 - 2012), a regular at the pub, sold his paintings to Butch in exchange for a bar credit before he became one of the 20th century's most famous artists. Sometimes, Neiman would sit at the bar and sketch the interior. Here, one of his sketches that adorns the Chicago Room.

LEFT: Butch McGuire loved antiques, especially those with nautical themes. At one time he operated an antique store in The Antique Room which opens onto the main bar area.

A staircase leads down to the only underground pub in Los Angeles.

Casey's

LOS ANGELES, CALIFORNIA

Subterranean Oasis

The problem with some people is that when they aren't drunk, they're sober.
 -William Butler Yeats

By most estimates, more movie scenes have been filmed at Casey's Irish Pub than any other pub in the United States, but that is only part of what makes this pub so special. Casey's is a story of renewal, adaptation and consistency. Where others have come and gone, Casey's just keeps rolling on.

For more than forty years, Casey's was the only Irish pub in downtown Los Angeles. Through economic boom and bust and modern urban renaissance, Casey's has always provided a place of comfort and refuge, whether patrons come in shorts or three-piece suits. Co-owner Mike Winn says, "In Los Angeles we love our space, our cars, our homes. We are very independent, yet we crave that indefinable human connectivity that only a good Irish pub provides. People come here to be with other people, to interact, to be themselves."

Today Casey's is the only remaining single story structure in a sea of modern high-rise buildings in downtown Los Angeles. The building dates back to 1916, when it housed a general store on the first floor and a Turkish bathhouse in the basement. In 1924 the business was converted into a cafeteria. Food was prepared in the basement and moved upstairs on dumbwaiters. In 1930 the building became La Palma Spanish restaurant. More change in 1962 when Sumitomo Bank took over the ground floor, and the basement was converted into a private

The outer entrance to the pub.

dinner club. In 1969 Frank Lawry purchased the building to put together an Irish pub, sparing no expense to create a 1920s-like interior. He purchased a complete stateroom from the RMS Mauretania, a majestic ocean liner that sailed the seas for the Cunard Line for 28 years through peace and war until 1934 when she was scrapped. William Randolph Hearst bought some of the ship's furnishings and fittings and sold one first class stateroom to Lawry which today forms the Captain's Room library of Casey's. Lawry also moved the building's façade back forty feet from the street to create an elaborate wrought iron encased entry that leads to the patio and pub entrance below the sidewalk.

The interior is huge, 10,000 square feet of mysterious recesses and crannies, making Casey's one of the largest pubs in the country and one of the very few subterranean businesses in Los Angeles. On special occasions when the furniture is removed, the facility can accommodate more than 1000 people. The interior boasts a beautiful mahogany bar, dart and billiards rooms and expansive W. F. Norman hand-pressed tin ceilings. With its black and ivory color scheme, the patio looks like a pint of Guinness. To the rear, the Jameson live music stage is testimony to the important role Jameson Irish Whiskey has played at Casey's throughout the years. They paid for the stage and, for several years, the top-rated musical talent that the pub presents. According to Mike Winn, Casey's is one of Jameson's largest US accounts.

The pub is around the corner from Los Angeles Center Studios, a major independent studio for film, TV and commercials production, which may help explain Casey's popularity with the 1000 or so location managers in Southern California. More than 200 productions have been filmed in the pub in the past decade. Being production friendly means no bragging, no signed pictures of movie stars displayed on the

walls and no gawking at notables who frequent the pub. "It's not in our nature to boast. We are an Irish pub where everyone is welcome," says Mike Winn.

A wee bit of boasting is in order, however, when describing Casey's annual St Patrick's Day celebration. Two blocks of Grand Avenue are shut down to accommodate the party's 20,000 celebrants, and the event is bigger every year. That is a far cry from the time when Mike purchased the pub in 2002, when it closed at 9:00pm and did not open on weekends. Downtown Los Angeles had been in decline, and everyone went home to the suburbs at night. Mike's close friends advised him not to buy the venture. Fortunately, he is a fearless entrepreneur, who mortgaged his house and worked 18 hours a day to resuscitate the business. Mike's vision and sacrifices paid off and today Casey's is open seven days a week and can rightfully claim leadership in bringing downtown Los Angeles back to prominence.

In 2005 Mike and his co-owner Mark Verge joined forces with Cedd Moses of 213 Spirited Ventures, a development company dedicated to the revitalization of downtown Los Angeles. While maintaining the independence of their company, Mike and Mark also benefit from belonging to an influential group.

ABOVE: View from inside the outer entrance. The main bar is to the left; games are to the right.

A Favorite Location for Movies and Television

Over the years Casey's has been a favorite location for movies and TV shows. Following are some of the productions.

Film

2011	It's Always Sunny in Philadelphia
2010	Date Night
2008	Eagle Eye
2007	Mad Men
2007	Charlie Wilson's War
2007	License to Wed
2006	16 Blocks
2005	Good Night and Good Luck
2005	Miss Congeniality 2: Armed and Fabulous
2002	Mr. Deeds
2001	Good Avice
1999	The Deep End of the Ocean
1998	Fallen
1998	X-File

Television

2009-2013	Castle
2004-2013	CSI:NY
2010	CHAOS TV pilot
2009	In Security
2005	Numbers TV series
2002	Bones TV series
2001	The Agency TV series

Coleman's Irish Pub has two entrances side by side, one of which is for leprechauns who also have their own phone booth.

Coleman's Authentic Irish Pub

SYRACUSE, NEW YORK

Tasteful Reminders of Ireland

I distrust camels, and anyone else who can go a week without a drink.   -Joe E. Lewis

Once the Erie Canal was completed in the 1800s, connecting the Hudson River with Lake Erie, many Irish canal workers and their families settled in enclaves along the canal in cities such as Syracuse. Their hilly neighborhood in Syracuse was called Tipperary Hill because so many of its inhabitants came from the Irish county of the same name. In the latter part of the 1800s many industries were established in and near Syracuse, providing jobs for the residents. These included salt mills, soda ash manufacturing, automotive, steel and pottery companies.

Over the years, Tipp Hill, as it is affectionately called, has retained a strong sense of self identity. Residents feel a deep attachment to the neighborhood and to their family roots. Not everyone on Tipp Hill is Irish these days, but Irishness runs deep. Helping to preserve Irish ways is Coleman's Authentic Irish Pub, owned and operated by Peter Coleman and his family.

Peter's father was the first to open an Irish pub on the hill. In 1933 he purchased Con Behan Grocery store and converted it to a small working man's saloon. Peter worked

with his Da as a youth and into his adult years. When his father passed away in 1963 Peter took over the business. Over time, Peter tripled the size of the building but never changed his father's commitment to serving the public with good cheer and good beer. Other members of Peter's family are deeply involved in the business as well. His son, also Peter, manages the rental properties. Son Dennis manages the pub and another family-owned bar.

ABOVE: The interior of the large pub features a bar inspired by the Jury's Inn in Dublin.

OPPOSITE, TOP, LEFT: An enclosed porch just off the main seating area is light and airy.

OPPOSITE, TOP, RIGHT: This appealing dining room is used for special occasions.

OPPOSITE, BOTTOM: The entrance to Tipperary Hill in the foreground with Peter Coleman next to a statue honoring Ukranian hero Taras Schevchenko. Coleman, owner of Coleman's Irish Pub, was the stimulus for the small park and many other enhancements to Tipp Hill.

Peter says, "everybody who walks into this joint is instantly comfortable. That is the key. Maybe the dark wood and stained glass help, but it is the people who make it all work. Pubs should be places where people meet and talk." Indeed, the interior of the pub is tastefully warm and friendly with a separate dining room and a notable bar. In 1979 Peter sent an architect to Ireland with instructions to find an ornate bar that could serve as inspiration for a bar in Coleman's. The bar selected was in the Jury's Inn located in Ballsbridge, Dublin. That inn no longer exists, but its spirit and "good pours" live on in Coleman's Pub.

Two long blocks up the hill from the pub is the famous green over red traffic light. In 1925 the city installed the first traffic signal on Tipperary Hill with the standard red light on top. A few local Irish youths, offended and irate at the notion of a light with the British red above the Irish green, threw stones and

broke the light. The city replaced it, but the youths repeated their act of defiance. After several rounds of tit-for-tat, the city gave in and the inverted light with the green above the red has been in place ever since. Thanks to Peter Coleman and other committed citizens, a small heritage memorial park was built on one corner of the intersection and a statue erected. Rather than show the stone throwers in action, the statue portrays a family with the father pointing to the traffic light, doubtlessly explaining its history. His small son is listening but has a slingshot in his back pocket, hinting that he might already be familiar with the history of the light.

Peter has devoted countless hours and financial resources to the preservation and improvement of the historic neighborhood. For example, he was instrumental in the creation of another small park down the hill from the pub in front of the St John the Baptist Ukrainian Church. A monument to

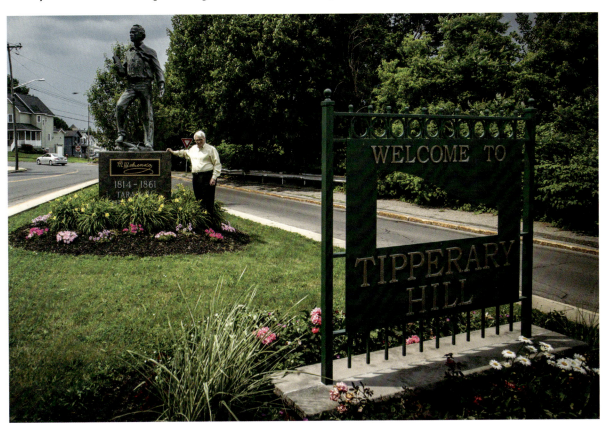

the Ukrainian poet, painter and freedom fighter Taras Schevchenko recognizes the contribution that Ukrainian immigrants have made to Tipperary Hill.

In his continuing efforts to enhance the neighborhood where he was born, Peter has purchased properties near the pub, rehabilitated them and rented them out to young couples. Peter's sister Mary Jo, runs an Irish gift shop in one of the houses across the street from the pub.

Peter's Irish sense of playfulness is everywhere evident. Next to the pub entrance for regular folks is a two-foot by one-foot door for leprechauns. Although the door has been stolen three times it always found its way back. Next to the bright red telephone booth by the entrance is a smaller booth so leprechauns can call home—or a taxi. Nearby, a four inch pipe rises 18 inches out of the ground surrounded by a protective fence. This is to receive the annual St Patrick's Day green beer delivered with much fanfare by a large tanker truck emblazoned with the pub's name. No one is certain how much green beer is actually delivered, but Peter, with a sly wink, says "a lot."

Emblazoned on the back window of one of Peter's pub trucks is written "Voted Best Bar in USA." Underneath, in small letters is "by owner." Now who could argue with that?

ABOVE: This statue in a small park at the site of the famous Tipperary Hill traffic signal light, memorializes a small group of Irish youths known as "The Stonethrowers." When a traffic light was first installed there in the 1920's, the youths forced the city to put the "Irish" green above the "British" red light by repeatedly breaking the light until the city relented.

The Irish and the Erie Canal

The Erie Canal was the engineering marvel of its time. Begun in 1817 and completed eight years later, the canal joined the Hudson River to Lake Erie. It was 363 miles long, 40 feet wide, and incorporated 83 locks to manage the 568 foot rise in elevation from the river to Lake Erie–plus numerous walls and aqueducts to allow the canal to cross rivers.

The route from New York City up the Hudson River to Albany and then to Buffalo on the canal cut travel time from three weeks by stage coach to one week for passenger packet boats. Slower-moving freight barges could make the voyage in two weeks because of waiting time for access to locks and weighing of cargo.

Many farmers along the canal route signed contracts to construct their own small portions of the canal. Resident Americans provided the muscle for the effort, some of whom were second generation Presbyterian Scotch-Irish whose parents immigrated from Northern Ireland. Irish and other Europeans with special skills were brought in to construct stone embankments, bridges, locks and aqueducts.

Ten years after its opening, enlargement of the canal was begun which expanded it to seventy feet wide and seven feet deep. Manpower for the 28 year-long project came largely from the 1.3 million poor Irish Catholics who immigrated to the United States between 1821 and 1841 due to economic and political conditions at home. Immigrants toiled with picks and shovels ten hours a day for about a dollar in wages, a place to sleep and a ration of whiskey.

Their diligent efforts stimulated a dramatic increase in commerce between the interior of the country and New York City and beyond. So in a real sense those hard working, good spirited Irishmen were responsible in no small measure for the opening of the interior of the United States to economic development.

ABOVE: The Syracuse Weighlock Building, constructed in 1850, was a specialized canal lock used to weigh barges on the Erie Canal so appropriate tolls could be assessed. When a barge entered the lock, gates were closed at each end and the water was drained out. The barge rested on an immense cradle suspended from a balance beam to determine the weight. Five weighlocks serviced the Erie Canal during the towpath era. This is the last of its kind and is listed on the National Register of Historic Places. Designed in the Greek Revival style, the former weighlock now houses the Erie Canal Museum. Gouache painting by John Batchelor. Image from the collection of The Erie Canal Museum, Syracuse, NY, www.eriecanalmuseum.org

Framed by autumn leaves in the heart of Cambridge, The Druid is a favorite of young professionals and students from nearby Harvard and MIT. The building is the oldest wooden commercial structure in the city.

The Druid

CAMBRIDGE, MASSACHUSETTS

Traditional and Unpretentious

I only drink on two occasions: when I'm thirsty and when I'm not thirsty. - Brendan Behan

DURING THE YEARS OF THE Irish potato famine, 1845-50, when more than a million people died of starvation, the Boston area was swamped with Irish immigrants seeking refuge from the deplorable conditions at home. A staunch Anglo-Saxon city of about 115,000 inhabitants, Boston did not put out the welcome mat for the 37,000 Irish Catholics who immigrated in 1847 alone. Cambridge, with a population of less than 13,000, was no more hospitable. Irish enclaves along the Boston waterfront and in East Cambridge were transformed into crowded tenements with poor sanitation where cholera ran rampant. Many immigrants worked in the clay pits and brickyards in Cambridge or labored in the glass works and furniture factories. Growing anti-Irish and anti-Catholic sentiment led to decades of friction with the local population fueled by competition for low paying jobs. Family ties and close friendships helped the immigrants endure the harsh conditions. Gradually, the Irish were assimilated into society while maintaining their ethnic identity, and their leaders were recognized for their contributions to the area and to the country. Today nearly a quarter of the Boston area population are first generation Irish or of Irish descent. To be Irish in the United States is to be part of a great success story.

As one might expect, the Irish brought with them their rich culture and institutions, sports, music, literature and, to everyone's delight, the Irish pub. The Druid, named for the ancient Celtic Druid priests, is a prime example of how family linkages came together to create a vibrant and successful business. It is the story of how a group of young men from one county in Ireland came to Cambridge and established a pub, bringing traditional Irish hospitality to one neighborhood.

John Blake, general manager of the Druid and the first to arrive in the United States, comes from Liscannor, a coastal village of some 200 inhabitants in County Claire. Owner Mikey Crawford is from the nearby and slightly larger village of Ennistymon. The four other staffers also come from villages in County Claire. All knew of each other in Ireland, and some were linked through family friendships.

In 2004, Mikey purchased the building constructed in 1902, the oldest wooden commercial structure in Cambridge. Mikey was careful to recreate an "old style look, just like the pubs back home." The atmosphere is non-pretentious, where "everyone is a friend," says John, who realizes that the patrons "pay our salaries."

Situated a stone's throw from Harvard University and close to MIT, the pub's regulars are a mix of young professionals, professors and workers. With a seating capacity of 99, the pub is small, typical of the area and relies on fresh, healthy food. "There are no food deliveries here," John proudly reports. "We go to the market every day." The menu is small to help assure quality. Mikey's mother's memorable brown bread is made fresh in the kitchen every day.

The cluttered entrance window entices passersby.

The colorful entrance is a local landmark.

Sturdy high back chairs extend the length of the bar. Purse hooks are at every seat.

Celts and their Druid Priests

The Celts, pronounced Kelts, were a group of tribal societies spanning much of Europe beginning more than 1000 years before Christ and lasting through the Renaissance. After the Roman expansion in the first century AD, Celtic societies became concentrated in certain areas, handing down their traditions and languages through the centuries. Today, separate Celtic languages are most commonly spoken in Ireland, Scotland, Wales, Brittany, Cornwall, the Isle of Man, Cape Breton, with revival efforts underway in Spain. These correspond to the seven Celtic nations which were based on common cultural characteristics rather than on sovereign nation-states.

The ancient Druids acted as a sort of priesthood in Celtic regions, especially in Ireland, Britain and France. Very little is known about them since they left no written accounts of their history. It is known that they believed in reincarnation and a plethora of pagan gods. Many ancient Irish texts refer to them as the mystics, educators, doctors and philosophers in Celtic society. To the Irish, the Druids were highly respected sorcerers who could cast spells and turn people into animals or stones. With the advent of Christianity in Ireland in the 5th century, the influence of the Druids gradually declined.

The Dubliner

WASHINGTON, DISTRICT OF COLUMBIA

A Place for Politics— And Peace

There's no friends like the old friends.
—James Joyce, *Dubliners*

THE DUBLINER SO RESEMBLES A Dublin city pub that it could just as easily occupy a corner of O'Connell Street in Dublin as a busy corner in the nation's capital. Many of the staff are fresh from Ireland and are as colorful as any character in James Joyce's Dubliners, for which the pub is named.

Owner Danny Coleman was raised in the pub business. Irish pubs are in his blood, so to speak, because his father opened an Irish pub in Syracuse, NY, where Danny was born, a few days following the repeal of Prohibition in 1933. After being discharged from the Army in 1964 Danny moved to Washington where he worked as a barman and manager of many of the new Georgetown and downtown saloons opening in the late 60s and early 70s.

During the tragically short Kennedy era, legions of well educated Irish Americans had migrated from Boston and elsewhere to the Washington area, establishing a firm foundation for expanding the concept of Irish hospitality in the city. They were Danny's target audience when in 1974 he opened The Dubliner in a converted German restaurant. It occupied part of the first floor of the historic Hotel Commodore, built in 1922 by noted developer Harry Wardman who was responsible for many Washington DC

Early morning at The Dubliner on a gray December day. In an hour, the chairs and tables will be made ready for the busy lunch crowd. Above the pub are the rooms of the luxury Phoenix Park Hotel.

landmark buildings. Danny later purchased the hotel and renamed it The Phoenix Park after Dublin's famous park of the same name, the largest urban park in Europe.

For almost 40 years, politicians from both Ireland and America have gathered at The Dubliner to negotiate deals, write legislation and even help find a way to end the Troubles in Northern Ireland. The Committee for a New Ireland was formed in late 1970s by a group of Irish Americans in Washington and Boston at the suggestion of Senator Ted Kennedy and Speaker of the House Thomas "Tip" O'Neil. Consisting of lawyers, lobbyists, and Congressional staff, the group worked closely with Kennedy, O'Neill, other key members of the House and Senate, the US, Irish and British Governments and those in Ireland and Northern Ireland seeking peace through nonviolence.

The Dubliner served as a neutral and friendly venue for Irish and Northern Irish politicians to meet with their US counterparts and others interested in supporting the Peace Process. Many of those meetings could not have taken place in Northern Ireland and were facilitated by Danny Coleman who gained the trust and friendship of all who met him. When the Irish coined the phrase "a stranger is a friend you've never met," they must have had Danny in mind.

Following the successful negotiation of the 1985 Anglo-Irish Agreement, the first of a series of agreements aimed at achieving a permanent solution, the Committee for a New Ireland disbanded and evolved into the Congressional Friends of Ireland. This bipartisan group of Senators and Representatives is dedicated to this day to sustaining peace in that part of the world.

Throughout the arduous peace process, Irishmen of both traditions could be found at The Dubliner enjoying a pint of Guinness or a meal at this neutral location. Gerry Adams, Martin McGuinness, Lord John Alderdice, Gusty Spence as well as Nobel Peace Prize winners John Hume and John Trimble were frequent guests. Every Irish Prime Minister since Jack Lynch in 1974 has visited the Dubliner on their annual St Patrick's Day visits to DC. It was the obvious choice for President Barack Obama to entertain his eighth cousin Henry Healy from the tiny village of Moneygall, County Offlay, on St Patrick's Day, 2012.

The Dubliner has provided nightly live Irish musical entertainment for 39 years and has introduced many famous Irish musicians to America. It is one of a very few pubs anywhere open for breakfast. It is a family affair. Daniel owns The Dubliner, while his brother, Peter, owns Coleman's Authentic Irish Pub in Syracuse [see page 40]. Daniel's son Gavin and Peter's son Danny, manage The Dubliner. The pub accommodates 150 patrons inside and an additional 75 on its sidewalk patio. Bric-a-brac and curiosities fill the shelves and cover the walls. The tile floor in the bar dates back to the building's original construction. Well-worn tables are at least 75 years old, and the Chicago rail on the oak bar has been flattened from countless elbows. "When you put your arms on it, it feels perfect," says Gavin.

While Danny has become the Publican Emeritus, he is still around almost daily. But for the next forty years or so, you will more than likely be welcomed by Gavin or by Young Danny. Their presence will ensure that in this wonderful family owned institution you will realize that, in the words of the great 19th century Irish statesman Daniel O'Connell: "The hospitality of an Irishman…springs, like all his qualities, his faults, his virtues, directly from the heart."

RIGHT: One of three cheerful entrances to The Dubliner. It has been a Washington landmark since 1974. Many Irish American politicians over the years have made it a second home.

Speaker O'Neill and President Reagan

In the 1970s the Dubliner became home base to a growing coterie of Irish-American politicians. Thomas "Tipp" O'Neill visited the pub with his wife Millie soon after his election as Speaker of the House of Representatives in 1977. Thereafter, whenever Congress was in session, the Speaker came to the pub two or three times a week. One day he was scheduled to go to the White House and told Dubliner publican Danny Coleman that he hated to go there because President Reagan "keeps talking me into doing things I do not want to do." Staunch political foes during the day, the two men enjoyed a solid friendship "after 6:00pm."

ABOVE: The pub's logo was designed by a pub server and student at Catholic University. It is based on the *Book of Kells*, produced by Celtic monks circa 800 AD. This magnificent illuminated manuscript is one of Ireland's greatest national treasures.

LEFT: The Chicago rail on the slightly tattered oak bar in the principal drinking area has been worn smooth by generations of elbows of the famous and not-so-famous. A separate breakfast room opens every morning at 7:00am.

Durty Nelly's

SAN FRANCISCO, CALIFORNIA

*Enter as Strangers;
Leave as Friends*

God made yeast, as well as dough, and he loves fermentation just as dearly as he loves vegetation.   -Ralph Waldo Emerson

SAN FRANCISCO'S HISTORY AND MULTICULTURAL heritage is showcased by its many Irish pubs. Whether large or comfy-small, each has woven its story into the tapestry of a great city. Unpretentious by design and not the oldest nor the most famous pub in town, Durty Nelly's is the oft-heard story of Irish immigrants who came to America in search of a better life.

So come on in, pull up a stool and be prepared to be entertained and fortified. Settle in to a welcoming booth by the open fire, have a pint or two and listen to the music.

Named in honor of the world famous Durty Nelly's pub which sits just outside of the 17th century Bunratty Castle in County Clare, this San Francisco neighborhood pub carries on the hospitality and musical traditions of the original. Since 1995 it has served as a home away from home to the local Irish community. Owner Odhrán McLaughlin tells the story of a pub regular

whose house burned down. He came into the pub that same day and proclaimed, "I just lost my house, but not my home."

The business was started by Odhrán's uncle Fergus McEleny of Donnegal and his partner Owen Conway of County Cork. After immigrating to the US, they made their way to San Francisco. Fergus worked as a bartender; Owen was a musician. They met up and eventually created a pub in the Sunset district,

PREVIOUS SPREAD: This small, unpretentious pub could be mistaken for a pub in the Irish countryside.

ABOVE: Good vibes–owners Karolina and Odhrán welcome patrons with a smile.

OPPOSITE, TOP: Previous owner Fergus McEleny purposely misspelled the name of one of the Irish counties on this large wooden map to give patrons something to gab about. Can you find it? Answer: County Laois in the Midlands Region appears on the map as Laios. The beautiful area is a popular tourist destination.

OPPOSITE, BELOW: The one-room interior can be very crowded on trivia night. The picture on the left is an Irish version of the Last Supper, with noted Irish men of letters at the table.

catering to the heavily Irish local community. Over the years of urban realignment, the area has been absorbed into the sprawling Asian community and most of the once-common Irish pubs have closed. The partners sold the pub in 2005 to Vivian Walsh of County Galway, who sold it in 2012 to Odhrán and his wife Karolina, bringing it back into the original family.

Odhrán was born in Derry City in County Derry and graduated from the Magee campus of the University of Ulster in Derry. At the urging of his uncle, he graduated on a Monday, arrived in the US on Wednesday and started working as a bar back in his uncle's pub on Thursday. Blessed with a powerful baritone, he doubled as a bartender and entertainer for ten years before buying the pub.

The building dates back to the 1940s and previously housed at least two Irish pubs, The Irish Embassy followed by The Irving Club. An eclectic assortment of odds and ends contributed

The Story of Durty Nelly

Durty Nelly was a toll-bridge keeper about 1000 years ago on the River Owengarney which flows into the mighty River Shannon in County Clare. She was a comely and resourceful lass who operated a wee sheeben in the rear of the gatehouse where a jug of whiskey was always available for friends and travelers. One dark night a recipe for a mysterious concoction came to her in a dream. She found the ingredients and filled her earthen pots with the mysterious brew and put them on a shelf where they sat undisturbed.

One morning she discovered a Wolfhound near death's door on her front stoop. For some unknown reason she rubbed some of her potion on his worn muscles and he slowly came to life. She determined to give him a small amount to drink, and the next morning the big dog was jumping and cavorting on the lawn. Word quickly spread in the village and beyond that Durty Nelly had the gift of life. The sick and lame, human and animal, came to her door. Best of all, perhaps, husbands' powers increased when they took a dram from her pot, and Durty Nelly went from rags to fame and riches. Today, we remember her for the drink that made her immortal, Irish Poteen, the elixir of new life and hope.

by regulars clings to the narrow shelves just below the ceiling. Musical instruments, ceramic mugs, jugs, a collection of silver mugs and a 1920s Underwood typewriter are among the "treasures" to be found. In keeping with Uncle Fergus' motto "enter as strangers, leave as friends," on Christmas Karolina cooks dinner for anyone who wants to join the Nelly's family for the day.

A third of the clients are regulars who stop by at least once a week. They can expect a phone call if they do not appear by 5:00pm on their normal day—to see if everything is all right. That is what makes a matchless neighborhood pub.

Emmit's Irish Pub

CHICAGO, ILLINOIS

Neighborhood Reborn

This fine turn of the century brick building has a colorful past. The brass plated revolving door entrance once ushered ladies and gentlemen and even Presidents into the famed Ambassador West Hotel. The hotel was gutted in 2002 to make way for condos.

I can think of no more stirring symbol of man's humanity to man than a fire engine.
-Kurt Vonnegut

CHICAGO'S RIVER WEST NEIGHBORHOOD IS considered trendy these days, but it was not always so. Where sleek restaurants, condos and high rises attract a young, affluent clientele today, a few decades ago stood rough and tumble, derelict flophouses and dive hotels housing the city's less fortunate. Chicago's infamous West Loop skid row, which in 1949 Time Magazine called "The Land of the Living Dead," was just a few blocks to the south.

When Chicago firefighters Ron Halverson and Kevin Doherty bought an abandoned and condemned building in 1993, the bank insisted that the former SRO (single room occupancy) rooming house on the upper floors be rehabilitated and converted into six two-bedroom apartments. The bankers were more confident in apartment rentals as a source of revenue than Kevin's plan to open an Irish pub.

The building which probably dates back to the 1890s originally housed the Italian Trust and Savings Bank, reportedly a favorite of Chicago's notorious mafia dons. The original

vault with its two-foot thick walls is in the basement and makes a fine wine cellar.

The basement was at one time the main floor of the building. Chicago had been built on marshy ground near Lake Michigan just slightly above water level. As a result, there was virtually no natural drainage. Standing water, mud and disease were serious problems. In the second half of the 19th century, Chicago gradually rose from the muck. Many buildings, large and small, were jacked up as much as 14 feet and new foundations put under them. Then, the land was filled in to the new first floor levels of the buildings and new streets were put in. Some building owners chose not to bear the cost of raising their homes or businesses. They created a new entrance on the second floor, making the first floor into basement storage once the land around them was filled in. The Italian bank chose the more economical course.

The neighborhood was settled by Sicilians beginning in the 1850s. The Sicilian mafia operated with impunity, and the Chicago police department was hesitant to enter the area. The Sicilian immigrants policed the neighborhood themselves. The situation became even worse during the Great Depression. Housing continued to deteriorate, and crime levels rose.

Several businesses occupied the premises over the years. In the 1980s, O'Sullivan's Tavern occupied the ground floor. By that time the Chicago police were in firm control of the neighborhood, and O'Sullivan's became known as a place for off-duty police to hang out. One night in 1985, proving that being bright is not a prerequisite for being a crook, two men with shotguns attempted to hold up the bar. One entered the front door, the other burst through the side door. "This is a hold up," they yelled, not realizing that the bar was filled with off-duty police. The outcome was distinctively negative and fatal for the would-be assailants. It took quite a while to count all the bullet holes in their bodies.

What could be more quintessentially Irish in Chicago than having a pub owned and operated by firefighters? From the earliest days of Irish immigration to Chicago and other large cities, the Irish found employment as firefighters and policemen. Kevin and Ron opened their pub in 1996. Kevin's cousin Chris Clyde joined the two friends as general manager. All three are firefighters and of Irish descent. Ron is now retired from the Elk Grove Village fire department. Kevin works as a relief officer (Captain), and Chris is assigned to Engine 125, both in the 2nd District. With more than 4,300 firefighters and well over 600 paramedics in the city, Chicago has one of the largest and oldest—established in 1833—fire departments in the country.

The first thing one notices when approaching the pub is its revolving door entrance. The door came from Chicago's famed Ambassador West Hotel, once a favorite stopping off point for presidents and celebrities. In 2002 the hotel was gutted to make way for high-end condos and all its furnishings were liquidated at auction, ending a proud 80-year history.

The second impression is that of the angles inside the pub, particularly the zigzag bar, portions of which Ron built himself out of Philippine mahogany and oak. Then there is the striking copper etched ceiling which dates back to the original construction. A small low-ceiling balcony is used for special events. The flatiron exterior is noteworthy for its lovely brickwork and white limestone trim.

Emmit's is named after Robert Emmet, an Irish rebel leader who was captured a few weeks following a failed rising he had organized in Dublin in 1803. He was tried, found guilty of high treason and hanged. When Ron attempted to register the name of the pub, he was told that Emmet's was not available. So, he changed the spelling to Emmit's and replaced the dot over the letter "i" with a shamrock, thus creating a distinctive logo.

Several films, TV shows and commercials have been produced in the pub because of its unique layout and high ceiling. Ron and Kevin have never marketed their business as a star-studded locale. They know that in a neighborhood bar, their customers and any drop-in celebrities just want to have a well-pulled pint and not be bothered.

THIS PAGE: The building that today is home to Emmit's was constructed in the late 1890s to house the Italian Trust and Savings Bank, reportedly a favorite of Chicago mobsters. The bank's sign is shown in the lower right corner of the photo. Photo courtesy of Emmit's Irish Pub.

OPPOSITE: Vintage dark wood, exposed brick walls, original tin ceiling and an old time tile floor evoke memories of decades past and qualify Emmit's as a classic Chicago pub. It has an enthusiastic and passionate following.

Fadó Irish Pub

CHICAGO, ILLINOIS

In with the old—in with the new

*The road to success is
always under construction.*
-Lily Tomlin

FADÓ IRISH PUB IS SIMPLY beautiful and fascinating, illustrating what knowledge of the business coupled with commitment and resources can accomplish. One of fourteen Fadó pubs in major cities around the United States, Fadó in Chicago combines the best of traditional Irish pub culture with modern knowhow and sophisticated business practices. Fadó Pubs, Inc, headquartered in Atlanta, and founded by a small group of Irish and Irish-American entrepreneurs in 1996, proves that there can be success in numbers.

The pub, in the River North Neighborhood, reportedly occupies one of the first buildings to be built after the Great Chicago Fire that destroyed more than four square miles of the city in 1871. It was possibly a tavern and boarding house which gradually became a brothel. Fadó CEO Kieran McGill purchased the building in 1995 and opened the pub two years later.

The interior of the pub was designed, milled and built by The Irish Pub Company of Dublin which has designed more than 1000 pubs and built more than 500 throughout the world. Their work is based on extensive research into old and new pubs in Ireland, which explains their great success in helping make the Irish pub concept a global phenomenon.

Visual delights abound wherever one casts an eye. The Irish Cottage is reminiscent of a modest but cozy rural Irish dwelling. The Shop and Post Office illustrates the multi-functional role Irish pubs played historically. Some provided groceries, hardware, a post office and even undertaking services. Some of the walls on the first floor are painted images from the Book of Kells, the world-famous 9th century illustrated gospel manuscript written by Celtic monks. It is Ireland's finest national treasure.

Saint Brendon's ship tells the story of the patron saint of travel, St Brendon of Clonfort, known for his legendary journey in a currach (lightweight boat covered with animal skins) to the Promised Land somewhere in the Atlantic. Some people believe that the legend is based on fact and that St Brendon actually discovered America hundreds of years before Columbus.

The Purty Loft features a priceless century old bar from The Purty Kitchen pub near Dublin. The pub is one of the oldest in the Dublin area, dating to 1728. Many Irish bands had their start there.

A warm Irish welcome is guaranteed at Fadó—which means "long ago" in Gaelic. A visit to the pub can be educational and provides a comfortable spot for some friendly conversation as well as a good pint or two or three.

ABOVE: The Purty Loft features a priceless century old bar from The Purty Kitchen pub near Dublin. The pub is one of the oldest in the Dublin area, dating to 1728. Many Irish bands had their start there.

OPPOSITE: An inviting corner, one of several in the pub, is a favorite meeting place.

Did the Irish Discover America?

Suspended from the ceiling at Fadó Irish Pub in Chicago is a currach, a type of small fishing boat with a wooden frame, over which animal skins are stretched. For hundreds of years the lightweight craft has been used for fishing and transportation among the islands off the western coast of Ireland.

The currach in Fadó is a tribute to Saint Brendan the Navigator (484 - 577) an Irish monk whose 6th century voyage across the Atlantic Ocean in a currach was first described in a 9th century book, *Navigatio Brendani*. It was written by a monk based on oral traditions handed down through the generations. The seven year voyage reportedly took St Brendan and a small group of fellow monks to Iceland, Greenland and the North American continent. His crossing is considered by some scholars as proof that the earliest voyage to America took place almost 1,000 years before Christopher Columbus. References in the book to a vast land and an impassable river suggest that he may have discovered the Mississippi River. When he returned to Ireland he had with him plant species unknown in Europe.

To others, the voyage by St Brendan in search of the Promised Land, or Paradise, is simply a colorful legend that cannot be proved. In 1976-77, Tim Severin, a British explorer and adventurer, built a replica wood-and-leather currach and crossed the Atlantic under sail and oars from Ireland to Newfoundland to see if St Brendan's legendary trip could have occurred. His successful effort was the subject of a National Geographic feature.

St Brendan established numerous monasteries in his long life and is remembered for the beautiful Clonfert Cathedral in county Galway built on the site of a monastery he founded in 563 and where he is buried. St Brendan's Feast Day is celebrated on May 16.

Whether legend or reality, the journey of St Brendan the Voyager, the patron saint of seafarers and travelers, poses a question for the ages, did he or did he not discover America?

The Field

DANIA BEACH, FLORIDA

Totally Special

Too much of a good thing can be wonderful.
 -Mae West

THE FIELD HAS TO BE one of the most unusual and special pubs in the united States, if not the world. Where else can you find a pub built under and inside a tree? In the case of The Field, a 120-year-old banyan tree engulfs the pub and creates an atmosphere like no other. Twisted and shadowy branches cast a spell at night and create an oasis of cool during the day.

Jay O'Hare opened The Field in a small cottage dating back to the 1920s or 1930s that at one time housed a popular restaurant. Over the years, additions to the cottage, first on one side, then on another, created a delightful, haphazard assemblage of spaces. The pub resembles an Irish farmhouse, warm, friendly and full of laughter and chatter. Meandering from room to room, one appreciates the tasteful décor of the seven rooms and alcoves decorated with old-country antiques. Low beamed ceilings, dark wood and a giant working brick fireplace provide a sense of wellbeing. Here people borrow books from the shelves and relax in overstuffed armchairs—hardly the typical pub.

Squeezed between the Everglades and the Atlantic Ocean, the expansive area around Fort Lauderdale is a maze of canals, waterways and small islands. This is the edge of the tropics with palm trees, hurricanes and alligators. Quaint mid-20th century cottages and modern skyscrapers coexist in this lush green ecosystem. It is also home to a contingent of Irish immigrants. The Field fits comfortably into this setting.

Jay and business partner Hillary Joyalle opened The Field in 2001. The building had been vacant for several years after the restaurant closed. Jay, who began his career as a kitchen helper, waiter and bartender in Dublin, was determined to create a true Irish experience. For Hilary, the business is engrained into her being. "Everything is personal," she says. Many of the traditional relics and works of art came from her home. "I sit in every seat periodically and look at every view and say 'Oh my goodness, the customers won't like that.' So I change it." Jay sums it up this way, "We have grown our business organically. If you have a crowd of people and treat them right, they will come back and bring more people. We take care of the people who take care of us." Words of wisdom from someone who is passionate about life and the Irish way.

LEFT: The Field is under and partially within this huge banyan tree.

The Stately Banyan

The first banyan tree in the U.S. was planted by Thomas Edison at his winter estate in Fort Myers, Florida circa 1925. The tree, originally only four feet tall, now covers an acre of land on the estate. It was a gift from Harvey Firestone, founder of Firestone Tire and Rubber, who brought the tree from India for his friend. Edison and another close friend Henry Ford planted many exotic plants on their adjacent properties in Fort Myers in hopes of developing domestic sources for natural rubber. The banyan tree produces a white sap that the three friends hoped would yield commercially viable rubber, but their efforts did not succeed.

Native to India, the banyan is a type of fig tree and a member of the mulberry plant family. Birds disperse its seeds, which often lodge in cracks and crevices of other trees or buildings. The plant sends roots through the air down to the ground. These so-called aerial prop roots can grow to be as large in diameter as the host tree. Over time, the banyan can grow up to 100 feet tall with enormous limbs spread over several acres, sometimes strangling the unwitting host tree or encasing a building. Banyan trees are top-heavy. The tree at The Field must be trimmed so storms can blow through the dense branches. Otherwise, it might topple over. Banyan trees evoke images of Gautama Buddha seeking enlightenment while meditating under a banyan tree in India. The tree is sacred to both Buddhists and Hindus.

TOP: A corner with a nautical theme is a tribute to the seafaring ways of the Irish. Similarly, there are areas dedicated to horses and to music, which is the heart and soul of the business.

ABOVE: A popular spot in the pub, a fireplace is often considered to be the emotional center of a home. It projects a sense of light, warmth, comfort and safety.

RIGHT: The bar is strategically located in the midst of dinner tables. The pub is a dining destination.

The building housing Finn McCool's was originally constructed in 1909 as a bar. Shops located on neighborhood intersections often had the entry cut at a diagonal, making them distinguishable from nearby residential properties. The pub sits by a giant live oak tree. The building was totally destroyed during Hurricane Katrina in 2005.

Finn McCool's Irish Pub

NEW ORLEANS, LOUISIANA

Phoenix Rising

If you want love and abundance in your life, give it away. -Mark Twain

When Stephen and Pauline Patterson came to live in New Orleans, they could not have imagined the triumph and tragedy and renewed triumph that would await them. Theirs is a story right out of Hollywood.

The Pattersons are from Belfast and were sweethearts beginning in their teenage years. They visited Wildwood, New Jersey every summer while in college, together with, or so it seemed, half of Belfast, to work in the town's many beachfront hotels, restaurants and bars. It was love at first sight when they visited New Orleans on vacation. In 1990, with little more than what they had in their backpacks, they became permanent residents of the Crescent City, so named for the route taken by the Mississippi River as it courses through town. Stephen worked in bars and Pauline worked as a sculptor, teacher and bartender. Their dream was to save enough to own their own Irish pub.

Their dream came true in 2002 when they purchased a once thriving bar that had fallen on hard times in a working class, ethnically mixed neighborhood. New Orleans is a city of neighborhoods. The French Quarter is the most famous as the center of endless entertainment and fine dining, but there are neighborhood bars throughout the city within walking distance for many residents. Finn McCool's is such a place. Stephen and Pauline's sweat equity efforts to rehabilitate the old bar constructed in 1909 inspired many neighbors to improve their own homes.

Stephen and Pauline named their pub after the mythical giant Irish hunter-warrior Finn McCool who in medieval times accomplished many astounding feats—like the time he built the Giant's Causeway as stepping-stones to Scotland. This rare geological formation in County Antrim on the northeast coast consists of 40,000 interlocking hexagonal basalt columns that stretch out into the sea. Another legend recounts the time Finn McCool scooped up part of Ireland to throw it at an adversary. It missed, landed in the Irish Sea and became the Isle of Man.

The couple became active in the local community. As with many customer-initiated fundraisers, they sponsored St. Baldrick's Foundation, a childhood cancer charity. The first year they raised $12,000; five years later in 2012 they raised $130,000. They sponsored a volleyball, a cricket, a softball team and two soccer teams. They even managed to overcome the intense tribal rivalries that exist among soccer fans in Europe, and in the process became known as the soccer pub of New Orleans. "We wanted to emphasize the importance of getting along," recalls Stephen. The decibels were quite elevated during

televised matches, and supporters of opposing teams were even able to sit peacefully on adjacent stools.

Then there were the games, some silly, some challenging, all fun. Monday trivia nights, patterned after practices in many pubs in Ireland, became very popular. Give a silly answer and a participant had to wear a dunce cap. As many as 20 teams played each night, with team names that should not be repeated in print. The annual writing contest, where each writer had to use the same ten words in the text, led to publication of the results in book form due to the high quality of the entries. Weekly dart and pool leagues helped keep the place lively. More games on St Patrick's Day were uproariously entertaining such as the contest to see who could hold a full pitcher of beer at arm's length the longest and cabbage bowling in the street.

As with the public houses in the old days in Ireland, Finn McCool's was a gathering place rather than just a bar where people went to drink. It is fair to say that the Pattersons and their pub were well-loved in the neighborhood.

When Hurricane Katrina came ashore with devastating force early on August 29, 2005, the city was not prepared for the costliest natural disaster in the nation's history. The Mid-City neighborhood was severely flooded after the eye of the storm passed to the north of the city. Much of New Orleans had already flooded as the levees that separate New Orleans from

ABOVE: The walls are covered with memorabilia and personal souvenirs, some salvaged from Hurricane Katrina's waters. The Lee-Enfield rifle was a gift of a neighbor and gun collector who recovered the rifle after it remained under water for eight weeks. The Lee-Enfield rifle was used by British troops in the first half of the last century

RIGHT: McCool's sign represents the four historical Irish provinces: Ulster, Munster, Connacht and Leinster. Today they have no legal status having been replaced by a system of counties. They have significance in the sporting world, however, as some teams are associated with the provinces.

surrounding lakes failed one after the other, releasing torrents of water into the city. After the storm passed, surge levels in many parts of the city began to drop but Lake Pontchartrain remained swollen. Water continued to leak into the city until September 1 when the lake level was equal to the flood waters.

Finn McCool's had six feet of water inside and eight feet outside. The Pattersons were allowed to return to their neighborhood eight weeks later, once the water had receded. They had to gut the building. Stephen, his brother, Pauline and three friends started to gut the building at 8:00am; by noon 25 friends and neighbors were pitching in. After dark, neighbors' cars surrounded the pub with their headlights on as people worked through the night hauling mud and debris out of the pub and into the street for pick-up by the Federal Emergency Management Agency, FEMA. By December the building had been stripped to its frame and the owners threw a big snacks and warm beer party for the neighbors, warm because the electricity was not restored until mid-February. The gas was not turned on for more than a year. By the end of the party, there

were more beer and snacks on hand than they started with as residents contributed whatever they could muster.

Then, the phoenix began rising anew. The Pattersons did much of the work themselves because so few people had returned to the neighborhood after the storm, but those that were on hand pitched in. The pub reopened on Saint Patrick's Day, March 17, 2006, with, of course, a big celebration. The new bar stools arrived 90 minutes after the pub re-opened, so customers had to unwrap their own stools. For neighbors working on their own devastated houses, the reopening of their local, much loved pub was highly therapeutic.

Pauline and Stephen are still somewhat amazed at the extent to which their community pub has been adopted by Irish expats and New Orleans natives. Their generous spirit and genuine caring for others has endured through tragedy and triumph, proving the old adage that what goes around, comes around.

With 30 stools the bar can accommodate a goodly number of enthusiastic soccer fans. Supporters of opposing teams sit side-by-side peacefully watching televised games, something not often witnessed in Europe. Five TVs provide pub visitors with ample viewing choices. A dozen small tables scattered about the pub offer additional seating.

What We Love About Finns

WHEN WE ASK PEOPLE what they love about Finns they always come up with great lists. They include the excellent bartenders, the inexpensive drinks, the lively atmosphere and the community feel.

Rarely do they ask us what we love about it. Let me tell you. It's the customers. They are truly brilliant.

We know we have the best staff but we also know we have the best customers in the world.

They are more than customers they are friends. We love spending time with them and that makes our time at work actually not feel like work at all.

We have made lifelong friendships here and Finns would not be Finns without them.

Pauline Patterson
Co-owner

Four Green Fields

TAMPA, FLORIDA

It's about the roof

Is the glass half full or half empty? It depends on whether you are drinking or pouring.
—Bill Cosby

WHEN STOCKBROKER COLIN BREEN COULD not find any Irish music in Tampa 20 years ago, he solved the problem the old-fashioned way: he built an Irish pub. His parents were from Tipperary, and he grew up listening to Irish music. Famed singer/composer Tommy Makem was one of his favorites.

Colin knew exactly what he wanted: a true Irish pub with no TVs, where conversation would reign supreme. He says, "If a TV is on, people will sit around and stare. That's not what an Irish pub should be." Once the concrete slab was poured for his pub, Colin took a piece of chalk and marked off an irregular seven-sided bar that would encourage cross-angle conversation. In a pinch, as many as 60 stools can fit around the bar, each one with a clear sightline to the music stage. The roof had to be thatched, just like the country cottages in Ireland. Seminole Indians were hired to install the roof. The traditional Seminole dwelling is covered with palm leaves, and some of the Indians' skills could be transferred to thatching.

The pub quickly became a local landmark. In large part because of its unique roof, Colin has never had to advertise. Also, the pub is ideally located in upscale Hyde Park where it takes advantage of its eclectic surroundings. Across the Hillsborough River are the busy Tampa Convention Center, Tampa Bay Times Forum, Tampa Cruise Ship Terminal and Tampa General Hospital. Nearby is The University of Tampa and MacDill Air Force Base, home of the Central Command, Special Operations Command and US Marine Forces Central Command. These institutions provide a steady after-work crowd for the pub where promotions, retirements and birthday celebrations often take place.

The pub is known locally for its sponsorship of the Four Green Fields Running Club, started several years ago by a small group of dedicated military officers. Every Tuesday, some of the 4000 members enjoy a 5K run followed by a friendly pint at the pub. Usually some 80—130 attendees representing all ages and walks of life in Tampa take part. The pub also sponsors the Four Green Fields Ice Hockey Team.

Tommy Makem's haunting 1967 song *Four Green Fields* referring to Ireland's four provinces following the partition of the country in the 1920s served as inspiration for the pub's name. Both Dennis Lehane, author of Mystic River, and crime writer Michael Connelly have appeared at the pub, and Connelly has mentioned the pub in some of his novels.

The pub's interior consists of one large, dimly lit square room with numerous small round tables decorated with maps of Ireland and fitted out with wicker chairs. Hurling, Gaelic football and rugby jerseys hang over the bar. Windows are small, as befits an Irish country cottage, some clear, others with colorful stained glass designs. Hardly a bare spot exists on the walls. "You need to give people something to look at," says Colin. A long row of framed caricatures of

customers from the 1990s lines one wall along with dozens of old newspaper articles, many of which recite battles that occurred during the Irish Civil War and other encounters. While true that former activist and current Sinn Féin political party leader Gerry Adams spoke at the pub during Florida tours in 1995 and 1999 and is a friend today, times have changed, and Adams is an elected official in a peaceful land. "That period was part of our history," says Colin. "It is not being political to recognize it, and thankfully now we have peace."

The thatched roof is what people most remember about their first visit to the pub.* The original roof was replaced in 2010 by master thatcher Colin McGhee, member of the traditional guild, the East Anglia Master Thatchers Association in England. Working with one assistant, he replaced the original roof in about four weeks.

At the tender age of seven during a visit to Scotland, Colin saw the historic roof of poet Robert Burns being rethatched and decided then that a thatcher's life was the life for him. He left school in Cumberland, England at age 16 and worked for six years as an apprentice thatcher, before becoming a journeyman and ultimately a master. Today, Colin lives in West Virginia and is kept busy by those who appreciate the esthetic as well as economic value that a genuine thatched roof can bring to a property. Properly maintained, a thatched roof is as fireproof as a treated cedar shingle roof.

Colin used phragmites for the Four Green Fields roof. This is a common water reed that can easily grow to six or seven feet tall. The plant, which grows abundantly in many parts of the world including the New Jersey Meadowlands, is waxy and holds up to humidity. However, skilled reed cutters are lacking in the United States, so Colin imported the reeds from Turkey where they constitute an important cash crop. The result of his commitment to his unique craft is a beautiful, hand-built roof that if well maintained will last for more than half a century.

*The name Four Green Fields and the pub's thatched roof design are trademarks of Four Green Fields Holding, LLC.

Nothing Can Match Thatch

Thatch is one of the most common roofing materials in the world, especially prevalent in parts of Africa, Asia and Latin America. Builders have installed thatched roofs routinely in Europe since early medieval times. Prior to the commercial availability of slate and metal in the 19th century, thatched roofs were the basis of rural European construction. After suffering a period of decline in popularity in the 19th and 20th centuries, thatched roofs have enjoyed a resurgence in Europe and to a lesser extent in the United States where they have become a mark of affluence, as they are more expensive than asbestos or slate roofs.

Almost any vegetation can be gathered, bundled and secured to a wood framework to create a thatched roof. A well-applied thatched roof can last for 70 years with minor maintenance every few years. Factors such as climate, material employed, pitch of the roof, topography and most importantly, the skill of the thatcher, will affect the roof's longevity. In modern times, old thatch is normally removed before applying a new roof. In Europe, however, thatch was traditionally applied over an existing roof. In some cases, centuries of accumulated thatch has resulted in roofs more than six feet thick. In developing countries, thatch provides weatherproof roofing, and sometimes walls, built with locally available materials at reasonable cost.

Today, thatchers commonly utilize tall-stemmed wheat straw and water reeds, which are harvested in winter when stalks are dry. Reed roofs generally outlast those made of straw. Some Indian tribes in the United States use palmetto leaves.

To make a thatched roof, the material is gathered, tied into bundles about two feet in circumference and wired to the roof structure in overlapping layers starting from the bottom of the roof.

Because it is dense like a book, a thatched roof does not burn easily. Also, reeds and straw are pretreated with fire retardants. Since it is so compact, a thatched roof is a natural insulator, helping keep a building cool in summer and warm in winter.

The Green Dragon Tavern

BOSTON MASSACHUSETTS

This is Not Your Father's Bar; It's Your Forefather's Bar

Beer, if drank with moderation, softens the temper, cheers the spirit, and promotes health.
     -Thomas Jefferson

SOME WOULD SAY THAT THE American Revolution began at The Green Dragon Tavern. Samuel Adams, Paul Revere, John Hancock, Daniel Webster and other revolutionaries were familiar faces at the tavern in the 1770s. They met there frequently to discuss resistance to the British Crown and Parliament. It was there that a 13-year-old kitchen boy overheard two British officers discussing plans to capture Sam Adams and John Hancock and to seize Lexington and Concord. The youth alerted the tavern owner who passed the intelligence to The Sons of Liberty, thus setting the stage for Paul Revere's famous ride and the Boston Tea Party.

Deemed the "Headquarters of the Revolution," The Green Dragon continued to play a role throughout the war. Redcoats of course, were no longer welcome once the war began. Although Irish immigration did not peak until the Great Potato Famine of the mid-1800s, Irish soldiers accounted for nearly half of General Washington's Continental Army.

The original pub was built in 1657 in the oldest existing section of Boston. The pub was razed in 1854 and was reestablished around the corner on the oldest street in Boston in a building dating back to the same period as the original. The new location had at one time been a tapestry shop. John Hancock lived next door. The neighborhood consists of narrow alleyways, even a secret passage way behind the pub. Corners were so tight that wheel-high cutouts were made in buildings to allow carriages to make turns. The pub is a favorite spot for locals, school outings and tourists who value the rich history as well as the decor. When he opened the pub in 1993, John Somers went to great lengths to fill it with authentic Revolutionary War relics. So many fascinating pictures and rare objects adorn the walls that the pub could be billed as a museum.

John came to the United States at the age of 20 from Finuge, a traditional crossroads village consisting of thatched roof cottages, a pub and general store, near Listowel in County Kerry. His father had owned a pub in London before moving his family to a farm in Ireland. John always had a knack for music and was blessed with a beautiful singing voice. He taught himself to play a range of musical instruments, and on St Patrick's Day he can be coaxed into entertaining pub patrons with a song or two at the Green Dragon or one of several other pubs he owns in Boston. With the pub's rich history, John is correct in saying "The Green Dragon is not your father's bar, it is your forefather's bar."

The pub is a family business. John's daughter Noelle manages some of the Somers pubs where in her words "pouring the proper pint is a beautiful process and is especially important since Boston is the Irish capital of the US."

ABOVE: It may be raining outside, but a warm welcome awaits inside in this inviting corner.

After a day of bringing the rebellious town of Boston to heel, a British soldier needed to relax. Here a red coated crown officer treats himself to a local libation at the Green Dragon. Michael Szkolka, a college professor who guides tours along the Freedom Trail, enjoys a pint in his battle uniform belonging to the First Regiment of Foot Guards, today the Grenadier Guards. British soldiers wore bright uniforms to be seen by their own soldiers. Muskets were not accurate, and a soldier's greatest risk was from friendly fire. Once war broke out, His Majesty's soldiers were no longer welcome at the tavern.

My Da

My Da has been in the pub business all his life. Born near Listowel, County Kerry, Dad spent his early years working in hotels and restaurants owned by his family in Kerry and London, where he was educated. After an exploratory year in The United States in 1971, he returned to Listowel and opened a pub before heading back across the pond the following year. His return was not quite career driven, "I had met a woman in Boston and I told her that I'd come back and marry her" he explains. "She had my heart and I loved her deeply." Ann and John have been married for thirty-seven years and have four children. They live in a 200-year-old farmhouse outside of Boston. The family keeps horses and Dad indulges in his favorite hobbies—collecting antiques and horseback riding.

On his return to America in the early seventies, having determined that the hotel and restaurant business was not for him, John put his talents for music to good use, touring the country with the renowned "Masons Apron," a career that he successfully followed for fifteen years. Finally, feeling a responsibility to his family Dad decided to settle in Boston and turned to the business that he knew best—the bar trade.

In 1991, Dad opened his first establishment, a traditional Irish bar called Mr. Dooleys in Boston's financial district. With a great leap of faith, he put everything that he had into the venture. It was so successful that two years later he was able to open his next venture, the Green Dragon Tavern. Since then he has opened a new business every three years.

Throughout his career Dad has received many accolades, notably "The most successful Businessman in Boston", The Irish Voice Newspaper; "The Boston Restaurant Magnate", The Boston Herald; and one of the top "Power Players in Boston", 2005 Stuff @ Night Magazine. In 2000, he was awarded the prestigious "Dreamer of Dreams" Award by the New York based Irish Voice.

When time allows Dad can be seen belting a tune or two in any one of his locations. A regular in Fenway Park, he has been called upon more than once to sing the National Anthem at the start of a game. But by far, his greatest mark of respect comes from his business peers and fellow Irishmen where he is hailed "The Dean of Irish Pubs!"

I am very proud of my Da.

Noelle Somers, COO
Somers Pubs

War Begins

After defeating France in the French and Indian War in 1763, the British Government wanted to provide peacetime jobs for thousands of its soldiers and have the American colonies pay for the program. The Parliament passed the notorious Stamp Act of 1765 to raise funds from the Colonies, which led to public demonstrations initially in Massachusetts but which quickly spread to other colonies.

That same year, a group of Boston shopkeepers and artisans called for organized resistance to the Stamp Act. As the group expanded, it became known as the Sons of Liberty. Soon similar organizations were set up in almost every colony, led overtly or behind the scenes by prominent men in the community. Over time, the various Sons of Liberty groups began to correspond with each other and established a larger, more cohesive organization. In 1767 the group adopted a formal flag consisting of five red and four white vertical stripes.

The seminal event organized by the Sons of Liberty was the December 16, 1773 Boston Tea Party led by Samuel Adams. It was a catalyst for the start of war and a principal reason why the Revolutionary War began in Massachusetts.

The Irish Bank

SAN FRANCISCO, CALIFORNIA

Away from the Frenzied Crowd

No poems can live long or please that are written by water-drinkers.
— Horace (65 – 8BC)

Turn into the narrow, shadowy alley in San Francisco's financial district, and you are unexpectedly transported to the Irish countryside. It is as if you stumbled upon a small cottage somewhere in the green hills of Ireland. The Irish Bank—we'll talk about its name in a minute—indeed is like a country cottage with its whitewashed exterior, low ceilings, well-worn floors, reclaimed bare brick walls and heavy wood beam ceilings. Yet it is just a few meters away from the jostling crowds of seriously suited bankers and investment advisors, tourists and shoppers on Grant Street.

The exterior is a work of art. The façade is festooned with an improbable collection of road signs from the Irish countryside, advertisements, brass plaques and flower pots. Elaborate iron gates guard the doors, and patrons can rest on sturdy wrought iron benches between the pub's two main entrances. A 19th century water pump sits in the alley, reminiscent of the type of pump once common in rural Ireland. In Ireland "rag and bone men" gathered these items and other collectibles found inside the pub. Long a tradition in

Ireland and some other countries, rag and bone men scavenged unwanted rags, bones, metal and trinkets and sold them to merchants. The interior consists of two rooms, kitchen and patio in the manner of an Irish cottage, and is jammed with antiques and collectibles throughout. It even has a confessional.

Every morning at 10:00, tables and chairs for the alfresco lunch crowd are placed in the alley, which only sees sunlight briefly during the summer months. After work, up to 200 patrons cram into the pub on their way home. The Irish Bank is a conversational bar. "People come in for lunch and spend the day," says co-owner Ronan O'Neill who with his partner Peter Friel and Peter's wife Stephanie Perry took over the pub in 2005. On the floors above the pub are 28 chic one-bedroom apartments. The neighborhood was not always upscale; in fact, when the pub was opened in 1996 by two gentlemen from Dublin, the area was quite rundown. In the past decade the neighborhood has experienced a rebirth.

The building was heavily damaged by and rebuilt after the great 1906 San Francisco earthquake, which destroyed 80 percent of the city and resulted in more than 3,000 deaths. The area surrounding the pub was once the purview of bootleggers. With the passage of the Eighteenth Amendment to the Constitution in 1920, sales of alcoholic beverages were illegal, giving rise to thousands of speakeasies throughout the United States, many in urban Irish and other immigrant neighborhoods. Bootleggers transported the moonshine to the speakeasies, sometimes called blind-pigs, evading police in the narrow alleyways of downtown San Francisco.

Ronan comes from Clifton, a town on Ireland's west coast in County Galway. His grandfather was a multitalented man: farmer, undertaker, politician, and owner of a bicycle shop and paint shop. He served on the Galway County Council for 25 years. Ronan's parents, brothers and sister still live in the town. Peter, a carpenter by training, is from the small village of Kerrykeel in County Donegal. This is the northernmost county in Ireland, where his ancestors have lived since the 5th or 6th century and where his brother operates the family farm. It is a small farm like all the others in the region, but farmers have free access to thousands of acres of hill country owned by the government for their cattle and sheep.

The first owners named their pub The Bank of Ireland. Back in Dublin, executives at The Bank of Ireland were not amused. They objected to having their distinguished name applied to a pub in America. On one side, a hallowed institution anxious to prevent dilution of its good name; on the other side, two young Irishmen anxious to introduce a bit of the old country to San Francisco. The Bank of Ireland went to court claiming the little pub in the alley was causing "irreparable harm" to the corporation. Net result, the name was officially changed to The Irish Bank Bar and Restaurant.

The favorite saying around the pub is Find the Soul of Ireland in the Heart of San Francisco—and with good reason.

OPPOSITE, TOP: The long bar.

OPPOSITE, BOTTOM: Early morning is time for cleaning the well-worn floors. Some of the tables were made from early 1900s Singer sewing machines from Ireland.

BELOW: The pub even boasts a confessional. Inside are a table and two pews for private dining.

The Irish Inn

GLEN ECHO, MARYLAND
Premier Location

Eat not to dullness; drink not to elevation.
-Benjamin Franklin

IT IS AN UNANTICIPATED PLEASURE to stumble upon a pretty Irish country cottage in the upscale neighborhood of Glen Echo situated at the end of Massachusetts Avenue, a main artery into the heart of the nation's capital. The area is home to many federal workers, making it largely immune to the vagaries of economic cycles, which is good for publicans Christy and Libby Hughes, owners of the Irish Inn at Glen Echo.

Even more surprising, the pub is comfortably settled on a small knoll a stone's throw from the entrance to a park housing one the best preserved Denzel carousels in the country. Five generations of the Denzel family have built carousels since the early 1800s.

Old-timers who frequent the pub proudly claim that little has changed in the neighborhood since the 1930s when a tavern was opened at the end of Prohibition. The neighborhood in this case includes the minute town of Glen Echo, population 255 in the 2010 census, and nearby sections of Bethesda. Well, some changes have taken place—occasional coats of paint or additions

ABOVE: The bar.

RIGHT: This 1921 Denzel carousel in Glen Echo Park is a stone's throw from the Irish Inn. It is called a "menagerie carousel" because it is made up of many different hand-carved wood animals: 40 horses, giraffe, lion, tiger, deer, four ostriches, four rabbits and two chariots. It is installed in a twelve sided canopy building. The Denzel family began making carousels in the early 1800s in Germantown, PA.

built on to the tidy pre-World War II slate-roofed houses, and a few new houses squeezed in, but little else.

The preponderance of light oak paneling, tartan backed booths, burgundy walls and white table cloths create a pleasantly airy interior that seats up to 190 for food or drink in the bar area and the two level restaurant. An additional forty patrons can take advantage of nice weather on the canopied deck.

Christy has been in the pub business for 47 years, so he appreciates the importance of regular customers, some of whom stop by three times a week. He was raised on a small farm in Ballymahon, in the southern part of County Longford. At the age of 16 he was awarded a scholarship to Saint Mary's Catering College in Athenry, County Galway, which helps explain why quality food preparation has always been a priority. "Irish cooking has come a long way from the early days, both in Ireland and abroad," he says.

It is said that the inn is haunted by the ghosts of a woman and her four children

tragically killed when the house that preceded the original tavern burned down in 1930. Since then the building has experienced several incarnations, first the tavern from 1931 to 1944, then Otto's Grill until 1964 when it became Trav's Roadhouse. In 1986 the space became a fashionable restaurant known as The Inn at Glen Echo. It closed in 2002 giving the Hughes an opportunity to open their pub the following year after extensive renovations to the building. Christy and Libby had previously owned and operated two Irish pubs, Ireland's Four Provinces in Washington, DC and Falls Church, VA.

The pub has won Irish Pub of the Year Awards from the influential Washingtonian Magazine several times and is a co-sponsor of the annual Labor Day weekend Irish Music and Dance Showcase in Glen Echo Park.

"Irish pubs are fun," says Christy. "You don't have to pretend that you are someone else. That is the secret of their success."

ABOVE: A dining room reminiscent of an Irish country inn.

LEFT: First introduced in 1914, this is one of three operational Wurlitzer Style 165 military band organs known to exist. The Glen Echo organ, installed in 1926, contains 256 pipes, including bass drum with cymbal, snare drum, crash cymbal, triangle, castanets, a glockenspiel, 88 violin pipes, 12 bass pipes, 14 viola pipes, 14 saxophone pipes, 6 trombone pipes, 14 trumpet pipes, 22 flageolet pipes, 22 flute pipes and 44 piccolo pipes. It is operated by perforated paper music rolls and compressed air generated by four leather bellows. John Philip Souza never sounded better!

Johnny Foley's Irish House

SAN FRANCISCO, CALIFORNIA

Urban retreat on a grand scale

Work is the curse of the drinking classes.
— Oscar Wilde

A SPRY MAN IN HIS early 80s, Johnny Foley is a living legend in the San Francisco Irish community, so much so that when Martin and Mary Connolly opened their pub they named it after Johnny. Folks tell many stories about Johnny and his beautiful tenor voice, like the time he sang his way out of jail by summoning up a tune for the judge.

The story goes like this: One night Johnny was singing the lovely Irish favorite, The Green Glens of Antrim, at a pub in the city's Mission District. Carried away, he continued for more than 20 minutes after closing time. The frustrated bartender finally got Johnny out the door into the street where he finished the song to the applause of the considerable crowd who had followed him into the street. The police were less enthusiastic, however, and arrested Johnny for disturbing the peace. Appearing the next day before the judge, Johnny told his story. The dubious judge demanded that Johnny sing for him and was so impressed that he banged his gavel and declared "case dismissed."

Sharing a pint with Johnny in one of the pub's small meeting rooms is one of life's pleasures. At 5'2" Johnny's improbably powerful voice can silence any room in seconds. He might have had a successful singing career had it not been for a stop at

a pub en route to sing on the famous Arthur Godfrey Television Show many years ago. When he finally arrived at the studio slightly inebriated, show producers would not allow him to go on the air.

Johnny was born and raised in Waterford City, famous for its beautiful lead crystal since 1793. (Lead crystal contains between 24 and 35 percent lead oxide, which gives the glass its well-known sparkle.) He worked as a typesetter for the Waterford News for many years for before immigrating to the US in 1953 via Canada. He first went to Chicago, then to San Francisco practicing his profession in the days when newspapers were still hand set using hot lead. Digital technology eliminated the need for typesetters, and Johnny at age 52 became a day laborer. "I never had to go to the gym to work out," he says with a grin.

Johnny Foley's is San Francisco's largest Irish pub. It occupies a choice location between fabled Union Square and downtown hotels, mixing old world Irish and new world visitors. On a busy night, the pub will fill its main floor, The Cellar—which hosts a dueling piano show, and its private room—The Parlour—with up to 400 people, accommodating both tourists and locals. Always loquacious and grinning, ever-present Johnny will burst into song with just a little prodding and a Guinness or two.

Built after the devastating 1906 earthquake, the building has known several incarnations.

From 1935 to 1947, Charles Fashion Store occupied the space. From 1947 to 1997, Bordelli's Italian Restaurant was a favorite evening destination. The upper floors were originally a 60-unit lodging house for shipbuilders and post-earthquake construction workers.

The ornate Victorian lathe and plaster ceilings and cornices are particularly noteworthy. Stained glass and wood panel partitions divide the enormous space into convenient seating areas. The black and white tile floor covering most of the first floor is characteristic of the era, and the wooden portions show the wear and patina of generations of foot traffic. The bar is divided into several sections which creates

visual interest and encourages conversation. A well-known portrait of the Mona Lisa holding a pint of Guinness fills one wall.

Owners Martin and Mary Connolly are natives of County Cork where Martin played football (soccer) at the county level for Cork and won two prestigious All-Ireland medals at the Under 21 level. They moved to the US and met in the Gaelic Park athletic facility in the Bronx, New York. In 1990 they ventured west to San Francisco where Martin worked for Guinness, and Mary worked in various hotels and restaurants. In 1998 they opened Johnny Foleys.

The business is managed by Kate Hickey who comes from the Cricklewood section of London, long a destination for Irish immigrants, first during the 1850s famine and more recently in the 1950s and 1960s recession that was particularly severe in Ireland. Kate's parents met at the Galtymore Dance Hall which was partitioned into two sections, traditional Irish music on one side and rock and roll on the other. For more than half a century, the dance hall was a home away from home for Irish immigrants until it closed for good in 2008.

If you want to experience a large urban Irish pub in the Dublin style, you can do no better than spend some hours at Johnny Foley's Irish House.

ABOVE: Johnny Foley's clock and sign are familiar San Francisco landmarks.

OPPOSITE, TOP: Johnny Foley enjoys a pint. His remarkable tenor voice and the Irish twinkle in his eye have made him a living legend in San Francisco.

OPPOSITE, BOTTOM Portrait of Mona Lisa enjoying a pint of Guinness. Is this why she is smiling?

Kells Irish Restaurant and Pub

PORTLAND, OREGON

At the Top of the List

Give my people plenty of beer, good beer and cheap beer, and you will have no revolution.
-Queen Victoria

FEW IRISH PUBS HAVE APPEARED on as many Top Ten lists as Kells, and with good reason. Its history is absorbing, the exterior and interior delight the eyes, and its entertainment is top of the line. It even has its own double-decker bus. Its success is an enduring tribute to the owners Gerard and Lucille McAleese.

To fully appreciate Kells, we must go back in history. Portland was founded in 1845 and quickly prospered, fueled by successful merchants catering to a population made wealthy from commerce and timber. Anxious to be the equal of the great cities of Europe and the Eastern United States, Portland's early leaders embraced cast iron-fronted architecture. Cast iron could be shaped into many intricate designs to create opulent facades more economically than traditional stone or brick. Between the 1850s and the late 1880s, 90 percent of commercial buildings constructed in Portland utilized pre-fabricated cast iron components, most employing decorative elements manufactured by local foundries. Only the Soho district in New York City has more cast iron buildings.

The craze eventually died out as Portland's architects adopted the Chicago style

The striking Kells façade is an outstanding example of late 19th century cast iron construction. Photo courtesy of Diego G. Diaz.

architecture with its steel framed buildings with masonry facades. The 1889 Glisan Building, which houses Kells, was the last cast iron building constructed in Portland and marked the end of an era. It was built by well-known physician Rodney Glisan who was married to the daughter of one of the founders of Portland. He was a pioneering surgeon who published widely and delivered lectures in Europe and elsewhere.

The Glisan Building is quite large, measuring 102 feet by 50 feet. The ground floor is divided into two main sections, a vast bar area and an ample dining room embellished with nine crystal chandeliers. Massive old growth fir beams are 8 by 14 inches by 52 feet long. The beautiful fir floor in the dining room is original, more than 120 years old, as is the ceiling. It was matched perfectly when the ceiling in the bar was replaced in 1990 due to damage to the wood over the years. It was Gerard and Lucille's goal to restore the ceiling to its previous grand condition. The 26 foot Honduran mahogany bar hugs the high five-shelf wall opposite a brick wall festooned with sports trophies and Irish memorabilia. The ceiling in the bar is covered with dollar bills contributed by patrons and "magically" stuck to the ceiling by the Kells staff. Once a year the bills are swept away and donated to charity.

A wide carpeted staircase leads from the street to the second floor. Dr. Glisan may have used the ample upstairs rooms for his offices, or, as some suggest, as a boarding house. The 1,500-square-foot ballroom, with its original pine floor and large skylights, provides banquet facilities for 120, or 250 standing. Three smaller tastefully appointed dining rooms and a large kitchen complete the setting.

Gerard notes proudly that the pub was smoke free before local ordinances required it; however, he is equally proud of the basement cigar room, which he labels one of Portland's coziest hideaways with its own cigar menu.

Portland is known as the brewpub capital of

"Green rain" falls from Kells' ceiling sweep every February. Dollar bills contributed by patrons and stuck to the ceiling are swept away annually with the money, matched by the pub, going to a local charity. The person guessing the closest to the amount wins a prize. Last year more than $8,700 was collected and matched by Kells, with an impressive $210,000 amassed over 15 years, thanks to the generosity of Kells' patrons and matching funds from Gerard and Lucille McAleese.

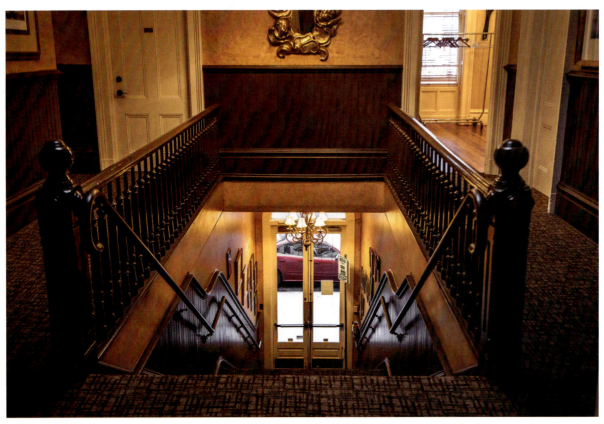

the world with more than 70 microbreweries and brewpubs. True to that tradition, Kells brews its own beers: Kells Lager, Kells Red Ale and Kells IPA as well as unique seasonal beers throughout the year at its new Brewpub in NW Portland.

Gerard was born in Belfast. He came to the US with his parents at age 20 and played semiprofessional soccer in San Francisco until he suffered an injury. He and his mother opened the first Kells in Seattle in 1983 two years after arriving in the United States. He and Lucille opened the Portland location in 1990. Gerard's brother opened a third Kells in San Francisco in 1998. Gerard opened the 4th Kells location, Kells Brewpub, in Portland in the spring of 2012, with his son Garrett.

Since childhood, Gerard wanted to own a double-decker bus. One day while on a trip to Mt. Hood, he passed a beat-up 1997 Bristol bus for sale. He immediately bought it, restored it and made it part of the Kells experience. He knew instinctively that the vehicle would be the perfect complement to the pub's sponsorship of serious amateur men's and women's soccer teams and youth soccer programs. The vivid green and white bus takes as many as 70 sports fans to every professional Portland Timbers soccer game and to Trail Blazers basketball games. When not used for games, the bus hosts private outings around the stunning Northwest region.

You don't have to be Irish to recognize that the pub's name is derived from The Book of Kells, the famous masterpiece of Western calligraphy produced circa 800 by Celtic monks. The lavishly illustrated manuscript depicts the four Christian gospels and is on permanent display at Trinity College Library in Dublin

OPPOSITE PAGE: The Kells bus is a familiar site at major sporting events. Photo courtesy of Andy Davies.

ABOVE: A stairway leads from the street to the second floor that was possibly a boarding house or doctor's office before the turn of the last century..

Kelly's Westport Inn

KANSAS CITY, MISSOURI

The Poor Man's Playground

Life itself is the proper binge.   -Julia Child

THIS IS AN INSPIRATIONAL STORY of how one Irish immigrant, blessed with personality and perseverance, came to America, married, raised a family and established one of the most successful Irish pubs in the oldest building in Kansas City.

The story really begins when the structure housing the pub was built in 1850 as a general store catering to the needs of wagon trains heading west on the Oregon Trail and Santa Fe Trail. The building has had many owners over the decades, including Daniel Boone's grandson Albert who operated a trading post in the late 1850s. Boone sold the store which had a succession of owners until 1904 when brothers John and Jake Wiedenmann opened a grocery which they operated for more than 20 years. After Prohibition ended in 1933, the Wrestler's Inn, which featured live wrestling matches, obtained a liquor license and became the first saloon to occupy the space. Following World War II three retired Kansas City police captains bought the bar and named it the Westport Inn. Westport, today a historic neighborhood in Kansas City, was originally its own town. Randal Kelly, a young Irish immigrant, was hired in 1947 as a bartender, and the family saga began.

Randal was one of those unforgettable characters whose personality added spice to the lives of everyone he met. The youngest of five children, he was born in 1905 in the small coastal town of Kilrush, County Clare. As soon as he reached 21 he headed to America and worked on the docks in New York City before heading to San Francisco where he found work as a bartender. He served as a mechanic in the Army during World War II. When the war ended, he stopped in Kansas City en route back to California, where he met his future wife Margaret, at a USO dance, and understandably decided to put down roots in that city which had a large Irish immigrant population.

After working in the Westport Inn for only seven months Randal bought out one of the partners. In 1977 he became sole owner and the name was changed to Kelly's Westport Inn. This was natural since people had been calling the business Kelly's informally for more than twenty years. Randal referred to his bar as the poor man's playground, remembering his own humble beginnings. He dispensed beer, wit and wisdom six nights a week behind the bar, kept his prices low and gave food and a sawbuck here and there to folks in need.

The bar became so popular that Randal closed the doors on St Patrick's Day—which attracts a quarter million people to the city—for many years because he was afraid someone would be hurt in the crush. Robert Briscoe, the Lord Mayor of Dublin, visited Kansas City in the early 1960s and couldn't get into Kelly's because of the crowd; Randal had to greet him in the street.

Randal's two sons, Kyle and Pat grew up working in the pub and showed a similar knack for making customers feel welcome. When Randal died in 1988, his sons took over the business. Kyle's daughter and son, Colleen and Mitch help run the business. One day it will be their turn to carry on the traditions that have made Kelly's a Kansas City landmark.

A Personal Reflection

On Christmas Eve 2012 I worked the day shift and then met up with my family to eat dinner. My Mom asked me how work was and I replied, "It was a lot of fun." My Aunt laughed and said, "I don't know if I have ever responded to that question with the word fun." It was an eye opener for me. I am so blessed. I love working with my family, my co-workers are my friends, and my customers remind me that in general human beings are good. On a weekly basis I walk into work and think, "I am one of the owners of Kelly's." I am Randal Kelly's granddaughter. While I have very few memories of him, I have heard 100+ stories that make me proud to call him my Grandpa. His legacy of being generous, down to earth and witty lives on through my Dad and Uncle and hopefully one day through my brother Mitch and me. I can only hope that decades from now I will have left a legacy that will make my grandchildren as proud.

Colleen Kelly

PREVIOUS SPREAD: The historic building that is home to Kelly's Westport Inn was constructed in 1850 and designated a national historic landmark in 1972. Some people believe the building is haunted because of the mysterious figures in two of the upper windows. In fact, they are paper mache Union and Confederate soldiers used in the annual Westport Parade in the 1950s. An all-weather patio was added to the pub a few years ago on top of a single story addition built in the late 19th century.

LEFT: View toward the front of the pub where covered wagons once passed. The first settlers arrived in the area in 1831, attracted by the location of a potential boat landing on the bend in the Missouri River where it meets the Kaw (Kansas) River. At the foot of dramatic limestone and loess bluffs, Westport Landing was an ideal location for outfitting fur trappers, Indian traders and immigrants heading west by covered wagon. In 1897, the town of Westport was annexed by Kansas City.

TOP: The main bar area. Patrons sit on high backed swivel stools. At work behind the bar is Mark Weber. Mark started at Kelly's on July 4th weekend, 1976.

The Kerry Irish Pub

NEW ORLEANS, LOUISIANA
Wears its History Well

The greater the obstacle, the more glory in overcoming it.   —Molière

HURRICANE KATRINA CHANGED THE LIVES of millions of people forever. It is an understatement to say that all residents of New Orleans, whether they evacuated prior to the storm as they were urged to do, or rode out the storm, have compelling, frequently nightmarish, stories to tell.

The Kerry Irish Pub owner Doris Bastiansen, a Louisiana native, chose not to leave town. After all, New Orleans had seen more than its fair share of tropical storms, and living with them was nothing new. When conditions rapidly deteriorated and staying behind was no longer feasible, she made her way to the Ursuline Sisters Convent, which dates back to 1752 and is home of the oldest girl's school in the United States. The refugees occupied themselves by rescuing elderly neighbors in untethered boats that the nuns snagged from the waters surrounding the convent. When the waters began to rise in their part of the city, the nuns moved food and water to the second floor where they took care of their "guests" for eight days.

As conditions continued to worsen, the Mother Superior ordered the nuns and evacuees to abandon the convent for their safety. Three boats took them to a bus which transported them to Baton Rouge where planes were waiting to take them to Ursuline convents in Illinois or Dallas. "It was an apocalypse," Doris recalls with tears in her eyes.

The city was under martial law. Doris was apprehensive when she was allowed to return to a city without electricity eight weeks after the storm. To her great surprise, she found that her pub was intact. It is in the French Quarter which is part of the 18 percent of the city that was largely undamaged by the storm. Looters had failed to gain entry thanks to the efforts of first responders who bunked in the fire station two doors down from the pub. You can imagine who were among the pub's first customers as soon as it was up and running!

Revival of the city was a tedious day by day process. Recovery workers frequented the pub to find solace amidst the tragedy, and many of them gratefully left their badges at the pub. These are displayed behind the bar.

Unfortunately, Doris and her entire family lost their homes in the Lakeview neighborhood, which became, in her words, "waterfront property."

The atmosphere after the storm was strange. There were virtually no children, houses were demolished, and no churches were open. So

---

OPPOSITE: The Kerry occupies a historic pre-Civil War building in the Greek Revival style. The exterior has been modified several times over the years. The upper floors are apartments.

BELOW: Hurricane Katrina relief workers found refuge in the pub during recovery efforts. Many left their badges behind the bar as a token of appreciation.

bars became surrogate churches, safe havens for people who spent their days trying to salvage their possessions. "They came at night," recalls Doris, "to feel normal. They spilled out their hearts here."

The pub is a New Orleans classic. Situated on the edge of the French Quarter near the docks, it is three blocks away from the madness of Bourbon Street. Non-descript on the outside and well-worn on the inside, it is small, subdued and intimate with a devoted following. The bar and brass foot rail have obviously enjoyed years of wear. Dollar bills signed by customers are tacked to the ceiling and walls above the bar. A small stage hosts musicians every night which makes it even better. It's the kind of place where a Brendan Behan or James Joyce would feel comfortable.

The entire French Quarter, officially known as the Vieux Carré, is historic. While difficult to determine the age of The Kerry building, early records show that it was sold in 1859 and served

as a rice depot in 1876. Property ownership records date back to 1722. The building reflects the Greek Revival style which was popular in New Orleans in the 1830s and 1840s antebellum period. The street was frequented by sailors, dock workers, some shady ladies and earlier by pirates. Before the Civil War the block where the The Kerry is located was opposite the docks, so it was frequented by people right off the boats. It was built on a swamp where there were no natural stones. When the Spanish galleons docked, they left behind stone ballast which was used to construct the first sidewalks in the city. The ships returned to Europe with cotton and sugar cane.

During the first half of the 19th century, many Irish immigrated to New Orleans drawn to the city to work on the construction of the New Basin Canal joining uptown New Orleans with Lake Pontchartrain. It was terrible work, and many Irish died of yellow fever during the construction. Immigrants could book direct passage from Cork to New Orleans, and many settled in the Irish Channel enclave. More Irish came during the great famine of the mid-1800s including Doris's great, great grandparents who met shipboard. The Irish are more scattered today, and the Irish Channel neighborhood is no longer predominantly Irish.

This little, some would say, hole-in-the-wall neighborhood pub has had its fair share of history and wears it very well.

ABOVE: Darts is a popular game. The alcove adds a measure of safety.

OPPOSITE, TOP: The Kerry is proud of its nightly music offerings. Here well-known artist Beth Patterson sings and accompanies herself on her electric Irish bouzouki performing her special blend of Celtic, Cajun, and original songs. Beth has been performing at The Kerry since 1994.

OPPOSITE, BOTTOM: The Kerry's well-worn bar has been a favorite around town since Kerry's first opened its doors in 1993. On the left is the bar with signed dollar bills on a column and the ceiling, pool table in the middle and music stage in the background. Note the original brick floor.

Kevin Barry's Irish Pub

SAVANNAH, GEORGIA

Required Stopping Off Place

I beg to present to you as a Christmas Gift, the City of Savannah with 150 heavy guns and plenty of ammunition and also about 25,000 bales of cotton.
  -General William Sherman, dispatch to President Lincoln, December 22, 1864

SAVANNAH WITHOUT KEVIN BARRY'S IRISH Pub is almost unthinkable. It is a link to another age, a spot that holds a special place of affection in the hearts of Savannah's many tourists, members of the military and the local population. A visit to Kevin Barry's is on just about everybody's must do list.

The pub's name is a tribute to an 18-year-old medical student from Dublin who was hanged in 1920 for his part in an Irish Republican Army operation in which three British soldiers were killed. Barry achieved iconic status due to his youth and his steadfast unwillingness to reveal IRA members who had avoided capture. Barry's story inspired Vic Power as he grew up in a mixed Irish/Italian neighborhood in Flushing, Queens in New York City. Vic and his friends often spoke of Kevin Barry and his fearless exploits during the Irish War of Independence. So, it was inevitable that when he opened his pub Vic

would name it Kevin Barry's.

Up to the time of the Civil War, Savannah was the center of East Coast cotton exports. General William Sherman captured Savannah in 1864 following his epic March to the Sea and offered up the city as a Christmas present to President Lincoln. Fortunately, since Savannah did not put up much resistance, it was spared the devastation Sherman previously inflicted on Atlanta and subsequently on Columbia, South Carolina.

Kevin Barry's pub occupies the lower three floors of one of Savannah's oldest buildings, originally a cotton warehouse dating back to the mid-1800s. The building faces the murky Savannah River and sits on a narrow strip of reclaimed marshland that was once used for rice cultivation seventeen miles upriver from the Atlantic Ocean. The top floor of the opposite side of the building opens onto the crest of a high cliff upon which rests the city of Savannah. Today, nine blocks of renovated cotton warehouses have been transformed into the city's most popular tourist attraction with hotels, restaurants, shops and an energetic nightlife.

Kevin Barry's Irish Pub opened for business in 1980. The historic brick walls had been hidden behind plaster, which was removed, and a second floor balcony was added. Four original fireplaces take the chill out of the air on blustery winter days. Iron-hard heart pine beams are original, and the 40 by 18 foot island bar is made of heart pine. Heart pine refers to the center portion of the pine tree, which is much harder than the outer sapwood. Due to its strength, heart pine was used extensively during colonial times for construction and shipbuilding, and vast forests were decimated. Today very few of the slow-growing trees remain, and most available heart pine is reclaimed from old structures.

There are no TVs in the three-story pub "so people will have to talk to one another," Vic

proudly proclaims. Irish music fills the pub seven nights a week. Noted Irish singer Frank Emerson who has sung there for 30 years says that the pub is a musical showcase, where "people truly listen to the entertainment, like in a concert hall."

One of the pub's proudest attractions is the second floor Hall of Heroes museum dedicated to members of the Armed Forces, Police and Fire Departments. The U.S. Marine Corps training facility at Parris Island is about 40 miles away, the U. S. Army 3rd Infantry Division at Fort Stewart is 30 miles away, and the 1st Battalion, 75th Ranger Regiment and 3rd Battalion, 160th Special Operations Aviation Regiment (Airborne) are headquartered in the city. These and other nearby military units appreciate the pub's commitment to the nation's service members. The POW/MIA flag flies prominently from the balcony between the US and Irish flags.

Savannah is the site of the world's second largest St Patrick's Day parade, outdone only by New York City. Savannah's parade dates back to 1813, less than a century after British General James Oglethorpe founded the Georgia colony as a haven for debtors and the poor. The three-hour parade includes more than 350 marching units and upwards of a million spectators in a city of only 140,000. Kevin Barry's is right in the midst of the fun.

ABOVE: The rectangular island bar is made of heart pine, the dense center wood of the longleaf pine tree. Vast forests of the tree once blanketed the Atlantic and Gulf Coasts. The trees were over harvested during colonial times, and few remain today. Faster growing, less desirable varieties were planted to replace the longleaf trees, which take up to 150 years to mature.

OPPOSITE: The second floor Hall of Heroes pays tribute to America's armed services from the earliest days of the nation to the present and to the nation's Police and Fire Departments.

SERIOUS MUSIC

The first time I played for Vic Power in July of 1981, I knew there was something special about Kevin Barry's, its staff and its owner. Not a television to be found. There was a large bar that promoted lively conversation about Ireland, America, religion, sex and politics. You know: all the non-controversial subjects.

There was a designated music room with a well-lit stage that showcased the musician. This was intimidating for a pub player of Celtic folk music, more used to competing for audience attention, until I realized that people were in that room because they wanted to be entertained. Chatter was at a minimum. People listened to the music. They were knowledgeable and made requests! This can put you on the spot sure, but for an entertainer—what a heavenly spot to be put on! I can tell you that after more than 40 years of performing, other venues pale beside it. This place is a reflection of the owner's convictions and beliefs in the culture and patriotic ideas and ideals of Ireland and the United States of America. That's not just my opinion. Every performer who has appeared at Kevin Barry's feels exactly the same.

Frank Emerson
Entertainer

Kevin Barry's pub occupies three floors of a historic former cotton warehouse. The American, Irish and POW/MIA flags fly from the balcony. The age-worn walls are constructed of bricks and English blue stone ballast from early ships which brought cargo to the Georgia colony. The ballast stones were dumped on the waterfront and were replaced with bales of cotton for the return trip to Europe. The building sits on a foundation of cypress logs; no steel was used in its construction. Cypress wood resists rot and was a plentiful and popular wood for building in Savannah.

The Local...

Admirable Craftmanship On A Large Scale

Quality tends to fan out like waves.
-Robert Pirsig
Zen and the Art of Motorcycle Maintenance

MINNEAPOLIS, MINNESOTA
FOR THE TRAVELER IN SEARCH of an Irish experience in Minneapolis, there is no better choice than a pair of spectacular pubs founded in the 1990s by Kieran Folliard, an enterprising young Irish immigrant from the small town of Ballyhaunis, County Mayo. Kieran's Irish Pub, which opened in 1994, was the first Irish pub in Minneapolis. It moved to its current location in 2010 in a space that had housed the famed Bellanotte Italian restaurant, once a favorite of Minnesota Vikings football players and Timberwolves basketball players. Like many nightspots in Minneapolis, the restaurant fell victim to the economic recession.

The Local followed in 1997. Known for its high ceilings and inspired decor, it is a brisk 15 minute walk from its cousin pub via the city's well-appointed skyway system. This intricate web of aerial footbridges, complete with shops and eating establishments, connects 80 blocks of downtown buildings to shield pedestrians from the city's harsh, blustery winters.

In 2011 Folliard sold his pub businesses to his longtime partners to devote his energies to his own brand of Irish whiskey which he calls 2 GINGERS. The following year, he sold this new, fast-growing company to Jim Beam Inc. and now serves as COO and Chief Irish Ambassador for the Kilbeggan Distilling Company.

The Minneapolis pubs are now led by CEO Peter Killen who grew up in troubled Northern Ireland before obtaining a degree in hotel management. He took a job with

Hilton Hotels, and during his travels around the world visited Minneapolis where he met Kieran. The two became fast friends and partners, and Peter became general manager of The Local before becoming CEO.

When it comes to sheer space, there are few pubs anywhere that can compare to Kieran's. With 10,000 square feet inside and an immense outside patio that holds 60 tables, up to 1,000 people can be accommodated comfortably. Kieran's is strategically located in the trendy Warehouse District, a block away from the First Avenue Event Facility, across from the Target Center Arena home of the Timberwolves, and a short distance from the Minnesota Twins baseball stadium. The pub can become very busy before and after major concerts and home games, says general manager Craig Wait, who worked his way through the University of Wisconsin as a bartender en route to a degree in business management. Says Peter Killen, "as an event-driven pub, sometimes 10,000 square feet is too big and sometimes it is too small."

The pub organizes numerous activities for the benefit of the community and pub patrons. Every Thanksgiving 300 of the city's needy and homeless are treated to dinner.

& Kieran's

LEFT: In the summertime people gather on The Local's sidewalk patio.

BELOW: The deceptively understated entrance to Kieran's, does not prepare one for the treasures that await inside.

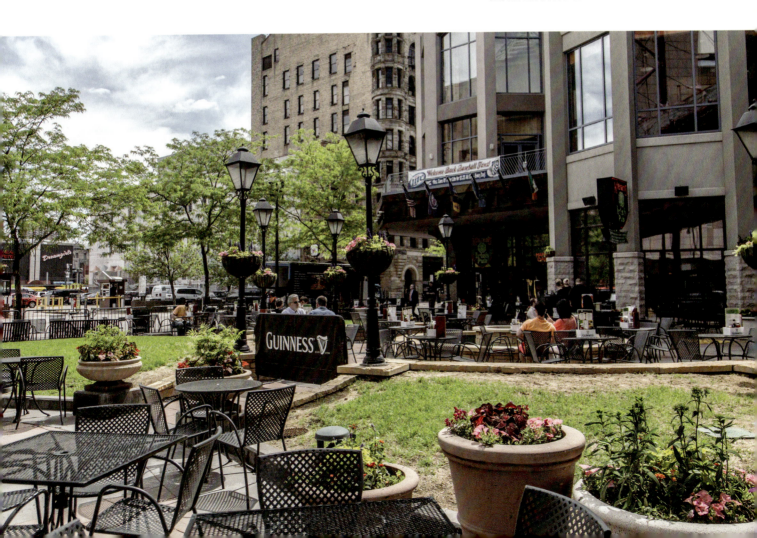

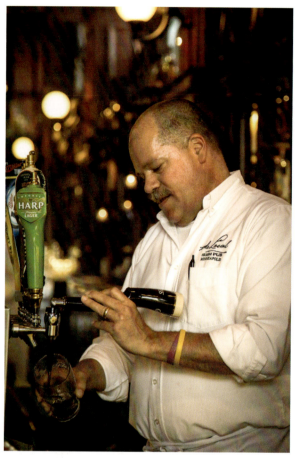

ABOVE: Bartender Todd Young has been pulling perfect pints at The Local for sixteen years.
RIGHT: The admirable craftsmanship of the long bar in The Local's Porter Pub encourages casual drinking and mingling.

The pub hosts monthly SlamMN competitive poetry slams where poets compete by reading their original poetry. Five judges randomly selected from the audience determine the winners. The ultimate goal is to compete at national poetry slams. Up to 200 people may attend a typical slam night. With no restrictions on content, one can only imagine what may pass for poetry during the annual two night Valentine's Day Erotica Slam.

The annual Get Lucky seven kilometer race is held the Saturday following St Patrick's Day for 12,000 runners. Since each runner receives a coupon for a free beer, the pub is

swamped with thirsty runners after the race.

While Kieran's is known as an event driven pub, The Local focuses more on its various beer and whiskey programs.

In Ireland the pub with the best beer and the most sought after patrons in town is referred to as The Local. General Manager Joshua Pepzel makes certain that The Local lives up to its name. Josh grew up in the Minneapolis area and began working at The Local in 2000.

The Local occupies a building that in 1899 was inhabited by a dentist, in 1905 a photographer, in 1910 a ladies tailor and from 1913 to 1916 a grocer. Then in quick succession, a Chevrolet showroom,

LEFT: One of many architectural delights of The Local is the copper-domed Bandstand featuring an early 20th century crystal chandelier. The Bandstand seats up to eight people.

ABOVE: The stunning interior of Kieran's with its sizeable long bar attracts visitors from far and wide who seek an "authentic" Irish experience.

Kelik Brothers Rug sales, Standard Tile and Marble, and Minnetonka Lumber. In 1923 Roy Bjorkman purchased a popular women's clothing shop, famous for its elegant walnut fixtures, from Martha Weathered, a well-known fashion importer with stores in Chicago and Minneapolis. Bjorkman, who was a civic leader for more than 50 years, operated his store at the location until his death at the age of 90.

Bjorkman's store closed in 1990, six years after his death, and remained vacant for a decade. It was slated for demolition when Kieran Folliard discovered the building and saved it from its impending fate. The enormous fur vault in the basement, the original terrazzo floor and two invaluable chandeliers dating back to the first part of the last century are the sole reminders of the building's early history. With 21 foot ceilings and an amazing 12,000 square feet of floor space, it, like its corporate cousin,

An 8' x 28' mural by Minneapolis artist John Erste adorns the walls of the plush Poets' Corner in Kieran's Irish Pub.

can accommodate huge crowds.

Initially, the pub was divided into a fine dining room on one side of a 15 foot high partition and an Irish pub on the other. The schizophrenic arrangement was doomed from the start. Tobacco smoke from the pub drifted over the partition and annoyed the elegant diners, so in 2001, the decision was made to be a pub.

The first pub installation was not up to The Local's high standards so in 2006 the pub was rebuilt by OL Irish Design and Build of Dublin, a leading provider of Irish pub interiors and exteriors throughout the world. The high partitions between snugs and dining areas are made of massive teak, creating a substantial and ultra quality look. The combined 150 foot bar featuring a hand-carved back bar is reportedly the longest bar of its kind in the United States. Gently curving surfaces predominate, somehow encouraging interaction among patrons.

The effect of curved lines cannot be easily exaggerated. They express joyousness, warmth and flexibility in nature and in architecture, whether the curves of a simple leaf or the complex beauty of a monumental building.

Each pub, in its own way, is a tribute to inspired vision, and represents a commitment to quality and to the Irish way. Sláinte.

A Leader With a Heart

Jacquie Berglund has always had keen business instincts. She also happens to have a big heart. As Director of Marketing at The Local, Jacquie knew she had a calling to help build a better world. Then, the idea hit her: sell a lot of beer and use the profits to help the needy. She figured out how to utilize a for-profit business model for non-profit purposes with a little Irish spirit. In 1999, with the support of The Local owner, Kieran Folliard, Jacquie created Finnegans Irish Amber, becoming the first known beer company in the world to direct all of its profits back into the community. (In fact, they called the first product Kieran's Irish Potato Ale, but the public did not warm to the notion of a dash of potatoes in the beer, so they changed the name and later, the formula.) In 2000 Jacquie wrote a check for $1 for the rights to the beer and left The Local to start Finnegans.

The Local's architectural design includes many soothing curves

The program works like this: Finnegans Inc., the beer company, sells its Irish Amber and Blond Ale brews in more than 1,500 restaurants, bars and liquor stores in Minnesota, North Dakota, South Dakota, Wisconsin and Florida. Because the beer is so good, it generates a nice profit, 100% of which is donated to the Finnegans Community Fund, a 501c3 nonprofit. The fund uses the money to buy produce through food bank partners from local farms, which is donated to food shelters.

This market-based approach addresses a prevalent social issue by supporting local farmers and helping alleviate hunger in communities throughout the Midwest.

Many volunteers help with the day-to-day operations of the two entities. Increasing beer sales and partnerships sustain the operation. There are no government grants.

When asked what she plans to do with Finnegans in the future, Jacquie simply states, "take it to the moon."

The Little Shamrock is an extremely popular neighborhood pub. A lot of fun is to be had inside.

The Little Shamrock

SAN FRANCISCO, CALIFORNIA

Historic Haven

I think this would be a good time for a beer.
-Franklin Roosevelt as he signed the 21st Amendment repealing Prohibition

IN DECADES PAST WHEN IT was time for lunch, semi-pro baseball players would run across the street from the Golden Gate Park to The Little Shamrock for a quick beer and beans before darting back to finish their games. They did not dare miss their turns at bat. The pot of beans was always ready for them. The tap has been flowing at The Little Shamrock since 1893 providing refreshment and fellowship for generations of sports enthusiasts and local residents.

The pub was opened by Antoine Herzo and his Irish wife Julia as San Francisco was in the throes of preparations for the California Mid-Winter International Exposition of 1894 in Golden Gate Park. The pub was the first address in the Sunset district to have a water meter, making it the oldest building in that section of the city. Immigrant workers of many nationalities would stop by the bar after long days of hard labor for a beer, a shot of whiskey and a free lunch or dinner. After Antoine died at the age of 38, Julia married J. P. Quigley, one of the workers from the park construction. Together they ran the business as San Francisco's urban population grew. Then at 5:12am on April 18, 1906, San Francisco came crashing down.

The earthquake measured somewhere between 7.7 and 8.3 according to the US Geological Survey. More than two dozen aftershocks quickly followed. Eighty percent of the city lay in ruins or was consumed by the fires that raged after gas mains exploded. Makeshift tents quickly covered Golden Gate Park, but The Little Shamrock survived and promptly became a destination for people grateful to be alive.

In the intervening years, Antoine's descendants ran the pub. Before the aging Tony Herzo Jr. sold the pub in 1969, the bean pot was never empty and reportedly never washed.

One day in 1974, Saeed Ghazi, walked across the Golden Gate Park heading home from St. Mary's Medical Center following the birth of his first son, Taymoor. He noticed The Little Shamrock and decided to have a beer to celebrate. Upon entering, he could not help but overhear an animated conversation between the owner and his accountant. The pub was in a crisis said the accountant. Business was slow and debts were rapidly piling up. "I don't know what persuaded me to do what I did, but I said to the owner, 'would you like to sell your business?' He agreed; we shook hands, and I was the owner of an Irish pub," recalls Saeed. Originally from Iran, Saeed has always appreciated all things Irish. His second wife, Ann Marie, is second generation Irish. Her parents hail from Dublin.

The Little Shamrock continues to be popular with locals. Novelist John Lescroart mentions the pub in many of his novels. Students at the University of California Medical Center live in small apartments nearby and are among the most loyal customers. They sit on sofas and overstuffed chairs and swap stories after long days at the hospital. Saeed keeps the volume on

In the back room a collection of board games, dice and dominos occupy a table by the comfortable sofa.

the five TVs low so patrons can converse and hear the music playing in the background.

George MacGlennon is typical of Shamrock loyalists. For the past 31 years, he has stopped at the pub almost every day. Initially its location mid-way between his home and work was a convenience; now in retirement it is an ingrained routine. "You always run into people you know at The Shamrock," he says. He remembers the volleyball games behind the Academy of Sciences in the Golden Gate Park and the pilgrimage to the pub afterwards. Val Markoff is another committed patron who has been helping out ever since Saeed purchased the pub, doing whatever chores he can to keep things running smoothly. As a sign of appreciation, a special stool is reserved for Val whenever he comes in.

No one could have imagined more than 100 years ago that this little working man's pub would last so long, firmly establishing itself as a local institution so important to so many.

ABOVE: The Little Shamrock circa 1905. From a photo on the Little Shamrock wall.

TOP: The clock on the wall in Jim O'Connor's Bar next door to The Little Shamrock stopped at 5:17 a.m. when it was thrown to the floor by the famous San Francisco earthquake. A few days later Jim gave the clock to The Little Shamrock where the octagonal Eclipse Regulator has remained, its hands forever frozen at that horrific moment in time.

Mac McGee

DECATUR, GEORGIA

The Poetry of Whisk(e)y

Why do I drink? So that I can write poetry.
-Jim Morrison

Meandering through the historic Decatur, Georgia city square, where people have congregated since the early 1800s, it is difficult to miss the fire-engine red exterior of Mac McGee Irish Pub, directly across the square from the century-old courthouse. Once you've entered the bar's cozy one-and-only room, you will know that you are a welcome guest. Even the bartender will shake your hand and introduce himself. It's like stumbling into a slice of Irish Public House utopia.

Although only three years old, the bar is unexpectedly authentic and just slightly scruffy, "still wagging its tail like a pup," according to manager Anthony Hogan. "It takes up to five years to become a fixture in the community. There's more than just being a namesake," he states. Anthony began his career as a young teen at Martins Pub on Ballygall Road in Dublin. Later, after traveling extensively, he turned up in Atlanta where for a decade he put his Dublin pub experience to good use at Fadó Irish Pub in Buckhead.

The Mac McGee location was "clouded with silhouettes of memories past" recalls Anthony when he was hired by owner Andy Anglin. "The interior brick walls strived for a new identity." Anthony suggested that they bring on board Casey Teague who was a former co-worker of his. Teague had his own passion for personal brewing and genuine love of the hospitality business. Andy and his wife, Courtney concurred and so a new foundation was set. In 2010 Anthony and Casey opened the door to Mac McGee, aptly named after Andy's Irish grandfather, whose photo hangs proudly on one of the pub's walls.

A morning ritual prepares the pub for the day's business. Employees polish the bar, set up the tables, clean the floor and write the menu on the chalkboard. Bright and early a local bakery delivers baguettes and the chef bakes soda bread in the kitchen. Many customers are regulars. "You know exactly where they will sit, but you can never take any patron for granted," says Anthony. "A good publican knows his patrons. The pub harbors on distinct characters." Their youngest staff member is 21 and their oldest fan is a mere 81. The pub accommodates up to 92 patrons.

While the pub serves a good assortment of beers, it is best known for its impressive selection of whiskies. With more than 400 brands on hand, Mac McGee offers more variety than just about any other pub in the Southeastern United States. The bottles are organized regionally and alphabetically behind the bar, starting with bourbons and rye whiskies on the bottom left shelf.

Monthly tastings, often with a distillery representative on hand, are popular with the pub's 1,000 strong member Whisk(e)y Club. (Spell Irish whiskey with an "e." Scottish whisky has no "e.")

"You will definitely find something in one of those bottles that strikes your persona," according to Anthony. "It may be a whiff-

RIGHT: It is hard to miss the bright red facade of Mac McGee across from the courthouse in this historic Georgia town.

of-smoke on the nose, a toasted haze of peat on the palate or a compelling finish involving oak and vanilla, but guaranteed there's a taste to be welcomed for all who are willing to try."

Hogan slips a parallel into the conversation between "the swirl of expression in a glass and the depth of impression from the patron. An element of subsided imagery is a pattern of explanation," he says. "Ardbeg Alligator is similar to the gravelly voiced singer Tom Waits in a glass. The ebb and flow of poetry lingers in Cardhu and then you have Red Breast Cask-Strength that opens up a quaint tornado on the palate. It's full of all kinds of explosive tannins. A sip of Writers Tears harkens to a moment alone with William Butler Yeats. There is definitely poetry in every bottle. It's all about the nose, palate and finish, " he concludes.

"Whiskies should be savored and respected for their charm and elegance. But we should not take it too seriously. We are all legends on our own barstool."

In Ireland it's whiskey; in Scotland its whisky. Either way you spell it, the arcane world of whisk(e)y is complex and slightly bewildering. We will try to simplify the subject.

The Wacky World of Irish Whisk(e)y

Whiskey is produced throughout the world, but four countries account for the lion's share of legitimate production: Ireland, Scotland, the United States (Bourbon and Rye Whiskey) and Canada. The main ingredient is grain, most often barley, but also corn or other grains. It can be malted or unmalted, single malt or blended, with the flavor of peat (Scotland) or not (Ireland), aged for many years or consumed almost immediately, matured in old oak casks previously used to store American bourbon, or Spanish Sherry or Madeira, with each imparting its own unique characteristics to the golden liquid. Distillation methods also differ between countries and among whiskey producers.

Here are a few things to note:

No one knows for certain who first distilled whiskey, but it is known that in 1608 a license was granted by King James I to distill whiskey in the area of Northern Ireland where Bushmills Distillery is located today, making it most likely the oldest licensed distillery in the word. It is also known that as far back as the 13th century distillation of spirits took place in the area.

In the late 1800s, with some 30 distilleries in the country, Irish whiskey was the world's most popular alcoholic beverage. The 20th century saw a rapid decline in the industry, due to the loss of the vital English market following Ireland's War of Independence, 1919-1921, the loss of the US market during Prohibition, 1920-1933, and the rise of the Scottish whisky industry. Today, only three distilleries remain in the Irish Republic. All are owned by foreign corporations.

Midleton, located County Cork in the southern part of the country, produces Jameson (established in 1780), Paddy's, Tulamore Dew and several other brands. Today the French multinational company Pernod Ricard owns the distillery.

Bushmills, located in Northern Ireland where the Bush River flows, produces several whiskeys under the Bushmill name such as Black Bush. It is owned by the UK multinational firm Diageo.

Cooley, located in County Louth in the northeast, was the first new distillery in more than 100 years when it was established in 1987. It was the only remaining independent distillery until 2012 when it was acquired by the American spirits firm Beam, Inc. who pledged to promote its flagship brand, Kilbeggan, produced at the oldest distillery in the world, dating back to 1757.

Single Malt Irish Whiskey is made from 100% malted barley (partially fermented barley sprouts) from a single distillery in a traditional copper pot still. Grain whiskey is made from wheat or corn in column stills, which are more modern, cost effective and efficient but which produce a less subtle whiskey. It is usually mixed with up to 40 single malts to make blended whiskeys. Blended whiskeys account for about 90 percent of total worldwide production. Malt must be dried before it can be used in distillation. If it is exposed to peat smoke (Scotch whiskey) during the drying process, the result is a "smoky" or "peaty" flavor. Irish malt is not exposed to smoke –usually– which distinguishes it from its Scottish cousin. Jameson is by far the largest selling Irish whiskey. Uniquely Irish, pure pot still whiskey is a mixture of malted and unmalted barley distilled in a copper pot still, such as Green Spot by Midleton.

ABOVE: A bottle of Writers Tears single pot still whiskey made from a mixture of malted (partially germinated) and unmalted barley distilled in a pot still. It is unique to Ireland.

Who Was Mac McGee?

Clarence Rayborne "Mac" McGee was born in Richmond, Virginia in 1922 into a family whose ancestors immigrated to America from Ireland during the Great Potato Famine. He joined the Army at the beginning of World War II and was stationed in France. After completing his military service, Mac returned home and married Agnes Mae Ford. What had been a friendship when he departed for France blossomed upon his return. They had three children, the oldest being the mother of the owner of Mac McGee.

Mac was a strong, tough man with a sly sense of humor. While not prone to avoiding conflict, he was also compassionate and enjoyed Irish poetry and music.

Family gathering with his brothers and sisters would inevitably end in storytelling and sing-a-longs. Danny Boy, My Wild Irish Rose and Goodnight Irene were particular favorites. Ireland was in his blood and he loved all things Irish. He traveled to Eire many times.

His desire to move to Ireland was well known, but sadly he passed away before his dream was realized. He would have so loved going to Mac McGee, sitting at the bar, Powers in hand, soaking up the atmosphere and enjoying the craic.

Mac at Mac McGee...it would have been a beautiful thing.

Andy Anglin
Owner
Mac McGee

LEFT: The pub is not large but it is well-appreciated in part due to its extraordinary selection of whiskeys.

Maguires Hill 16

FORT LAUDERDALE, FLORIDA

A Great Place to Pull Up a Stool

He was a wise man who invented beer. -Plato

You know that you will enjoy a perfect pint if Jim Gregory pulls it for you. After 50 years in the Irish pub business in Ireland, New York and Florida, Jim's hands instinctively hold the glass under the tap at a precise 45-degree angle. They deftly apply just the right amount of pressure to the handle to control the flow of stout. Jim does not let the tap touch the tulip-shaped glass or beer. Allowing the dark velvety liquid to settle partially at just the right moment before topping it off, he creates a luscious, creamy head that barely tops the rim of the glass. Jim knows that pulling a pint correctly is an art, one of life's great moments, a prescribed ritual to be instilled with drama and showmanship.

Jim was raised in the village of Bessbrook in County Armath, Northern Ireland, once the scene of much sectarian strife. He and his wife, Martina, purchased Maguires Hill 16 pub in 1999 and ever since have divided their time between Florida and Ireland where they once owned five pubs. The Florida establishment is managed by their son James, while their remaining pub in Ireland is managed by their daughter Eugina. The Gregory Tavern

McGuire's Hill 16 is a large pub, holding up to 400 people.

is attached to a 17th century monastery in the town square of Kilcock, County Kildare, where Martina is from, some 20 minutes from Dublin by train.

The Florida pub takes its name from The Sam Maguire Cup awarded each year to the winner of the All-Ireland Senior Football Championship held in Croke Park, Dublin. The cup was first awarded in 1928 and is modeled after the famous 8th century Ardagh Challice, which along with the Book of Kells, is among the most important historic Celtic relics. Hill 16 refers to a terrace at one end of Croke Park stadium. A likely explanation for the terrace's name is that rubble from the 1916 Easter Rising conflict in Dublin was used to build permanent terracing where a simple grassy slope previously existed.

Winner of numerous "Best Of" awards, the pub was established in 1986. A major renovation four years ago expanded and opened up the facility. The local newspaper calls it "the real deal." Upon entering, one is impressed with the spacious main room with its ample central island bar, which encourages lively banter and camaraderie among patrons. Hanging Tiffany-style ceiling lamps shine down on eight comfortable booths along one wall. A smaller, more intimate special events room has its own bar and entrance to the popular outside patio.

The pub hosts parties several times a week and sponsors nine local football and softball teams. Proudly displayed on a wall is Jim's Irish Person of the Year Award, presented by the Emerald Society of Fort Lauderdale in 2011 for Jim's many contributions to the community.

The large island bar in the main room is a popular gathering place.

Lovely Lace
(NOT THE KIND YOUR GRANDMOTHER WORE)

Many terms are used to describe a glass of beer: rich, creamy, velvety, malty, strong flavored to name a few. Add to the list the word lace or lacing as in beautiful lacing with every sip.

When beer is poured, a head of foam is created at the top of the glass. Lacing is the pattern left by the foam on the inside of the glass as the beer is drunk. With each sip, the head moves down, leaving a ring of foam, or lace, on the side of the glass.

Lacing is important for several reasons. First, it is aesthetically pleasing. Part of the beer drinking experience is visual, and a beer that looks good inspires confidence. A nice latticework of foam adds to the pleasure of the pint. Second, foam that lingers suggests that the beer is fresh and of good quality. Third, beer that clings means the glass is clean because soap or oils will prevent beer from adhering evenly to the glass. Lace should not be confused with clusters of bubbles on the glass, which are a sign of an unclean surface.

Not all beers lace the same way. Some types of beer will lace more than others, and factors such as the amount of carbonation and temperature can have an effect. Even though the rules are not hard and fast, be sure to notice the lacing the next time you sink into your seat to enjoy a pint at your favorite pub. It will enhance the experience.

RIGHT: After 50 years in the business, Jim Gregory knows that pulling a pint is a true art form.

McGillin's Olde Ale House

PHILADELPHIA, PENNSYLVANIA

Where the Past and Present Meet

Beer is living proof that God loves us and wants to see us happy. -Benjamin Franklin

A GOOD WAY TO SPEND an unforgettable afternoon or evening is to wander down a quaint side street—some would say alley—in Philadelphia and enjoy a few beers at McGillin's Old Ale House, acclaimed for its support of the local craft beer movement. When Chris and Mary Ellen Mullins purchased the pub in 1993, only a handful of micro beers were brewed in Philadelphia. Today there are dozens of microbreweries and beer pubs serving the community.

Even in Colonial times, before awareness of germs as a cause of illness, each household brewed its own beer, somehow knowing that it was safer than drinking water which could lead to sickness. Because Pennsylvania is blessed with an ideal climate for growing beer's key ingredients, hops and barley, over time Philadelphia became a center of beer production, only to be decimated during Prohibition. It was not until the microbrewery movement began in the 1980s that Philadelphia re-entered the brewing community in earnest. McGillin's offers three specialty beers, McGillin's Genuine Lager, McGillin's Real Ale and the unfiltered McGillin's 1860 IPA, which are brewed for the tavern in Adamstown, PA by Stoudt's Brewing Company, itself considered to be a microbrewery.

The historic old tavern has been pouring beer since 1860—the year of Abraham Lincoln's election—qualifying it as the oldest continuously operating tavern in the city and one of the oldest in the country. William "Pop" McGillin emigrated from County Tyrone, Ireland during the Great Potato Famine in the mid-1800s and set up his tavern in a small row house. He and his wife Catherine lived upstairs with their thirteen children. William expanded the structure to incorporate the two adjacent buildings including the oyster house next door. According to his obituary in the Philadelphia Times in 1901, William took great pride in his floors even after the wear and tear of workers' boots. "None of the floors were ever torn up. They were merely covered over with other floors, until now they are in triplicate," according to the obituary.

Situated in the old theater district, the pub was noteworthy for the many actors who let down their hair in the upstairs speakeasy during Prohibition. The flamboyant, amazingly ornate Garrick Theater was nearby. The theater, built in 1901, was popular with theatergoers and in the words of the contemporary The Theater magazine attracted "the best people of every class."

The elaborate façade is a tribute to mid-19th century Philadelphia architecture.

LEFT: A copy of the April 7, 1933 Philadelphia Inquirer announcing the end of Prohibition. The photo caption reads "Reviving an old Philadelphia spot and custom is this crowd in "Mom" McGillan's famous ale house on Drury St., which reopened at midnight after 13 quiet, beerless years."

In 1907 Catherine, who took the reins after her husband's death, extensively renovated the combined properties, adding the classic pub exterior and the beautiful tile flooring, which is still in use. Catherine died in 1937. Sadly, due to a flu epidemic during World War I, only two of the children outlived their mother.

The Ale House was owned by the McGillin family for nearly 100 years. In 1958, Mom and Pop's youngest daughter Mercedes McGillan Hooper, then 72, sold the Philadelphia landmark to brothers Henry Spaniak and Joe Shepaniak (yes, with different last names). Henry's daughter, Mary Ellen Spaniak Mullins and her husband Chris, who is third generation Irish, are the current owners. Chris and Mary Ellen's son Chris Jr. is general manager.

The spacious bar area, with rows of small wooden tables, crafted from hulls of ships which sailed up the Delaware River, greets patrons when they enter. The long bar runs down one side of the room. Walls and pillars are covered with photos and memorabilia including a collection of framed liquor licenses dating to 1871 and a metal signature sign from the Wanamaker Department Store, a Philadelphia landmark for a century. When the building was sold executives gave the sign to the tavern. Climb the stairs to find a large special events room featuring a rare late 19th century Brunswick-Balke-Collender bar.

The secret to the tavern's long success,

according to Chris Sr. is four fold. First, own the real estate. When you rent, the more you succeed, the more the rent increases. Second, be consistent in projecting the image of the business; always use the term Ale House. From the very beginning, William McGillin preached the gospel of constant repetition, making him an early marketing guru. Third, be involved. Family members are in the pub every day attending to the myriad details of pub ownership. Mary Ellen doubles as kitchen supervisor. Fourth, adhere to the old adage: early is on time, on time is late, and late is unacceptable.

OPPOSITE, TOP: Originally called "The Bell in Hand," the tavern was nicknamed McGillin's by laborers who frequented the tavern in the 1860s. The nickname stuck. The walls and pillars of the large, dimly lit main bar area are covered with historic memorabilia. Guess which NFL football team the pub and its patrons support.

OPPOSITE, BOTTOM: An original Wanamaker department store logo patterned after John Wanamaker's signature hangs in the main bar area along with other memorabilia. In 1877, Wanamaker opened a department store in Philadelphia, one of the first in the country. When the store was sold in 1978, the logo was gifted to McGillin's. The building was designated a National Historic Landmark in 1978.

ABOVE: A beautiful late 19th century Brunswick-Balke-Collander bar highlights the large second floor bar.

The Cradle of Liberty

Philadelphia is known as the Cradle of Liberty because of the major role it played in America's independence. The great Benjamin Franklin was a resident and early proponent of independence. The Declaration of Independence was adopted in Philadelphia on July 4, 1776 by the Second Continental Congress, and the first Constitution was written there in 1787. It was the nation's first capitol until 1800, and the American flag was designed there. By 1750, Philadelphia overtook Boston and New York to become the second largest English-speaking city in the world, after London.

The 20,000 square foot establishment has a staff of more than 200.

McGuire's Irish Pub

PENSACOLA, FLORIDA

So Much to See; So Much to Do

Make sure that the beer—four pints a week—goes to the troops under fire before any of the parties in the rear get a drop.
       -Winston Churchill to his Secretary of War (1944)

The inside clutter of McGuire's Irish Pub feels like a history lesson taught in a folk art museum. Not an inch of wall space is spared from all manner of framed—often signed—pictures of politicians, sports figures and entertainers, clever sayings, wood carvings, Irish knickknacks, even 12 moose heads. It would take years to absorb it all and would be well worth trying. McGuire's is one of those places people never forget.

McGuire and Molly Martin opened their pub in 1977 as a small neighborhood watering hole in a shopping center, the Town and Country Plaza, where McGuire did the cooking and Molly waited tables. McGuire was making a steamed sandwich one day when Molly earned her first tip. She tacked the two one-dollar bills on the wall for good luck. A liquor salesman tacked up another. As the oft-told story goes, a Federal judge and some pals noticed the dollar bills a few days later and decided to add their own dollars to the wall. The magistrate suggested they write their names on their bills so in the unlikely event the pub would ever fail, they could recover their investments. Thus, a tradition was born, and today well over a million signed dollar bills adorn the ceiling and rafters. Each year the pub pays taxes on the increased number of bills, with

The exclusive Irish Politicians Club provides members with a quiet retreat away from prying eyes.

the difference from the prior year calculated by means of a complex formula and certified by an accounting firm.

In 1982 having outgrown their original location, the Martins purchased Pensacola's historic 1927 Old Firehouse No. 2 and moved everything to the new location, including the dollar bills which were transported by armed Brinks guards.

Since its beginning, the pub has been creating traditions left and right.

First-time visitors and patrons who cannot keep time with the live music are strongly encouraged to "kiss the moose" to the accompaniment of loud applause. Moosehead McGuire, a large stuffed moose head mounted over a fireplace near the music stage has endured countless kisses over the decades.

A restroom signage controversy has added to McGuire's renown. Since first opening, its restroom signage has been mischievously misleading. The sign on the women's restroom states "Men's Room" with small text above "This way to" and an arrow pointing to the adjacent men's room, and vice-versa. Many people do not notice the small text and walk into the wrong restroom. This ongoing joke was the subject of a formal complaint to the authorities a few years back, and the pub was required to remove the confusing signage. More than 3,000 people signed a petition to have the signs returned, and the story made national news. Finally, an agreement was reached with the powers that be, and the pub was allowed to keep the signage with the installation of a set of swinging doors between the famous signs and the restrooms. When McGuire and Molly opened a second pub in Destin in 1996, they maintained the same restroom signage.

More than 5000 personalized green and white ceramic mugs hang from the ceiling and cram shelves along the walls. Members of the McGuire's

The microbrewery, just off the main floor, uses two copper pots–a mash-lauter tun and a brew kettle, five fermentation tanks and one bright beer (carbonating) tank in the brewing process. Copper is for appearance only; the interior of the tanks are stainless steel.

Family Mug Club use them when they visit the pub. Some dating back to the 1970s bear the scars of multiple vigorous drinking sessions. Even after long absences, patrons can always locate their mugs thanks to modern computer technology.

A popular item on the menu is Senate bean soup, the same navy bean and smoked ham soup that has been served in the US Senate since the early 1900s. The price today at McGuire's is 18 cents, the same as it was in the Senate Dining Room and McGuire's in 1977. On Capitol Hill, the price is $6.00 today—so who says there is no inflation?

The McGuire's Irish Pipes and Drums band has become a fixture in Pensacola. Established in 1988, the band wears the MacDonald Lord of the Isles tartan. The group plays throughout the Southeast and has won numerous awards. They dress in the ancient tartan worn by the mighty clan MacDonald, Middle Age rulers of the remote Western Islands off the coast of Scotland, also known as The Outer Hebrides.

As the business grew, wings were added to the McGuire's building. They contain delightful medium-size themed rooms that glow in a warm rose/pink light: the Pipers Den, the Irish Links Room, the Notre Dame Room ("Every pub should have a Notre Dame room," says McGuire) as well as a brewery and well-stocked wine cellar. A special room is reserved for the very private Irish Politicians Club, a group of local power brokers who make deals and otherwise have fun at secluded tables in nooks behind green velvet curtains. The more than 200 members pay a yearly membership fee to belong, and there is a waiting list for membership.

A number of Irish pubs brew their own beer off-premises, but it is unusual that a pub brews it adjacent to the main drinking lounge. Perhaps anticipating the current microbrewery rage, McGuire's opened Florida's first microbrewery in 1988. Head brewer Mike Helf produces

six beers and one non-alcoholic root beer, all consumed in-house. There are 33 recipes in his collection. He uses only two-row barley without adjunct grains such as corn, rice or oats which are sometimes added to reduce costs.

It is an unexpected pleasure to find a first rate wine-cellar in an Irish pub, but why not in a pub otherwise so full of surprises? In 1996 McGuire and Molly built an addition to accommodate an 8,000 bottle cellar. They cleverly recessed into the wall two huge oak casks from Bartel's, a local winery that was in business for fifty years beginning in 1925. The room's vaulted ceiling, granite walls and two twelve-foot stained glass windows from a Masonic hall in Philadelphia give the illusion of being in an ancient European monastery. A complete collection of Chateau Mouton Rothschild artist label vintages reposes in climate controlled comfort in racks behind large display windows. To celebrate the liberation of France after World War II, beginning in 1945, Baron Philippe de Rothschild commissioned a leading painter or sculptor of the day to design a label for each year's vintage. The bottles are highly collectible and full sets are indeed rare.

The pub is a family business. McGuire and Molly's son Billy and daughter Amy manage the day to day operations. McGuire's Irish-born grandfather operated a pub in Philadelphia in the 1920s. McGuire grew up around his father's saloon in the Pennsylvania Dutch Country and is a proud third generation saloon keeper.

McGuire likes to say that his pub is an ongoing celebration, "a never ending family party." Even its logo, a leprechaun sitting on a stump holding a shillelagh suggests mischievous fun. And that's no blarney.

OPPOSITE: One of five buses owned by McGuire's used to take patrons to sporting events. This one is a 1945 Bristol.

THIS PAGE: "Every pub should have a Notre Dame room," says publican McGuire Martin.

Do the Irish Wear Kilts?

While kilts are most often associated with Scotland, the Irish also wear them. The history of the Irish kilt is subject to much interpretation, which is another way of saying that misinformation abounds.

Kilts probably originated in the Scottish Highlands in the 16th century or earlier. They were wool garments worn by sheep herders to protect against the cold, damp climate. The bottom half of the "great kilt" was pleated and belted at the middle with the upper half thrown over the left shoulder as a cloak for added warmth. The shorter "walking kilt," worn slightly above the knee to allow more movement was probably developed in the 17th century. In the 19th century clans began to use individual tartans (patterned cloth). Some Scottish military units wore the kilt in combat during World War I.

Several conflicting versions exist about the origins of Irish kilts. Some say immigrants from the Scottish Highlands as far back as the 16th century brought their tartans and kilts with them. Others say some Irish nationalists first wore the kilt at the end of the 19th century as a mark of cultural independence from British rule. Irish pipe bands of the early 20th century often wore solid saffron kilts, using a dye extracted from the crocus flower and used by Celts of northern Europe for two thousand years. The bands became important recruiting instruments for nationalist forces. The most popular Irish tartans are a recent phenomenon. In 1966 the House of Edgar woolen mills in Scotland designed tartans for each of the 32 Irish counties.

The most distinctive kilt accessory is the *sporran*, a pouch worn in front of the kilt and used to carry personal items since the kilt has no pockets. Some sporrans are highly ornate.

The main bar. More than $1 million in one-dollar bills covers the pub's ceiling, each signed by the person posting the bill. The pub pays taxes on the increase in bills every year.

RIGHT & BELOW: An extensive wine cellar with a complete collection of Baron Philippe de Rothschild post World War II artist vintages.

BOTTOM: At the entrance to the wine cellar a barrel from a former local winery.

McGurk's Irish Pub & Garden

ST LOUIS, MISSOURI

Largest Small Pub You'll Ever See

The light music of whiskey falling into a glass—an agreeable interlude. -James Joyce

MCGUIRK'S IRISH PUB AND GARDEN has so many rooms and nooks and crannies, one could almost hide there forever. The pub consists of a series of adjacent town houses strung together over a 35 year period. It began in 1978 when local attorney Jim Holloran bought a small corner property in a tired neighborhood burdened with a surplus of vacant buildings. It consisted of one small room, a few tattered tables and a stage.

Like all of the empty townhouses in the block-long building, the badly deteriorated property required extensive rehabilitation. Two years later, as his business began to prosper, Jim rented the adjacent town house. The brick wall separating the townhouses was in poor condition, and the owner allowed Jim to knock down a major portion of the wall and build an archway between the rooms. Every three years Jim rented another townhouse and constructed a new archway. In 1988 he bought the four townhouses he had restored. Soon thereafter he bought townhouse number five, giving him ownership of the entire building.

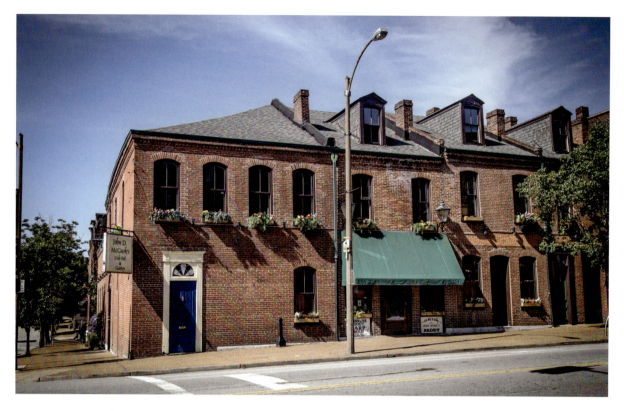

Immigrants from Germany, Ireland, France, Croatia, Lebanon and a mix of other countries settled St Louis in the 19th century. Ethnic neighborhoods fostered strong ties among people with similar backgrounds. McGurk's is situated in Soulard, a French neighborhood noted for its Mardi Gras, one of the biggest celebrations in the country, and for its Bastille Day parties. Turn of the century brick homes with hidden courtyards, Mansard roofs and elaborate terra cotta ornamentation recall the area's halcyon days. The pub's vicinity has been dubbed "steeples of Soulard" because it is dotted with ethnic churches including the Croatian Catholic Church across the street. After suffering through the economic recession and consequent population decline, Soulard is currently in recovery mode, alive with restaurants and music clubs that bring people to the area in the evening.

However, it is not just the architecture that attracts a loyal clientele and out-of-towners to McGurk's. Rather, it is the garden, lovingly maintained and constantly changing, which on a warm, sunny summer day provides a sanctuary for the soul, a bite to eat and a friendly pint. Jim built the original garden with a fountain twenty years ago. About eight years later he added a covered pavilion and a waterfall. The garden has become a popular spot for weddings and rehearsal dinners. By creating the 10,000 square foot garden, Jim doubled the overall size of the pub.

Jim, raised in South St Louis, is one of ten children of 4th generation Irish immigrants. His son Patrick manages the pub. His brother, Michael, is a contractor and works full time maintaining and improving the property, which is always in a state of flux. His sister Maureen is the bookkeeper assisted by sister Martha. Sister Maggie is responsible for the garden.

Traditional Irish music is a big draw for the pub. Bands are frequently brought over from Ireland and housed in "The Palace," a three bedroom apartment above the pub making for

an easy commute for nightly music sessions.

The pub takes its name from the traditional Irish song *The Irish Rover* about a mystical ship with 27 masts that comes to an unfortunate end. The name refers to one of the crew members, "Johnny McGurk who was scared stiff of work."

The line in the song clearly does not apply to the modern day McGurk's where years of hard work have obviously paid off. For Jim, the pub is serious business, but it is also his hobby and passion. He says jokingly that in his younger years he and a friend were doing estate planning and realized that a fair amount of their expenditures were dedicated to drinking. So, rather than take the traditional approach to estate planning, they decided to buy a little tavern so they could "drink wholesale and play gin rummy on Saturdays." Whatever the motive, the plan was sound. The pub flourished, and the people of St Louis have plainly adopted this great neighborhood institution.

ABOVE: Behind the pub an enchanting and well-tended garden delights the eyes.

TOP: It is called the million dollar garden for good reason. With a waterfall, koi pond, fountain, exotic plants and covered patio life in the garden is good on a bright summer day.

OPPOSITE: The pub occupies most of a block-long building.

PREVIOUS SPREAD: These brightly painted doors are all part of McGurk's Irish Pub and Garden. At one time each door opened to a separate town house. They are inspired by the famous Doors of Dublin posters.

LEFT: The lovely brick arches between rooms are appropriate in a city made famous by its 630 foot high Gateway Arch built as a tribute to westward expansion in the United States. The superb interior is an architectural treasure.

BELOW: A wall lined with straight-backed booths, typical of those found in Ireland.

BOTTOM: Employee Cindy Biggers pulls a pint of Schlafly, a local brew.

McSorley's Old Ale House

NEW YORK, NEW YORK

Enduring Traditions

Entering McSorley's one seems to leave present day New York to find oneself in a quieter and more aesthetic place
  -Hutchins Harpgood, *Harpers Weekly*, October 25, 1913

As soon as the door opens at 11:00am, a steady stream of characters starts to wander into the oldest and most famous alehouse in New York City. And characters they are! Some have rested their feet on the brass foot rail at their special spots at the bar since the 1970s. Regulars don't necessarily come every day, but when they do it is like coming home, and because there are no stools at the bar, they stand glued to their preferred spot for hours. In fact, when Old John McSorley opened his saloon for Irish working men in 1854, he called it The Old House at Home, a tribute to a public house in his hometown of Omagh, in County Tyrone. Little has changed since then.

If a regular customer fails to show up for a week or more, legendary barman and general manager Steve "Pepe" Zwaryczuk will give him a call "just to be sure everything is okay." The pub is a destination for locals and tourists. "You can't fall down here on a Saturday," says Pepe who has worked in the pub since 1977.

The place oozes authenticity. Everything is dark and worn. No piece of memorabilia has been removed from the walls since John McSorley's death in 1910. Sawdust covers the floor, originally because patrons tracked mud in from the street just outside the front door. Tradition has its practical side: sawdust absorbs spilled beer and is a natural abrasive cleaner.

The potbelly stove is vintage. In the old days, a warm kettle of soup was always kept on the stove to feed many poor souls living in the Bowery. There is no cash register. Only cash is accepted and is kept in a box behind the counter. Harry Houdini once left a pair of handcuffs on the bar after escaping from them on a dare from John. Someone long ago attached the cuffs to the brass foot rail, another historic memento among the hundreds in the pub. The treasures on the walls include copies of several paintings of McSorley's by turn-of-the-century artist John Sloan of the celebrated Ashcan School, a group of painters who depicted the rougher side of New York. Sloan was a regular at the pub.

McSorley's has occupied the same location since its beginning in the storied Bowery section of Manhattan. Generations of immigrants, through peace and war, have lived in one of the eight rooms above the bar. They came to the US to find a better life or to escape persecution. They worked hard, became affluent enough to move to the suburbs and were replaced by subsequent generations. The first wave of Irish immigration began in the 1840s. More than 200,000 Irish lived in New York City when McSorley's first opened, many of whom lived in the pub's neighborhood. They were poor and lived in squalid conditions, but McSorley's was open to them. Then came the Russian Jews and other ethnic groups. After World War II large numbers of Ukrainians moved into the neighborhood. The First Ukrainian Assembly of God church across the street caters to the large Slavic local population. Local schools teach the Ukrainian language, similar yet different from Russian. You can tell that the Blue and Gold Bar down the street is Ukrainian because blue and gold are the colors of that nation's flag.

McSorley's was the only pub in New York City that remained open during Prohibition because it sold only "near beer" with a miniscule alcohol content. The concoction was made in the pub's basement since all breweries were closed.

Every period of the pub's history has its own collection of stories. Abraham Lincoln visited the pub in 1860 when he was an unannounced candidate for President. John McSorley's close friend Peter Cooper—who had his own chair in the pub—allowed the future President to use the Great Hall in the recently opened Cooper Union to deliver his famous "right makes might" anti-slavery speech. His eloquent words may have played a pivotal role in his road to the White House. In one of the pub's greatest moments Lincoln went behind the bar to pour his own glass of beer. Lincoln was reportedly the only person John McSorley ever permitted behind the bar because people called him Honest Abe. Industrialist Cooper established the Cooper

BELOW: Owner Matthre Maher takes a quick break from the hectic pace of the day's activities.

McSorley's Bar, 1912 (oil on canvas) by American realist John Sloan (1871-1951). Sloan was a regular patron of the pub. Detroit Institute of Arts/ The Bridgeman Art Library

A Regular's Tribute

McSorley's has been like a second home to me since 1964, the same year that current owner Matty Maher began working there as a bartender. Three of my college friends and I had heard about this great drinking establishment in Manhattan where the waiters transported as many as 20 mugs in their two hands. As a student at the RCA Institute in the West Village, I took my lunch there every Monday through Friday. The waiters never seemed to mind how much you consumed, but they admonished you to "be good or be gone," which was founder John McSorley's motto.

McSorley's was always strictly men only. During the winter months, the college men would sneak girls into the bar wearing long coats and hoods. After quite a few ales, the girl would stand up, remove her coat, let down her hair and reveal that she was wearing a dress. The bartender would reach behind the bar and feverishly ring an old fire alarm bell, which is still there, and the waiters would duly escort the young lady to the front door, with the attending customers cheering, laughing and clapping in enjoyment of the escapade. In 1970, the U. S. Supreme Court granted access to women; however, it was 16 years later before a separate ladies room was installed.

Things are always constant and never changing at McSorley's, which is just the way I like it to be.

-Joe McKiernan

Union for the Advancement of Science and Art the year before Lincoln's appearance to provide educational opportunities for working class children free of charge. It is today considered one of the nation's finest educational institutions.

While McSorley's remains committed to its past heritage, it also has had to adapt to the modern world. In 2011, the NYC Department of Health banned Minnie the cat, the latest in a long line of resident cats dating back to the pubs first days. In the same year, the DOH mandated the cleaning of dozens of dusty wishbones hung over the bar by soldiers departing for battle in World War l. Soldiers collected their bones upon returning from war. Remaining wishbones belonged to soldiers who failed to come back. As a final tribute, no one had ever cleaned the bones.

When John McSorley established his pub, he made a commitment to sell only beer. When he retired, John turned the pub over to his son William who made the mistake of introducing whiskey to the pub's customers. A very upset John came out of retirement and fired his son, who again took the reins after his father's death at age 87. This time he honored his father's commitment, and to this day McSorley's serves only two kinds of beer: McSorley's Cream Ale and McSorley's Black & Tan. The F. X. Matt Brewery in Utica, NY brews the beer under contract with Pabst Brewing Company which owns the McSorley's brand.

At the beginning of the last century, the pub was one of the busiest places in the city and it has never slowed down. *The New Yorker* writer Joseph Mitchell raised the pub to stardom in 1943 in his book titled *McSorley's Wonderful Saloon*. He chose his article about a visit to the pub as the title for his bestselling compilation of essays penned over the years. Mitchell said of the pub, "It is a drowsy place, the bartenders never make a needless move, the customers nurse their mugs of ale, and the three clocks on the walls

The legendary coal fired pot belly stove has been burning for almost 160 years.

have not been in agreement for many years."

The pub's current owner is Matthew Maher who hails from the town of Kilkenny in the county of the same name. His is an inspirational story of how Irish immigrants made good in America. He came to New York in 1964 because he had stopped to assist a stranded motorist vacationing in Ireland who happened to be Harry Kirwan, the owner of McSorley's at the time. Impressed with the young man, Harry offered Matthew a job as a waiter and bartender, and Matthew soon joined the ranks of Irish immigrants who began life in America living in a room above McSorley's. Matthew worked hard, learned the business quickly and in 1977 purchased the pub.

Bill McSorley said it best, "New York can go its wanton ways, but change stops here." McSorley's really is a historic and treasured relic of the American past.

RIGHT: Harry Houdini's handcuffs have been chained to the foot rail ever since he escaped from them on a dare by John McSorley.

LEFT: This strategically placed corner table is one of the most popular with regulars because of its excellent view of the bar and front door.

FOLLOWING SPREAD: Early morning getting ready for business. The chair in the doorway blocks the entrance during the morning ritual. Historically, sawdust helped protect floors from patrons' muddy boots when it rained.

Meehan's Public House

ATLANTA, GEORGIA

A Neighborhood Pub Downtown

Not a shred of evidence exists in favor of the idea that life is serious. - Brendan Gill

Upon entering Meehan's Irish pub on the premier street in downtown Atlanta, you would never guess that it was once the site of the Macy Department Store's women's shoe department. Famous for its two-story arched openings, marble floors and 14-foot high crystal chandeliers, the iconic building was constructed in 1927 during the glory days of downtown shopping. A victim of tough economic times, the landmark structure closed in 2003 and remained dark until 2009 when a group of investors gave it a new lease on life by creating a magnificent meeting and special events facility.

Tucked away in a corner of the building, adjacent to the 73-floor Westin Peachtree Plaza Hotel, is Meehan's Public House. When the circular glass tower hotel opened in 1973, a few

Located in one of Atlanta's landmark buildings, the former Macy's Department Store, Meehan's Public House is popular with Atlanta's thriving convention trade.

steps connected it to the former department store constituting what is now the rear entrance to Meehan's.

Irish pubs are all about the comfort factor, "like your Mom's food," says Meehan's co-owner Phil Roness. Before heading out to a $20,000 wedding at the nearby Ritz Carlton, wedding party members will hang out at the pub to relax. Or, if a group of diners can't decide whether to eat Italian, Chinese, or Mexican, someone will say, "Oh, well, we can all agree on one thing, let's meet at Meehan's." Phil takes pride in the pub's menu of classic Irish dishes "elevated to the gourmet level," giving lie to the common misconception that "pub grub" is mediocre at best. Chef Jordan Wakefield studied at Atlanta's famed Le Cordon Bleu culinary school.

Phil grew up in the Bay Ridge neighborhood of Brooklyn, NY, where pub goers know a well-poured Guinness when they see one. Successive waves of Dutch, Norwegian, Danish and Irish immigrants settled Bay Ridge, leaving an appreciation for all things Celtic, and leaving Phil with a lifelong desire to own an authentic Irish pub.

Partner Ian Macken is from Dublin, just a stone's throw from the city center. As a young boy, he was not always invited when his father went to the pub. "I always hated seeing my Da and uncles sneaking off to the pub on Sunday evening for a few pints," he recalls." On his 18th birthday, his Da took him to a nearby pub for his first legal pint. Now he and Da enjoy a pint or three within the walls of Meehan's on Peachtree, some three thousand miles from his hometown. "The pub is coming on three years now," says Ian "and I love seeing the shock on guests' faces when they ask how long we have been here. 'Wow' they reply "we thought you'd been here for 30 years."

A long hallway leads to the well-appointed rear private events room.

The bar surface is inlayed geometric parquet, a technique dating back to the 17th century. Usually stalled as flooring, parquet surfaces are extremely durable and look better with time. Since bars take quite a beating, few surfaces will be as robust as this one.

Students, families, hard hats and lawyers join the convention and luncheon crowds at the long parquet bar in the dimly lit main room. The parquet bar is unique and over time will age to a beautiful deep, golden patina. The floor came from an old textile mill in Thomaston, GA, at one time a leading producer of cotton fabrics and tire cord. Light floods into the private events room through a 120-year-old stained glass ceiling that once graced a chapel in Savannah.

One long time patron says, "Meehan's is like a second home." That compliment is music to a publican's ear.

TOP: Beautiful 14-foot high teardrop chandeliers that once graced Macy's department store now illuminate weddings and other notable occasions in a special events facility. A team of investors converted the three main shopping floors of the vacant downtown showpiece store in 2009 to help revive this storied part of downtown Atlanta. Tucked away in a corner of the former Macy's building, Meehan's occupies space that was at one time a movie theater lobby and subsequently a woman's shoe department.

LEFT: A bird's-eye view of selling floor crowded with Christmas shoppers. Davison-Paxon Company, Atlanta circa December, 1941. This photo was taken from the same vantage point as the photo above. Photo courtesy Georgia State University Library.

OPPOSITE TOP: Light floods into the private events room through a 120-year-old stained glass ceiling that once graced a chapel in Savannah.

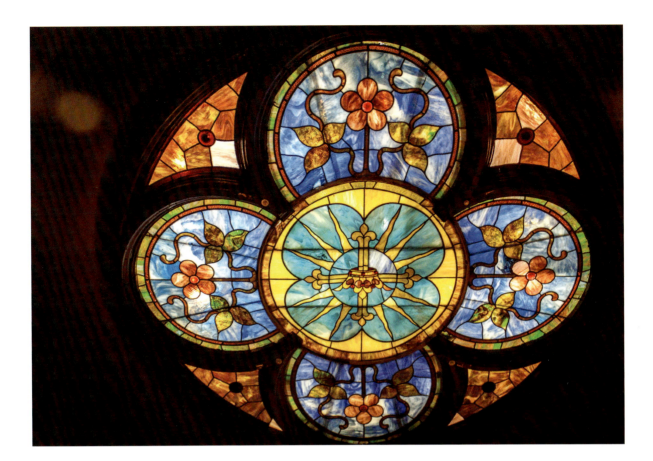

The More Things Change… Many years ago in small towns across Ireland, farmers spent the days toiling and working the land. It was back breaking labour and a tough existence to be sure. There wasn't much to look forward to, except perhaps the chance to gather at a neighbor's house for a pint of stout and a chat. "Let's meet at Kay Meehan's this evening, as it is central to us all, and there's a few extra chairs for us to sit on." Perhaps Kay would put out sandwiches for supper. The farmers would compensate their hosts for the hospitality and nourishment. As this became common practice, the crowds grew and more space was needed. Maybe a wall or two were removed. The residents of the houses would move upstairs, leaving the downstairs as the lounge area with tables and a bar. Travelers passing through would be directed to the "Public House" to wet their beak and get their bearings. The Pub became central to the community, a forum to air your grievances or counsel your friends. The pub provided an early form of therapy, pints being the couch and the ear of a friend playing the therapist.

Today, things have not really changed. Office workers and college students have replaced the hard working farmers. The weary traveler passing through town is now the happy vacationer or the conventioneer. Find your way to the pub and you'll be welcomed, offered a seat, a pint and bite to eat, just as in days of yore. And, although I don't live above the pub like my predecessors, I have been known to spend a night or two on a dusty mattress in the wee loft.

Ian D. Macken
Partner, Meehan's Public House

Molly's Shebeen

NEW YORK, NEW YORK

Where Conversation Reigns

There is nothing which has been yet contrived by man, by which so much happiness is produced as by a good tavern or inn. -Samuel Johnson

"Molly's is a conversation pub, a community pub, a local pub," says co-owner Peter O'Connell who goes out of his way every day to make sure all comers are welcome. Through all the hustle and bustle of a great and vibrant city, Molly's maintains its Old World charm thanks in large part to the gracious hospitality of Peter and his long-serving Irish staff.

Molly's is a neighborhood tavern, held in warm esteem by residents of Gramercy Park, a community of 19th century brownstones and tree-lined streets. This venerable place attracts an eclectic clientele as well representing New York's wonderful tapestry of cultures. People keep coming back to "the same old Molly's" where drinking a pint by the log fireplace is a grand way to thaw out on a cold winter evening.

The son of a farmer from Ballinglough, County Meath, "a small village with a pub, a church and a post office," Peter learned the value of "natural" and "organic" before they became all the rage. His parents raised sheep, cattle and barley in the 1950s and were totally self-sufficient. His father believed that tractors would damage the land so he planted his crops with horse and plough. Believing farming to be "a spiritual exercise, he sought a balance between his compassion and love of nature with what was needed to run the farm," says Peter, whose brother still operates the farm "with no telephone."

The building that houses Molly's dates back to 1820 and has experienced various incarnations including a bar beginning in 1895, grocery store during Prohibition and a rough gin mill or "beer and ball joint" in the 1940s and 50s. In 1962, the property was converted into an Irish pub designed by Stanley Franks, an architect whose footprints are seen in many Irish pubs in the city. It was named Molly's after the traditional Irish folksong Molly Malone. Peter acquired the pub in 1991 and renamed it Molly's Shebeen, a reference to the illegal drinking establishments once common in Ireland. John Ronaghan, from County Monaghan, joined Peter in operating the pub in 1995.

Molly's is a New York stalwart. It's long and narrow shape, low beamed ceiling, row of well-worn wood booths across from the bar, and dim lighting encourage intimacy and warmth. A person can disappear comfortably there for hours on end.

One secret to Molly's success is the long tenure of the staff. Peter believes it is important to "leave a bit on the table for everyone." Treating staff like family, attending baptisms and weddings and nurturing long-term relationships with vegetable, meat and other suppliers is the Irish way, and it works in the US too. A good example is barman Jim Gallagher who began his career working in the Favorite Bar None pub, owned by a bookmaker in the ancient walled city of Derry in County Ulster. Jim came to the US and began working in Molly's in 1996. The following year he came down with cancer, and again in 2000. "Peter and John took care of me every time I was out sick," Jim, who is now cancer free, recalls. As Teddy Roosevelt once said, "Nobody cares how much you know, until they know how much you care."

One of the joys of New York City is discovering precious little gems like Molly's Sheeben. Here co-owner Peter O'Connell stands in front of the pub's familiar white and black façade, ready to greet patrons, old and new.

SHEBEEN,
an Irish Speakeasy

Shebeens were unlicensed, untaxed and illegal drinking establishments in Ireland. The word derives from the Gaelic word sibín, originally meaning "little mug" that was a measure of ale and which later came to mean "illicit whiskey." Their heyday was in the 17th and 18th centuries when English officials in Ireland regulated and taxed distillation, leading to extensive illegal production and excessive consumption. Poor, exploited, and living in a chilly, damp climate, people resorted to alcohol for warmth, comfort and comradeship. Often, the relatively few legally licensed pubs and the more common shebeens offered more agreeable environments than the inadequate housing most inhabitants endured. Over time, shebeens became the central social centers in towns and villages all across Ireland. Even today, occasional illegal shebeens are raided and closed. The term has entered into colloquial speech and spread across the world wherever Irish congregate, becoming synonymous with the notion of Irish hospitality and craic.

SWEET MOLLY MALONE

Molly Malone is the title of a traditional folk song that tells the fictional tale of a beautiful and voluptuous 17th century Dublin fishmonger who died at an early age of a fever. It is the official anthem of the city of Dublin and has been recorded by many famous singers including U2, Sinéad O'Connor and The Dubliners. June 13 is Molly Malone Day in Dublin. Few occasions can stir the emotions more than hearing Molly Malone sung by 80,000 fans in Croke Park Stadium during an Irish football game. Here are some of the famous lyrics:

In Dublin's fair city,
Where the girls are so pretty,
I first set my eyes on sweet Molly Malone,
As she wheeled her wheel-barrow,
Through streets broad and narrow,
Crying, "Cockles and mussels, alive, alive, oh!"
…
She died of a fever,
And no one could save her,
And that was the end of sweet Molly Malone.
Now her ghost wheels her barrow,
Through streets broad and narrow,
Crying, "Cockles and mussels, alive, alive, oh!"

RIGHT: What could be better than to warm oneself by Molly's welcoming fireplace with its blazing fire on a cold winter day?

Murphy's Bar & Grill

HONOLULU, HAWAII

Irish Oasis

May your home always be too small to hold all your friends.   -Irish toast.

An island in the middle of the Pacific Ocean may appear to be a strange place to find an Irish pub. After all, Hawaii is about as far from Ireland as it is possible to be. Yet, that is the case, illustrating that there is something wonderful and almost magical about Ireland that makes the Irish pub take root almost anywhere in the world. There seems to exist a universal urge to be Irish if only for a few minutes or for a day.

When the bubonic plague struck Honolulu's Chinatown in December 1899, the fire department attempted to burn down buildings that were exposed to the disease. Unfortunately the prevailing winds out of the east gained control of the blaze, resulting in most of the Chinatown buildings being burned to the ground on January 20, 1900. Fortunately, a few brick buildings on the edge of the district escaped the inferno. One of the surviving structures, constructed in 1890 to house The Royal Saloon, has been home since 1987 to Murphy's Bar and Grill, owned by Don "Murph" and Marion Murphy.

The building was constructed on the waterfront with bricks made in Maryland and used as ballast in the ships of the day. Worthless

Murphy's Bar and Grill occupies a historic late 19th century brick structure originally built to house the Royal Saloon.

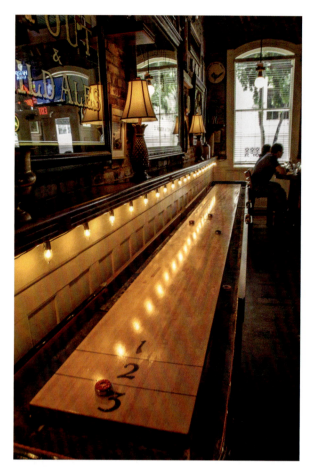

and abundant coral was used as ballast for the return voyages. The sidewalks surrounding Murphy's are made of ten-inch-thick granite blocks, also used as ballast, in this case on ships returning from China in the 19th century when Hawaii sold sandalwood to the Chinese market. The Chinese used the fragrant wood for incense, as medicine and for carving.

The pub shares the so-called "Irish Corner" with O'Toole's Irish Pub across the street. Celebrants typically visit both pubs during an evening out, and the two friendly competitors often collaborate on projects.

Murphy's has two claims to fame. First, according to Murph, it is the home of the biggest

---

ABOVE: Table shuffleboard is popular at Murphy's.

RIGHT: The interior of Murpy's is light and comfortable with original exposed brick walls. Here, one of two bars with a variety of interesting bric-a-brac on the walls.

St Patrick's Day party thrown by any single Irish pub in the US. Second, it has received much recognition for its extensive charitable works.

A few statistics will point up the size of its St Patrick's celebration: 2,500 pounds of corned beef, 6,000 plates of food, 4,000 oysters, 200 kegs of beer, 90 bartenders, upwards of 15,000 attendees, 60,000 square feet of serving area, and more than a dozen tents.

Murphy's pub raises more than $200,000 per year for local charities. The Pigskin Pigout has raised more than $1.5 million over 15 years to support the University of Hawaii football team. Twenty five years of annual gift wrapping parties to benefit the Ronald McDonald House and annual outdoor white table cloth dinners for the Hawaii Children's Cancer Foundation are among other events organized by the pub.

In 2011 Murph and two partners purchased John Ferguson's Irish Pub. John and Murph were long-time friends and when John died, his widow asked Murph if he would carry on her husband's legacy. The pub is housed in the splendid Italian Renaissance style Dillingham Transportation Building, constructed as an office building in the late 1920s by industrialist Walter Dillingham. A portion of his immense wealth came from managing a business founded by his father, the Oahu Railway and Land Company, which connected sugar and pineapple plantations with the Honolulu docks.

ABOVE: Murphy's annual St Patrick's Day block party is billed as the largest celebration of it kind hosted by any single Irish pub in the United States. O'Toole's, on the left of the intersection, and Murphy's on the right, constitute "The Irish Corner." Photo courtesy Jo-Ann Smith.

LEFT: Ferguson's Irish Pub is tucked beneath the arched arcade of the striking Dillingham Transportation Building. The building is listed on the National Register of Historic Places.

Murphy's Grand Irish Pub

ALEXANDRIA, VIRGINIA

Steeped in History

It takes only one drink to get me drunk. The trouble is, I can't remember if it's the thirteenth or the fourteenth.
— George Burns

ALEXANDRIA, FOUNDED IN 1749 AS a seaport, has played host to visitors and travelers from around the world. As a busy trading post, the city became a major port of entry for imports of manufactured goods and a center for exports of agricultural products to Europe. George Washington's home at Mount Vernon was nearby, and Washington was active in the management of the city. When Virginia seceded from the Union in 1861, Federal troops occupied the city within a matter of days and operated a supply center there throughout the Civil War. Thus, Alexandria was spared much of the destruction suffered by other cities in Virginia. During World War II, the population swelled. After the war, the once-sleepy southern town began to modernize. Today the city is home to thousands of Federal employees, many national associations and corporate headquarters. The Old Town along the Potomac River retains many of its charming historic buildings, including some warehouses and townhouses dating back to the eighteenth

Old Town Alexandria is decked out for the holidays. Murphy's has been a favorite spot since 1978 where everyone is a neighbor or friend or needs one.

The pub attracts a loyal following.

ABOVE, RIGHT: Murphy's has long supported police and firefighters who have contributed more than 1000 patches to the pub.

and early nineteenth centuries—a perfect setting for an Irish pub.

A true Hibernian welcome awaits anyone who enters Murphy's Grand Irish Pub, a staple in Old Town since 1978. Tom Mooney, one of the owners, can probably name half of the people at the bar at any given time. Tom retired in 2007 following 40 years working in the US House of Representatives, serving as General Counsel for the House Judiciary Committee and lastly for the House International Relations Committee.

Tom and his wife Melinda, a registered nurse, were honored to be Grand Marshals of the 2012 Alexandria St Patrick's Day Parade, an annual event that kicks off Irish-American Heritage Month. Tom's grandparents came to the US in 1883 from County Mayo on Ireland's west coast which boasts the highest sea cliffs in Ireland. Melinda's ancestors also came from County Mayo.

The pub has an intensely loyal following of mostly local residents. A strong measure of Irish-American politicians and tourists are

also drawn to the famous pub by its staff and warm fireplace. Thirty miles to the south is the Quantico US Marine Corps Base. During the first ten years of the pub's existence, most New Year's reservations were made by officers from Quantico. Tom recalls that if the crowd became a little unruly, all the band had to do was play the revered Marines' Hymn, the oldest official song in the U.S. military, and the revelers would immediately snap to attention.

New England Patriots football fans in the Washington metro area have adopted Murphy's as their official Patriots Irish pub. Since the early 1990s, the pub has televised every Pats game on their upstairs screen to a large and enthusiastic crowd of supporters.

Murphy's has never closed due to inclement weather. During blizzards, pub employees are put up at local hotels. The pub shows its commitment to people in other ways as well. More than 1000 police and firefighters' patches adorn the walls, contributed by their grateful owners. "We go out of our way to show our appreciation for their service," says Tom. Pub employees wear blue ribbons during Washington's Police Memorial Week every May honoring officers killed in the line of duty the previous year. Murphy's recently conducted a memorial service for fallen firemen.

The building housing the pub dates back to 1816. At one time it was a Salvation Army distribution center. It is located near what was once part of the underground railroad, the secret network of routes used to move escaped slaves from the south to Canada during the 19th century. Paradoxically, it is five blocks away from a pre-Civil War era slave auction facility. With its location on the railroad and the Potomac River, Alexandria was an ideal spot for receiving and shipping slaves to the deep south. A former World War ll torpedo factory, now a museum, is nearby. Photos on the walls of are VIP visitors including most U.S. presidents.

A place with a sense of closeness where friends are made and stories are shared—that is the essence of a true Irish pub. If that is what you are looking for, you cannot do better than Murphy's, a vibrant business in a heritage location. They even have purse hooks under the bar.

Even the Irish harp above the fireplace is ready for the holidays. The Celtic Harp is the national emblem of Ireland. It first appeared on coins in the 1500s. The harp symbol was used by The Irish Brigades that served in the Union Army in the American Civil War.

Presidential Proclamation—Irish-American Heritage Month, 2013 Excerpts

For more than two centuries, America has been made and remade by striving, hopeful immigrants looking for a chance to pursue their dreams. Millions among them were born in Ireland, separated from our shores but united by their belief in a better day. This month, we celebrate the Irish-American journey, and we reflect on the ways a nation so small has inspired so much in another.

Generations of Irish left the land of their forebears to cast their fortunes with a young Republic. Escaping the blight of famine or the burden of circumstance, many found hardship even here. They endured prejudice and stinging ridicule. But through it all, these new citizens never gave up on one of our oldest ideas: that anyone from anywhere can write the next great chapter in the American story.... So as we celebrate Irish-American Heritage Month, let us retell those stories of sweat and striving. And as two nations united by people and principle, may America and Ireland always continue to move forward together in common purpose.

NOW, THEREFORE, I, BARACK OBAMA, President of the United States of America, by virtue of the authority vested in me by the Constitution and the laws of the United States, do hereby proclaim March 2013 as Irish-American Heritage Month. I call upon all Americans to observe this month with appropriate ceremonies, activities, and programs.

Barack Obama

Nallen's Irish Pub

DENVER, COLORADO
Wedding Pub

You never want to be the first to leave an Irish conversation. —John Nallen

THE AIR IN THE MILE High City is crisp, clear and invigorating, befitting a city on the move. Once blighted areas have given way to breathtaking skyscrapers. A new generation of shops, restaurants and businesses has reinvigorated run-down neighborhoods. Public art abounds, invoking civic pride and proclaiming the city's importance. (More than 300 pieces of public art have been constructed under a program mandating that 1% of major capital improvements be set aside for art.)

The LoDo district is a prime example of urban revitalization and renewal. LoDo is the affectionate term for the Lower Downtown area of Denver, once the city's Skid Row. It is where Denver began in 1858 and is today a designated historic district. Much of the area's rebirth occurred after the opening of Coors Field, home of the Colorado Rockies baseball team, in 1995. (A home run travels 10 percent farther in Denver's thin air than it would in Yankee

Stadium.) Coors Field injected a new sense of excitement into the decaying area, which translated into new businesses, art galleries, restaurants, condos and a very active night life.

Nallen's is a family-run business. It is one of 42 Irish pubs in Denver according to proprietor John Nallen, who with his wife Una, runs the operation on a daily basis. Son Sean at 24 works to attract the younger crowd with his texting and Facebook activities. Daughter Katie's fiancé Keith Lawler is the manager. He hails from the seaside town of Malahide, County Dublin, famous for its 12th century castle.

The pub occupies a well-designed space in the heart of now chic and trendy LoDo, in one of 125 brick buildings constructed between the 1870s and turn of the last century. The two-story blond brick commercial style building has a typical recessed entrance with bright red doors, rectangular windows with flower boxes and a wrought iron fence that claims part of the sidewalk.

Nallen's is the oldest Irish pub in the city, opening in 1992 and transferring to its current location in 1996. John is a friendly face who warmly greets everyone who enters and claims

OPPOSITE PAGE: The bright red door at 1429 can't be missed. Behind it is the oldest Irish pub in Denver. It is situated in a two-story commercial building dating back to the late 1800s in the historic LoDo district. Numerous weddings have taken place there.

BELOW: Good advice.

A well-deserved award. A Guinness "double pour" (the first pour to settle the brew, the second to top it off) should take exactly 119.53 seconds. The head must protrude above the rim but never spill over. The beer should be served at 42.8 degrees Fahrenheit. Each sip must leave a ring on the inside of the glass. Creating a perfect pour is an art.

to know 90 percent of his weekday customers by name. Some younger regular patrons visit the pub before going to local nightclubs and then return to the pub at 1:00am. Other clients have been dropping by for years. One 94 year old gentleman comes in from his retirement home by bus two times a week for a pint or two. The weekend crowd has a more suburbanite character and fewer regulars. The busiest days are St Patrick's Day and opening day of the baseball season.

The decor is all business, no frills, with thick, well-worn wooden tables and dark wood throughout. That is part of its charm and character and may help explain why it is known as the wedding pub. Twelve weddings have taken place there, often between people who have met at the pub. They inevitably return for anniversary celebrations.

John Nallen came to the US in 1973 from the tiny village of Belderrig, located on the rugged Atlantic coast between Ballycastle and Belmullet in County Mayo. His home town has "a church, post office, pub and commonage," lands used by local farmers for sheep and cattle. John's brother still runs the farm where John grew up. He and Una visit the farm from time to time. Una comes from the similarly diminutive Stonefield Village, some 15 miles from Belderrig. The two met at a local dance, and as the saying goes, the rest is history.

Before settling in Denver, in both Ireland and New York, John was a middleweight and light heavyweight amateur boxer, skills that can come in handy for any publican.

RIGHT: The suitably-worn bar is not large, but it is well loved in Denver.

From the Owner:

When I was boy working on the farm tending to the cows and sheep I often dreamed about moving to America. I aspired to make something of myself in land of opportunity. When I turned 21, my dreams came true, and I headed across the Atlantic and landed in New York City. I packed my bags with the gift of the gab I was blessed with and utilized the work ethic I learned back home. I made a living working hard knowing that one day I would like to open an authentic pub of my own. After spending time in New York and becoming familiar with the nightlife, I headed to beautiful Colorado with my wife. After several years of owning my own landscaping business, I decided it was time to embark on my dream and open a pub. Twenty-one years later, I'm blessed to have had the opportunity to open my doors and share stories with friends and patrons from all over the world.

- John Nallen, owner
Nallen's Irish Pub

Nine Fine Irishmen

LAS VEGAS, NEVADA

Unexpected Pleasure

I can resist anything except temptation.
 -Oscar Wilde (on the threshold of Nine Fine Irishmen)

WALK THROUGH THE GAPING ENTRANCE, go past the blackjack tables, slide between endless rows of blinking, whirring slot machines and suddenly it is right in front of you, unmistakably green—a totally perfect Irish pub in the middle of one of Las Vegas's largest hotels. It is an unexpected pleasure for some and the object of a purposeful trek for others.

Nine Fine Irishmen is one of America's best known Irish pubs and certainly one of the most frequented. It is an example of the new Las Vegas, a city of celebrity chefs, family entertainment and enough neon to be seen from outer space. Gone are the days when gambling was the only attraction. Today, many of the world's largest and most elegant hotels and hundreds of restaurants line the extravagant 4.2 mile Las Vegas Strip. Forty million visitors descend upon Las Vegas every year. No wonder Nine Fine Irishmen is the largest purveyor of Guinness in the country.

The pub is in the New York New York Hotel which belongs to MGM Resorts International,

Las Vegas is glamorous and exciting. What better place to find an Irish pub than under the dazzling lights of a vast casino?

a global operator of luxury resorts, including several of the finest hotels in Las Vegas. New York New York opened in 1997 and features a 150 foot replica of the Statue of Liberty in front of the property. Following the September 11, 2001 attacks, people spontaneously sent tributes to fire, rescue and police departments from around the country, creating an impromptu memorial in front of the statue which eventually reached the height of three stories. Later, a permanent memorial was created on the site.

Nine Fine Irishmen was designed and installed by The Irish Pub Company of Dublin, a firm that has built more than 450 Irish pubs in 47 countries. Many would say that the firm deserves a great deal of credit for the enormous success of the Irish pub concept globally.

Nine Fine Irishmen is proof that a new enterprise can be created with authenticity. Every item in the pub comes from Ireland and was placed for a reason. The bar was made and assembled in Ireland, then disassembled and shipped to Nevada. Areas of the interior were designed to replicate the traditional functions of a typical Irish cottage, for example the scullery, a room used for washing dishes and laundering clothes, and another room used to store everyday hand tools.

Executive Chef Mitchell Roberts is typical of the new breed of topnotch chefs who exemplify how cuisine has come to the fore in modern Las Vegas. A graduate of the rigorous and prestigious American Culinary Federation, Mitchell manages all food operations, employee training and recipe development. He has won significant awards over his fifteen-year career and brings his own style of cuisine to the kitchen. Pub food has come a long way.

The pub's name honors nine young idealists, leaders of a group known as Young Ireland who

argued and fought against British rule in the mid-1800s. Inspired by the French Revolution and provoked by the desperate conditions of the Great Irish Famine, a group of the revolutionaries led a small band of coal miners and farmers in an ill-conceived uprising in July 1848 in the village of Ballingarry, County Tipperary. The men fought unsuccessfully against some 50 local police, reportedly unfurling for the first time the green, white and orange tricolor that would become the Irish national flag. Captured and tried, some of the patriots were condemned to be hung, drawn and quartered until Queen Victoria herself objected to the harshness of the sentences. The men were sent to a penal colony in Australia instead. Eventually, most of the men became very successful in Australia, the United States and Canada. Today, the farmhouse where the rebellion took place is an Irish national monument.

ABOVE: The pub is named in honor of nine Irish revolutionaries who led an ill-fated uprising against British rule in 1848. In this Currier and Ives print, Trial of the Irish Patriots, circa 1848, several of the rebels, standing right, receive a death sentence from Lord Chief Justice Doherty, standing left.

OPPOSITE, TOP: The 9000-square-foot pub is spectacular.

THIS PAGE, TOP: The New York New York Hotel and Casino lights up the Las Vegas skyline.

Olde Blind Dog

MILTON & BROOKHAVEN, GEORGIA

A Tale of Two Pubs

When a man's best friend is his dog, that dog has a problem. -Edward Abbey

There is a story behind the name of just about any Irish pub, but it would be hard to top the saga of Olde Blind Dog. Local businessman and pub co-founder, Ron Wallace, spent years developing the one-of-a kind concept behind his two pubs in the Atlanta suburbs, but a meaningful and memorable name for the business escaped him and his partner Joe Creamer. Desperate, Ron sent several hundred emails to friends soliciting suggestions. It came down to ten potential names. Late one night in 2008, with his faithful 125 pound, blind-in-one-eye female American Bulldog on the floor beside him, Ron was ready to send out a final email asking his friends to select the best name from the finalists. Just before hitting the send button, Ron said to Peaches, "Ok, old blind dog, let's go to bed." For a joke, he added the name "Olde Blind Dog" to the list. You guessed it; respondents overwhelmingly selected that name.

Olde Blind Dog Irish Pubs are located in Milton, Georgia, and 25 miles away in Brookhaven on the outskirts of Atlanta. Milton is a new city, incorporated in 2006 and positioned in the midst of gently rolling hills and equestrian estates. Brookhaven is also new, incorporated in December 2012 as an upcoming neighborhood of young professionals on the move. It is home to Oglethorpe University, a liberal arts school founded in 1835. Inside the pubs, a wonderland of imported antiques, artifacts and authentic Celtic food transports visitors to 18th century

Olde Blind Dog in Brookhaven is situated on a large brick patio in an up and coming new community. It provides room service to residents of the chic apartments above it. On the next page is Olde Blind Dog in Milton.

Ireland and other old-world Celtic nations.

Nineteenth century advertising mirrors, signs, stained glass, hand carvings and furniture are each unique. Two examples: a bookcase that spans an entire wall was once part of Napoleon III's library. A massive two hundred year old hand carved panel that embellishes the back bar framed the entrance to the grand ballroom of the King George hotel in Paris. Both pubs include cobblestoned floors and neatly tucked away snugs for private dining.

The bars serve many whiskeys and numerous types of beer, but the featured brew is treated like royalty. A special cooler is reserved exclusively for Guinness, to maintain the ideal temperature standards set by the Guinness Company. According to Guinness's Global Ambassador, Olde Blind Dog is one of a handful of pubs worldwide that really does serve the perfect pint.

OPPOSITE: Dublin's famous 18th century Temple Bar is affectionately reproduced inside the Brookhaven location right down to the cobblestone street in front. Patrons can enjoy a measure of privacy inside the bar.

RIGHT: Life size replicas of Braveheart are featured in both pubs. William Wallace, known as Braveheart, was a 13th-century Scottish warrior who led the Scots in a war against King Edward I of England. Photo by Leslie Watson.

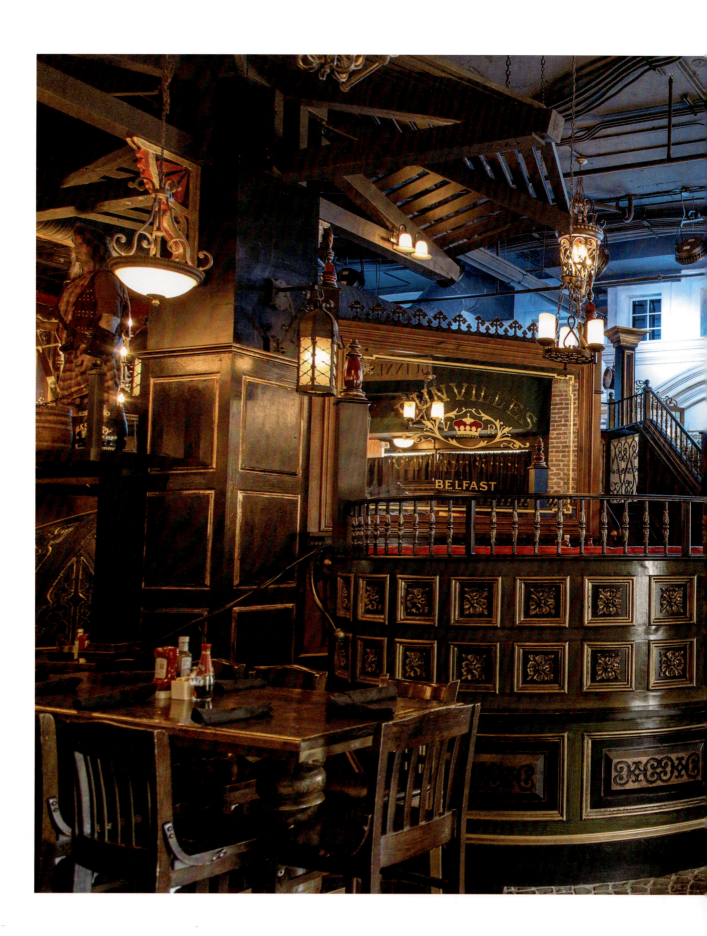

The elegant three level central tower in Brookhaven offers small, semi-private areas for dining and drinking.

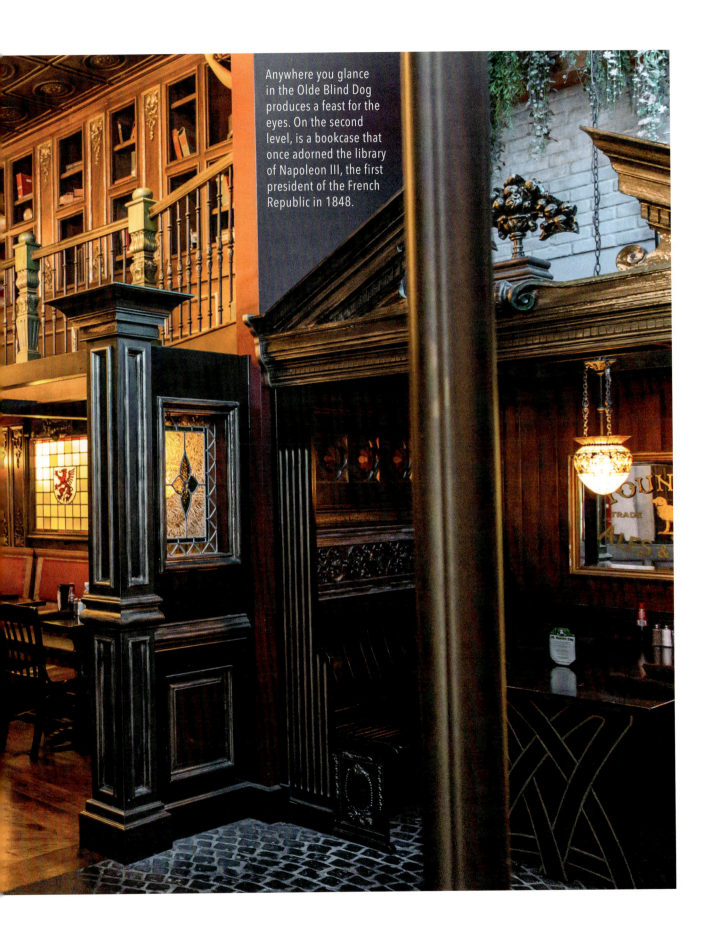

Anywhere you glance in the Olde Blind Dog produces a feast for the eyes. On the second level, is a bookcase that once adorned the library of Napoleon III, the first president of the French Republic in 1848.

Is it a museum or a pub? Photo by Leslie Watson

The True Story (more or less) of the Olde Blind Dog

The following story appears on the cover of the pub's menu to explain the origin of the name of this pub.

Not so very long ago in the green hills of Ireland, a young pup named Caden (meaning Spirited Warrior) shared a cottage with his master, Sean. Each day, the little white bulldog would rise before sun up and accompany Sean as he tended to his sheep.

At the end of each day, Caden would faithfully follow Sean to their favorite pub. The dog would sit under the bar patiently while Sean enjoyed a pint (or two or three) and traded stories with the locals.

Early evening became late night and in true Irish tradition the music grew louder, the patrons sang and the Guinness flowed. These were happy times, especially for Caden, as he enjoyed table scraps and was lavished with more attention than any dog could want.

Legend has it that late one night as they made their way home, they were suddenly attacked by a pack of wolves. Without hesitation, Caden bared his teeth and the fur flew. Although outnumbered, he fought off the pack and sent them howling into the canyons below. Bloodied and bruised, they arrived home only to discover a wound to one eye that eventually caused blindness.

Word spread like wildfire. Caden had rid the village of wolves, like Saint Patrick had rid Ireland of snakes. He became a hero overnight. Glasses of stout were lifted and songs were sung in his honor.

After that night, when it was time to head to the pub, Sean would say, "C'mon old blind dog, let's have a pint."

As time went on, Sean looked far and wide to find an easier life for him and his faithful dog. They found the perfect place —no sheep, no wolves, but green as an Irish pasture. And that place was Milton, Georgia.

Moved by the story of the legendary dog, a few local friends decided to bring a wee bit of Ireland to this side of the pond. They established an authentic Celtic pub in the heart of Milton and named it in his honor.

Welcome to Olde Blind Dog

- Ron Wallace, Co-founder
Olde Blind Dog

O'Reilly's

SAN FRANCISCO, CALIFORNIA

Keeping Traditions Alive

Strangers are friends we have not yet met.
         -William Butler Yeats

SEVEN OF IRELAND'S GREATEST INTELLECTS greet visitors to O'Reilly's Irish pub in the heart of San Francisco's North Beach neighborhood, once the epicenter of the beat generation. Seán O'Casey, William Butler Yeats, George Bernard Shaw, Oscar Wilde, Samuel Beckett, Brendan Behan and James Joyce are ranged along the railing at the end of the bar eager to engage in discussions about literature or politics.

The splendid life-size mural of Ireland's most famous literati was painted by local muralist Vranas Van Hoyt and is entirely appropriate in Myles O'Reilly's pub, where all are welcome, none are judged and where conversation flows like the River Liffey, especially if the effusive and ever-cheerful Myles takes part. Hundreds of photographs, documents and other conversational memorabilia adorn the walls, assuring that there never need be dull moment and that every pregnant pause can be filled. The beautiful bar comes from a guest house in Kanturk, a small market town in County Cork, and dates to 1825. The German stained glass behind the bar is from the same period.

Myles was born in Dublin where he attended Belcamp College, a novitiate of the Oblate Fathers in the Balgriffin section of the city. He intended to become a priest until age 20 when he transferred to a more traditional school. His grandfather owned a pub on Cooper Street in Belfast aptly named O'Reilly's. His father was a bodyguard for the President of Ireland Éamon DeVelara.

Expect a warm welcome in this charming neighborhood pub in the heart of North Beach.

"I was raised on herring and offal," Miles recalls. After college, Miles worked for CIA International Tours, a semi-state body, promoting Ireland as a place for visitors and investors. Seized with an incurable wanderlust, he traveled to Thailand where he taught English to hill tribes and then to Australia where he worked as a jackaroo in northern Queensland before eventually ending up in San Francisco in 1989. When not working in his pub, Myles enjoys horseback riding, fine food and falling out of airplanes, having made more than 300 sky dives to date. He is well-known for wearing green shoes every day for the past 25 years.

O'Reilly's is one of the most popular watering holes in the city. Regulars and tourists know they will find a friendly and pleasant environment. They know that maintaining the traditions that made Ireland great is important there. Charity is one of the traditions, and the pub supports local charities because even if poor, "the Irish just can't say no, no matter how little they have to give," says Myles, whose mantra is "sharing is caring."

The luscious oyster is Ireland's favorite bivalve, a fact not lost on Myles who started an annual oyster festival extravaganza 15 years ago. Every May thousands gather for the O'Reilly's Oyster and Beer Festival in Golden Gate Park to down Guinness stout, brown bread and 55 thousand oysters, a combination "made in heaven," Miles enthusiastically asserts. If you are among those for whom eating the slippery mollusks is a challenge, imagine the festival's competitive consumption record of 75 oysters swallowed in five minutes. Part of the proceeds from the festival's $10.00 admission is donated to the Silesian Boys and Girls Club of San Francisco. Never at a loss for trivia, Myles reports the oyster was fast food in Lincoln's time. Transportation in sawdust kept the little creatures fresh.

LEFT: The early 19th century long bar comes from a small town in County Cork.

Eternally cheerful Myles O'Reilly at the entrance to his pub. He has worn green shoes every day for 25 years. It doesn't get more Irish than that.

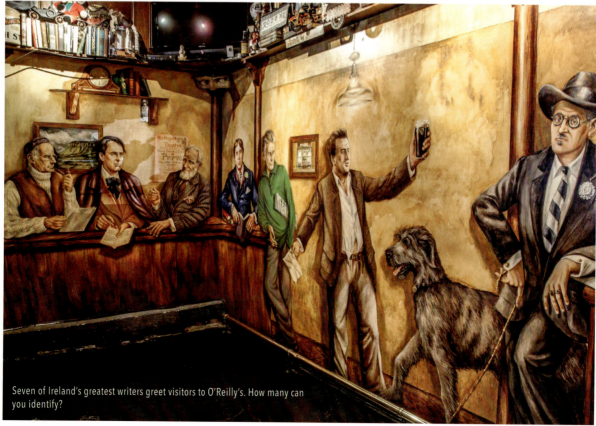

Seven of Ireland's greatest writers greet visitors to O'Reilly's. How many can you identify?

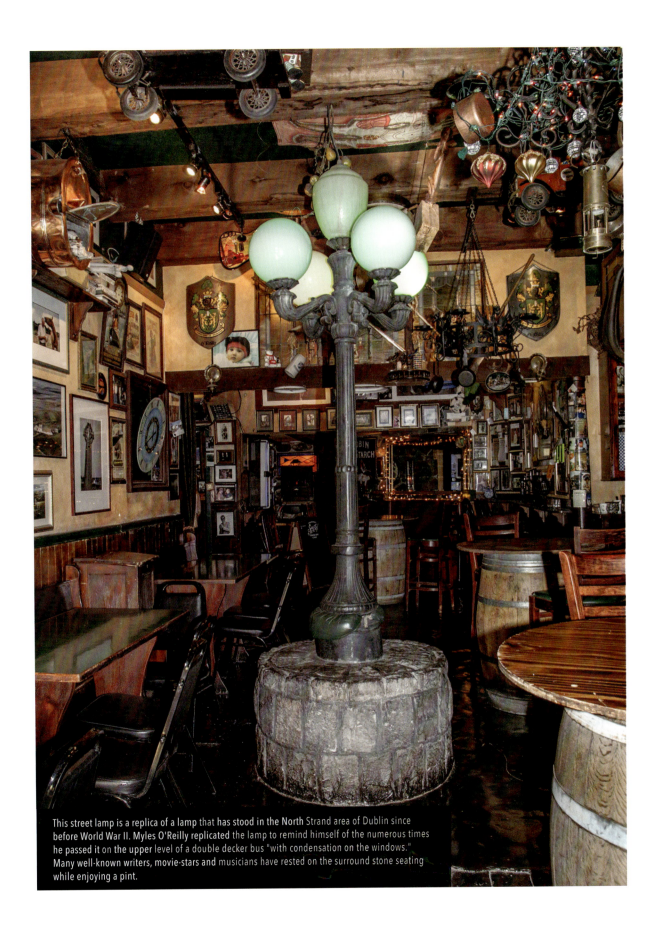

This street lamp is a replica of a lamp that has stood in the North Strand area of Dublin since before World War II. Myles O'Reilly replicated the lamp to remind himself of the numerous times he passed it on the upper level of a double decker bus "with condensation on the windows." Many well-known writers, movie-stars and musicians have rested on the surround stone seating while enjoying a pint.

O'Rourke's

SOUTH BEND, INDIANA

Where science, wisdom, and good times converge.

An atheist is a man who watches a Notre Dame-Southern Methodist football game and doesn't care who wins. -Dwight David Eisenhower

IT WOULD BE IMPOSSIBLE TO write a book about Irish pubs in America without visiting Notre Dame. Some institutions are simply Irish to the core; Irishness is in their genes. Such is the case with the University of Notre Dame du Lac, located on 524 lush acres just north of South Bend. The university is known best for two things, scientific research and football, not necessarily in that order.

Notre Dame was founded in 1842 by Father Edward Sorin, CSC (Congregation of the Holy Cross), who also served as its first President. Pioneering research was characteristic from the start. Notre Dame was the site of the nation's first wireless transmission in 1899, for example, and the formula for synthetic rubber was discovered there. Perhaps best known of the university's distinguished presidents is Father Theodore Hesburgh, CSC under whose 35 year tenure (1952 - 1987) the university's enrollment, faculty and degrees awarded doubled. Its research funding increased twenty-fold. Current President Father John Jenkins, CSC has continued the focus on research, academic excellence and religious faith.

O'Rourke's Public House is perched at the southern edge of the university campus, and while only two years old it takes being Irish seriously.

The straightforward exterior of this pub gives little clue of what awaits inside. It sits is across the street from the beautiful Notre Dame campus.

That is a weighty obligation with decades of tradition just across the street.

The pub takes its name from the proud O'Rourke clan. It is an anglicized version of an Old Norse name dating back to the 10th century. The family motto, Serviendo Guberno, I govern by serving, is totally appropriate for an Irish pub in close proximity to the university. The pub's logo is a modification of the O'Rourke family crest featuring two walking lions.

O'Rourke's main bar area is large. It has to be to accommodate the quantity of thirsty fans that squeeze in after a Fighting Irish football game or an important basketball or other significant game. The university is strongly sports oriented and participates in 23 NCAA Division 1 intercollegiate sports. Patrons love it when head

---

TOP: A complete set of John Ireland drawings depicting the "Gentle Art of Making Guinness" adorns one wall.

LEFT: The long bar with 23 taps and ample TV screens.

football coach Brian Kelly or basketball coach Mike Brey hold live radio or streaming internet programs at the pub. Notre Dame Football Fantasy Camp draws large, sometimes bruised, crowds to the pub every summer. In partnership with the university, the pub sponsors many athletic events throughout the year. When legendary Notre Dame coach Lou Holtz (1986 - 1996) visited the pub, it was "like a beam of light when he walked around," says Manager Andrew Pankowski.

Themed areas are decorated with Irish bric-a-brac. The shops section includes groceries and bags of flour as is common in rural Irish pubs. The iron and dark wooded Victorian area is warm and comforting. The brewery section of the bar is notable for its striking copper dome. One wall features a full set of humorous John Ireland drawings from the famous 1981 calendar depicting the "Gentle Art of Making Guinness." As in many Irish pubs throughout the world, Guinness advertising posters by John Gilroy adorn some walls. Gilroy, who died in 1985, produced some 100 ads and 50 posters for Guinness, many featuring animals and birds enjoying a pint.

General Manager Shelly Freitag believes that O'Rourke's absorbs and projects a special energy from being close to the university stadium, where so much emotion and excitement abound. It is an "awesome atmosphere," she asserts.

TOP: The beautiful interior is large enough to accommodate the crowds that pour in before and after Notre Dame football games. Spotted in this picture, at the table on the right, in the dark track suit jacket with red shirt, is former Notre All-American George Kunz.

LEFT: Small tables along the row of windows encourage conversation.

FOLLOWING SPREAD: Entrance to the main bar.

STAMPS 2¢ EACH

O'...arke's Public House

SALT TELEPHONE

COFFEE

GUINNESS

...CK DANIEL

Notre Dame's Hesburgh Library with Touchdown Jesus mosaic.

ABOVE: Notre Dame Stadium, home of The Fighting Irish. Photo by Matt Cashore/University of Notre Dame

Symbols of Ireland
Many symbols are associated with Ireland. Here are some of the best known.

THE HARP has been the official symbol of Ireland since medieval times. The current design is based on the 14th Century Brian Boru harp, which is housed in the Trinity Colleges museum in Dublin and is one of the country's national treasures. Those who played the harp in the time of the Celtic chieftains were highly regarded and often played for the nobility. Harpers would also lead the troops into battle. The harp appears on Irish coinage and on the Guinness label.

THE SHAMROCK, a trefoil, or three leaf clover, is an unofficial symbol of Ireland. According to tradition, St Patrick used the shamrock to explain the Christian doctrine of the Holy Trinity to the pagan kings of ancient Ireland. It was reportedly sacred to the Druids because it had three leaves, and three was a mystical number for them. The shamrock is worn on March 17, St Patrick's Day, the Irish national holiday, and has come to symbolize Ireland and Irish culture around the world.

THE CELTIC KNOT consists of a series of interwoven knots which have no clear start or end. They first appeared in Celtic art in the 5th century. There are many interpretations of the knots' symbolism, but generally the unending cycle of life and notions of interdependence and physical and spiritual connections are involved. Elaborate examples of knot work are found on many Celtic crosses and in the ornamentation of the 8th century Book of Kells.

THE CELTIC CROSS During his proselytizing in the 5th century, St Patrick reportedly was shown a sacred pagan stone that was marked with a circle, possibly representing the moon goddess. To encourage the union of pagan and Christian ways St Patrick marked a cross through the circle and blessed the stone. While these crosses are associated with all Celtic nations, they probably originated in Ireland. Today, some see the circle as representing Christ's halo or the endlessness of God's love

THE CLADDAGH RING was first created in Claddagh, a small fishing village just outside the Galway city wall. It consists of a heart held by two hands surmounted by a crown. The heart denotes love; the hands symbolize friendship, and the crown signifies loyalty. The Claddagh ring has become immensely popular as a friendship and wedding ring.

O'Toole's Irish Pub

HONOLULU, HAWAII

Ulysses *Hawaiian Style*

Good puzzle would be cross Dublin without passing a pub. -James Joyce, *Ulysses*

NEAR THE WATERFRONT WHERE THE giant cruise ships dock is situated a handsome brick building, named in honor of shipwright Thomas Foster, who made his fortune as founder of the Inter-Island Steam Navigation Company, the precursor to Hawaiian Airlines. Constructed in 1891 the building was originally a warehouse for Mr. Foster with a small adjoining stable separated from the main building by a brick patio.

Originally, ships docked at the Foster Building, bringing as many as 400 thirsty sailors per day to the harbor. The area since then has been extended several hundred yards into the ocean to accommodate the large cruise ships.

The Foster Building houses O'Toole's Irish Pub, owned by Bill Comerford and his business partner Fred Remington, who bought the pub in 2003. The business operated as a bar in the 1960s and was named O'Toole's in the 1970s after a favorite customer Jimmy O'Toole who worked at a local Ford automotive dealership until his retirement. For some committed regulars, O'Toole's is almost like Cheers where everyone knows your name.

O'Toole's occupies one half of the well-known "Irish Corner." Across the intersection sits a friendly competitor, Murphy's Bar and Grill. In reality, the two pubs complement

each other. Murphy's serves food but does not offer entertainment. O'Toole's does not serve food but provides music every weekend. The competitive side is best evidenced by the baseball teams that each of these pubs avidly supports. O'Toole's is partial to the Boston Red Sox, while it is best to root for the New York Yankees over at Murphy's.

O'Toole's is noted for its Bloomsday celebration which, along with select pubs throughout the world, observes the life and work of Irish writer James Joyce (see adjoining sidebar). Readings from his novel Ulysses, a pub crawl and mock funeral procession honoring Joyce's other great novel, Finnegan's Wake, are all part of the popular four hour event.

Bill Comerford is President of the Friends of St Patrick, a charitable organization that among other efforts organizes the annual St Patrick's Day parade in Honolulu. The parade includes bands, floats and marching groups and proceeds down Kalakaua Avenue, the main thoroughfare on Waikiki Beach. Bill proudly notes that it is the last St Patrick's Day Parade on that day anywhere in the world since the next one takes place on the other side of the International Date Line.

O'Tool's is divided into two rooms—a bar and a music room—separated by a brick arch.

Bloomsday

James Joyce's epic novel Ulysses, published in 1922, meticulously recounts an imaginary day in the life of an ordinary Dubliner, Leopold Bloom. He and a friend wander their way through the streets of Dublin, roughly paralleling the ten-year voyage of the Greek hero Ulysses in Homer's Odyssey. Each of the 18 episodes of the novel loosely parallels the people and events in Homer's classic.

The events are set on June 16, 1904, which corresponds with Joyce's first outing with his future wife. Each year on that date, Joyce devotees reenact key events of that imaginary day with readings, period costumes, walks and pub visits in an event known as Bloomsday. Although Joyce's prose is at times impenetrable, the celebration of the man, his work and the city of Dublin is very much down to earth -- particularly for those who enjoy a healthy pint.

Ulysses is considered one of the greatest novels of the 20th century.

Owl 'N Thistle

SEATTLE, WASHINGTON

Built on Solid Ground

If the facts don't fit the theory, change the facts.
-Albert Einstein

ON JUNE 6, 1889, JUST five months before Washington became a state, the Great Fire raced over a 30-block area, destroying the heart of Seattle all the way down to the waterfront on Elliott Bay. Most of the structures were wood, the cheapest raw material in a region of dense conifer forests—and the most flammable.

Gone was the structure known as the Colman Block, a wooden building constructed by engineer and businessman James Colman several years earlier on tons of fill dirt moved from the first of some 60 regrades that changed the topography of central Seattle. Hilltops were leveled off to make way for roads, trollies and commercial buildings, forever altering the terrain of the city.

Included in the land fill was the clipper ship Windward which had run aground in dense fog on nearby Whidbey Island in 1875. Colman purchased the ship, towed it, anchored it 150 feet from his dock and salvaged its usable parts, leaving the rest to slowly deteriorate. When he built the Colman Block in the early 1880s, he left the ship where it lay, adding dirt and concrete as foundation for his building.

When the city's citizens rallied to rebuild their devastated city after the Great Fire, they raised many of the streets by at least eight feet using a system of retaining walls which were filled in with dirt and debris from the fire and then repaved. In 1890 Colman erected a new building on his waterfront site in the Chicago School style, which became a landmark structure earning a listing on the National Register of Historic Places in 1972. The front of the building is on the upper level street; the rear, housing the Owl 'N Thistle is at the lower level. According to pub co-owner Jack Geary," the building sits right on top of the old ship." Over the decades, the six-story building has had a variety of tenants

including some who catered to miners heading to the Yukon gold rush in the mid-1890s.

The pub is much larger than it appears from outside. Normally, a pub has the bar up front so customers see it first. However, because of local liquor laws in the 1930s when the space served as a restaurant, the dining area had to be separate from the bar. The space was designed with two entrances, one with a passageway leading to the bar in the back, and a second opening directly to the dining room. The layout appears somewhat awkward by today's standards. Off to one side of the pub is a small library of law books donated in the 1970s by noted attorney John Henry Brown when he moved his office from the Colman Building. The pub attracts businessmen and attorneys from the nearby courthouse during the lunch hour and a mixed clientele at night enticed by the lively music. Ferry commuters going to Bainbridge Island and Bremerton often stop off at the pub on their way home.

Jack, son of a civil servant, studied to be a teacher. He and his business partner Declan Fury were fellow students at the National University of Ireland in Galway and remained in contact through the years. After graduating in 1968 Jack traveled to the US for the summer and, as fate would have it, decided to make his life in America. He landed a job as a musician catering to the large Irish-American community in the Irish Catskills. He and his friend Sean Tyrrell, who has since become a successful singer of traditional Irish songs, traveled around the country as the duo Freedom Folk. In 1970 Jack married a Seattle girl, Terri Warden, and took up residence there. Terry does the books for the pub. Their son Colin is the pub's general manager. Jack's wonderful singing voice and guitar playing regularly entertain pub patrons. He received the 2011 Irishman of the Year Award from the Irish Heritage Club of Seattle.

One oft-told story relates to movie star John

Wayne who was an avid boater. He and his buddies including Robert Mitchum, enjoyed sailing around the islands in Puget Sound. It is said that they painted their signatures in the pub's entrance hallway where they remained until one day some mastermind painted over them. Since Jack is also an avid boater, it is not surprising that the pub's decor has a nautical theme. Included are two model Irish fishing boats, a Claddagh Hooker, the traditional fishing boat of the Claddagh village in Galway, and a Currach, an animal skin covered wooden frame boat traditional to the west coast of Ireland for centuries.

OPPOSITE: One of three rooms in the pub. The corner library is a noteworthy feature.

TOP: The bar. Due to local regulations in the 1930s, the bar is located in the rear of the pub to separate it from dining areas.

Paddy Reilly's Music Bar

NEW YORK, NEW YORK

Come for the Music

Alcohol may be man's worst enemy, but the Bible says love your enemy.   -Frank Sinatra

PADDY REILLY HAS BEEN SINGING Irish ballads for forty years. His rendition of the beautiful The Fields of Athenry has become a classic and is a favorite of Irish footballers. No wonder that in 1986 Paddy decided to open his own New York pub dedicated to music. Although no longer active in the pub, his influence remains strong and traditional music continues to flourish at Paddy Reilly's. Many Irish bands of note had their start there, bands such as Black 47, The McCabes, The Mickey Finns and the Prodigals among others. Countless other Irish singers and bands have performed there, giants such as members of The Chieftains, members of The Dubliners and members of the Clancy Brothers. Members of U-2 used to hang out at the pub. No visit to New York City by an Irish band would be complete without a gig or a pint at Paddy Reilly's.

The pub is a magnet for celebrities as well. On any visit you might see the likes of actor Jason Patric, Chris Noth (Sex in the City), Daniel Craig (James Bond), model Naomi Campbell or Tim Flannery (San Francisco Giants coach). The pub is also home to some great American bluegrass music, which after all has its roots in the songs immigrants from Ireland and other countries brought with them to the American shores.

The pub is unassuming on the outside and unpretentious inside, a place where you make instant friends at the bar. After all, you came there for a frosty pint, for the music and conversation. When you are there you know that this is a good time to be Irish. Manager Steve Duggan loves the business. He recites words of wisdom from his grand uncle in Ireland who said, "For people who know the pub business,

LEFT: Unassuming on the outside and filled with music on the inside, Paddy Reilly's occupies a special place in the lexicon of Irish pubs.

RIGHT: Wednesday is open mike night when any accomplished musician is welcome to play. The music goes on for most of the night.

NEXT SPREAD: The slightly cramped but warm environment attracts well-known and aspiring musicians as well as Irish and bluegrass music lovers.

AN IRISH STORY

I grew up on a farm in Kilkenny in the southeast of Ireland. One day an American drove by where my father was cutting a ditch. The American asked my father for directions, and they got into a conversation. They found that they had much in common. The American was a rancher in Texas; my father was a farmer. The Texan asked how big my father's farm was. Dad described it in personal terms: it goes from that tree over there over the hill to the pond and then to the other hilltop, etc. The American asked, "Is that a big farm in Ireland?" Father said, "About average." The Texan said that he gets up in the morning, climbs into his car and drives from dawn to dusk and still cannot circle his entire ranch. Dad was not about to let that go by and responded; "We had a car like that once. We had to get rid of it."

-Steve Duggan, Manager, Paddy Reilly's

no explanation is necessary; for those who don't know it, there is no explanation possible." Steve comes from County Cavan where he was an all-star GAA (Gaelic Athletic Association) Gaelic football player. (He has also run 13 New York City and Irish marathons.)

If you are a Guinness fan, it is especially good to be in Paddy Reilly's since it is the first and only all-draft Guinness pub in the world, according to Steve, that is, the pub sells only Guinness on draft. They also sell a variety of bottled beers, liquors and wines. Steve firmly believes that the secret to serving Guinness is to move it quickly. Never keep the Guinness stout for more than two or three days once a keg is tapped. Use clean dry glasses and clean the lines once every two weeks. Keep the temperature as close as possible to the ideal 42.8 degrees Fahrenheit, maybe a tad cooler to accommodate American tastes.

A traditional Irish session takes place every Thursday night. A "seisiun" in Gaelic is an ongoing musical session that never really ends, and the seisiun at Paddy's has been going on since the pub was first established. The evening begins when someone starts a tune. Those who can play it join in with their instruments. Those who don't know it, sit it out according to long-standing rules of session etiquette. Common instruments are flutes, fiddles, tin whistles (feadóg), bodhran (Irish drum) and uilleann pipes (Irish bagpipe). Players generally play to entertain themselves although observers are welcome.

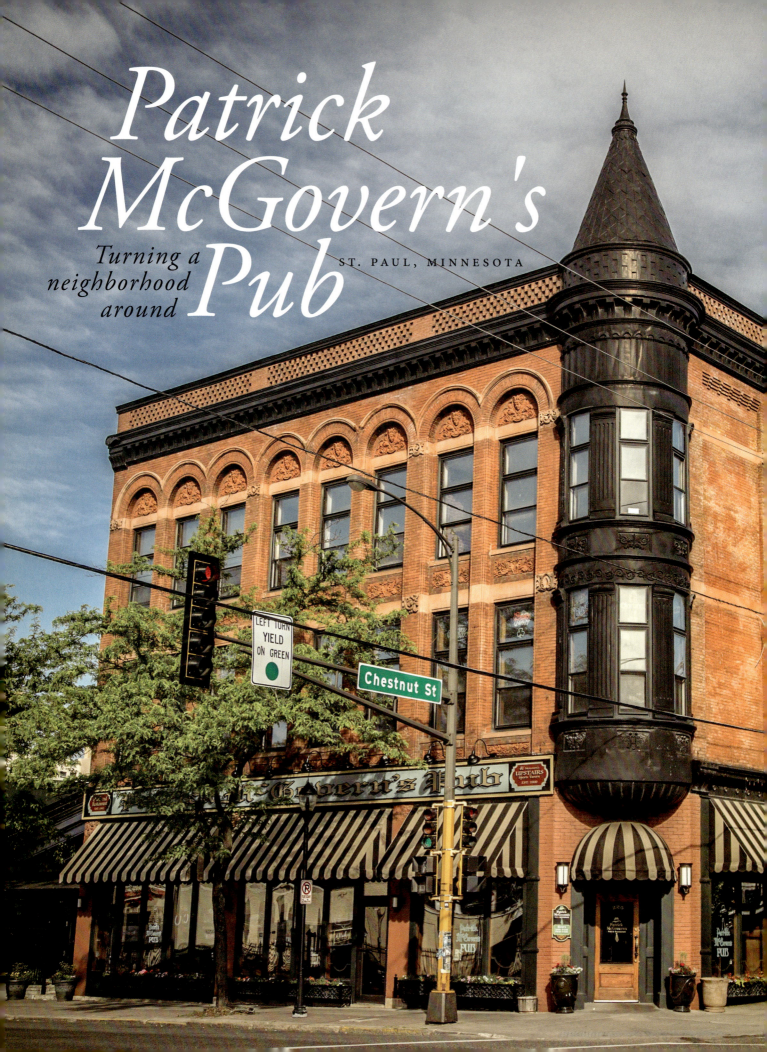

Patrick McGovern's Pub

Turning a neighborhood around

ST. PAUL, MINNESOTA

Patrick McGovern's Pub occupies the first and second floors of this magnificent example of late 19th century Victorian Romanesque Revival architecture.

May you live every day of your life.
                                                -Jonathan Swift

THANKS TO PROHIBITION, ST. PAUL once enjoyed a reputation for living on the edge. Prohibition was a free-wheeling era for the city, so much so that in 1925 Collier's Magazine ranked San Francisco and St. Paul as the country's wettest cities. Local moonshiners reportedly produced some of the country's finest whiskey which was in great demand by speakeasies coast to coast.

Life is calmer today in the state's capital, but its exciting past is still grist for tour guides and articles about its flamboyant days gone by.

In the midst of this colorful landscape, a beautiful building in a historic Irish and Italian neighborhood is home to Patrick McGovern's Pub and Restaurant. The lovely brick structure in the Late Victorian Romanesque Revival style popular in the 19th century was built in 1888 for Robert Smith, an important Democratic politician who served as mayor of St. Paul from 1887 to 1902. The building was designed by Edward Payson Bassford, one of the city's most prominent architects of that era.

During Prohibition and the Great Depression, St. Paul served as a refuge for gangsters when the heat became too intense in Chicago and elsewhere. St. Paul's deeply corrupt police department put out the welcome mat for the likes of Al Capone, John Dillinger, The Ma Barker Gang, Baby Face

Nelson, Homer van Meter, Machine Gun Kelly, Alvin "Creepy" Karpis and the Irish-American mob boss Roger "the Terrible" Touhy. The police offered amnesty as long as the underworld transplants stayed out of trouble and committed their mischief elsewhere.

Down the street from Patrick McGovern's Pub, lived "Dapper Dan" Hogan, known as St. Paul's Irish Godfather. He served as a go-between when police and gangsters needed to communicate. In 1928, a bomb planted in his Paige coupé in the garage behind his house exploded when he turned on the ignition. His murder was never officially solved. John Dillinger lived briefly near the pub in 1934 soon after the end of Prohibition as part of his brief but intense stopover in the city.

Irish immigrants have long called St. Paul home. The first settlers arrived in 1838. The early immigrants often worked as household servants, unskilled laborers and dock workers. Many became police officers or entered politics. In 1866, groups of angry Irish-American insurgents, some from St. Paul, attacked British forts in Canada as part of efforts to free their mother country from English rule. The raiders were members of the Fenian Brotherhood, a nationalist republican movement founded in 1858 by Irish-Americans. With the end of the Civil War, the ranks of the Fenian army swelled with former Irish soldiers from both North and South. The raids into Canada were poorly organized, and without the support of the United States government they ultimately failed. A smaller raid in 1870, planned in St. Paul, met a similar fate.

The limestone cliffs of St. Paul traditionally have provided foundation stones for the city's buildings. Their white chalky appearance is noted on exteriors as well as in basements, where it is sometimes mistaken for mildew. The basement of Pat McGovern's is typical of buildings of its era. There are even the remnants of a

The outdoor patio.

blocked-off tunnel. It was part of a labyrinth of multilevel, interconnecting underground utility passageways in downtown St. Paul. Beginning in the mid-1800s, tunnels were dug out by hand in the soft sandstone that sits under a layer of hard limestone. These tunnels carried gas, steam, sewer, water and telephone lines. The tunnel under Pat McGovern's was most likely used to carry power lines for the city's electric streetcar system that began operations in 1889.

Pat Boemer—the pub's name is a combination of Pat's first name and his former partner's last name—started his business in 1982 as an Irish pub "with a lot of brick and brass" in a very ethnic, rough neighborhood where homeless people roamed the streets. Pat bought out his partner in 1985 and began to grow his business, adding adjacent businesses whenever they became available. For the first twenty years there was only one other pub in the area. The two pubs prevailed, gradually turning the neighborhood around until it became the hot, thriving restaurant and bar scene that it is today. Pat runs the pub with his wife and business partner Dianne and their son Evan who is manager.

The pub is large with seven bars in various locations throughout the lower two floors of the building. An outdoor patio with a sliding glass roof keeps patrons toasty warm even in the midst of winter. Thirteen inch interior walls are constructed of dense Chicago bricks which were made in Chicago's Irish ghettos in the 1800s. Pat believes that every pub must occupy a niche to set it apart. Pat McGovern's niche is turkey, all manner of turkey dishes. Fifteen to twenty birds are consumed by appreciative patrons every day. So when in St. Paul, be sure to have a turkey platter with your Guinness.

ABOVE: The main bar area.

LEFT: Side entrance to Patrick McGovern's Pub showing the complex architectural details.

The Perfect Pint Public House

NEW YORK, NEW YORK

Perfection Starts in the Basement

If you drink, don't drive. Don't even putt.
-Dean Martin

IT'S A BRISK FIFTEEN MINUTE walk down 45th Street from one pub to the other, especially if you are being led by the energetic and enthusiastic Bernie Reilly who is synonymous with The Perfect Pint's two Manhattan locations. The pubs are shrines to Guinness. The color scheme of floors, bars, chairs, tables and walls is the unmistakable Guinness black and cream. Upon entering, one has the feeling of being suspended inside a pint of that magical brew. The atmosphere is so perfectly Guinness that many people are convinced that the brew tastes better here. No one told Bernie to make

The walls are adorned with large historic images of operations at the Guinness St James Brewery in the 1800s.

The distinctive façade of The Perfect Pint stands out along the cluttered streets of Manhattan.

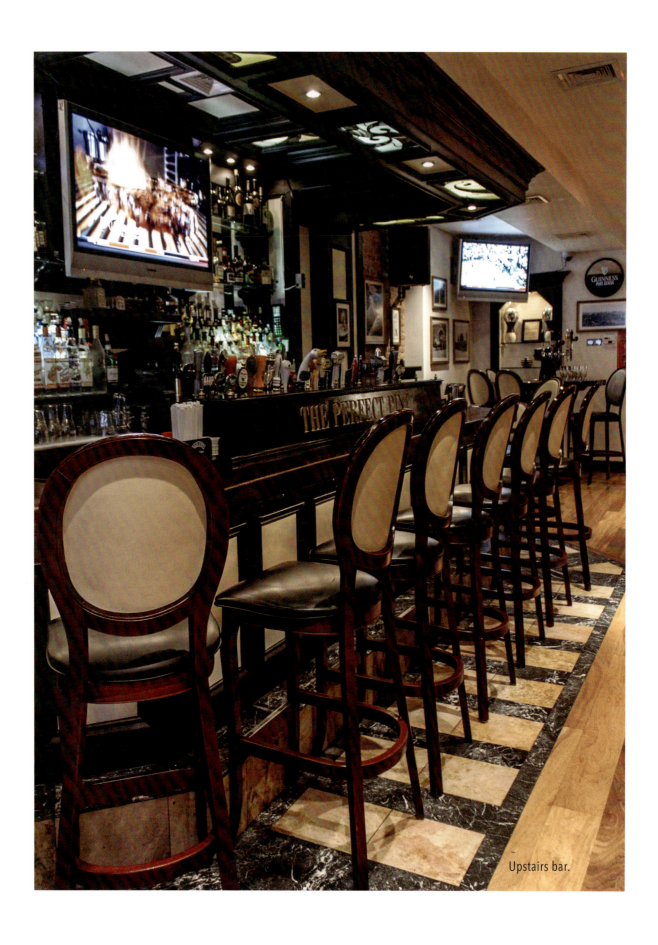
Upstairs bar.

these pubs places of pilgrimage; he did it because of his commitment to the product and because it made good business sense.

Bernie made many of the pubs' matchless curios and ornaments himself, which is understandable given his background. In 1980 he left Caherlistrane, a small village in County Galway in Western Ireland and headed to London where he worked as an auto body mechanic for seven years, perfecting the special skills that would serve him well in the United States.

In addition to the rooftop metal tables and beer barrel chairs, Bernie made the door handles from Guinness beer tap handles. Perhaps the most impressive expression of his handiwork is the elaborate systems of pumps and lines that lead from the basement of each pub to supply 40 beers on tap throughout the buildings. Maintaining the complex setups is a major responsibility, not to mention the effort that went into the design and construction of the systems. Bernie's personal slogan is "40 perfect pints on tap."

While both pubs have rooftop gardens, one pub is especially unique. Its rooftop garden is a veritable Irish country thatched roof cottage. Seated on converted beer barrels at diminutive round tables people just naturally engage in conversation, which after all is the *raison-d'être* of any pub. The view is of the iconic Chrysler Building with its shimmering terraced arches set on top of the world's tallest brick building.

ABOVE: Patrons pour their own beer at this self-serve bar. Kilkenny, Smithwick's, Harp and Guinness taps representing four Irish beers owned by Diageo Inc, and The Perfect Pint Golden Wheat, a craft beer brewed specially for the pub.

NEXT PAGE: In each of the Perfect Pint's two locations, an ingenious and highly complex system of pumps and hoses transports 40 kinds of beer from the basement to taps on four levels.

Technology and Ingenuity Meet the Perfect Pint

Some folks believe that pouring the perfect pint begins and ends at the tap, guided by the sensitive hands of a skilled bartender. That is just part of the story. Perfection starts at the keg and continues through the entire delivery system to the glass.

After a long hike up the narrow staircase to the fourth floor rooftop of The Perfect Pint, a patron expects the Guinness served there to be identical to the Guinness poured on the ground floor. He or she will not be disappointed, but that does not just happen. Four floors is a long way for beer to travel.

The cooling and distribution systems Bernie Reilly designed and built for his two pubs are identical works of art. They are crammed with trade secrets–real masterpieces that provide a constant flow of forty beers on tap to all floors of each pub. The systems' secret is an intricate arrangement of glycol cooling units, compressors, generators and pumps that maintain consistency of the product as it flows through a quarter mile of lines. The temperatures of the beer on the fourth floor and on the ground floor are identical.

The intricate pumping system connects each 175-pound aluminum keg to all four floors, assuring that the kegs drain quickly to ensure freshness. Kegs are changed out frequently, especially during the March St Patrick's Day celebration and the holiday season. Guinness is the largest seller, and its kegs are changed two or three times a day. Several other popular selling brews are changed almost as frequently.

Since the beer must travel long distances, the pub uses nitrogen and CO2 gas under pressure to push the beer through the lines. The Perfect Pint manufactures its own nitrogen, a highly technical and expensive process, but which is efficient and effective. It saves space by eliminating the need to store excess bulky nitrogen containers while assuring a steady supply.

It is important to keep yeast out of the lines because it attracts bacteria, which sour a beer. A special system cleans all 40 lines simultaneously and frequently. Specialized radio waves prevent yeast build-up between cleanings. A bartender activates the radio waves each time he pulls a tap handle.

Installation of the systems took about four grueling weeks, but they have been constantly modified and perfected for more than twenty years. They are a unique differentiator in the marketplace and help the pub justify its name, The Perfect Pint.

Raglan Road

LAKE BUENA VISTA, FLORIDA

Tradition on a large scale

Laughter is brightest where food is best.
       -Irish Proverb

RAGLAN ROAD, A REMARKABLE IRISH pub, is in the midst of the most celebrated family amusement park in the world. It is possibly the largest Irish pub in the United States with a capacity of 556 patrons. Like its much smaller brethren in the Emerald Isle, Raglan Road caters to families and children. Amazingly, in the midst of the millions of annual visitors to Disney World, thirty percent of the patrons of Raglan Road are regulars from the local area, a very high percentage for a resort environment. The pub also attracts many Europeans who easily identify with Irish pubs.

 Irish pubs are misconceived by the general public according to Sean Griffin, the pub's General Manager. "They think of St Patrick's day and beer," he says. Traditionally pubs have been the centers of Irish society, where families gather to celebrate life's essential moments—baptisms, christenings, weddings, homecomings, even deaths. "Irish pubs started in homes centuries ago," says Sean, "and the tradition of hospitality and friendliness continues today." This concept fits in well with the

This statue of poet Patrick Kavanagh is a replica of a statue on the banks of the Dublin canal. Before his death, Kavanagh asked that the statue include a place where passersby could sit with him to enjoy the canal. This statue is beside one of the pub's entrances. A Kavanagh poem provided the pub with its name.

ABOVE: A boardwalk over water runs along the exterior of the pub which consists of several buildings joined together to create a characteristic Dublin street scene.

LEFT: Portrait of the meeting at The Bailey pub in Dublin between famed poet Patrick Kavanagh and Luke Kelly of The Dubliners band which led to the The Dubliners' recording of Kavanagh's poem "On Raglan Road." The painting is by Irish artist Ann Marie Ryan.

Sean is from Glenbeigh, a sleepy seaside village in south County Kerry popular with vacationers, and the home of flamboyant celebrity chef Ernie Evans, whose Towers Hotel once played host to celebrities including Charlie Chaplin, John Wayne, Burl Ives, Joan Collins and many more.

Food plays an important role at Raglan Road due to the influence of financial partner and signature chef Kevin Dundon, owner of the exclusive Dunbrody House Hotel in County Wexford. Kevin is a household name in Ireland when it comes to cooking. The author of three cookbooks, he has appeared frequently on Irish, British, Canadian and American TV. His philosophy is to use only the freshest ingredients and not to hide them under fancy sauces. "He lets the food speak for itself," declares Sean, who notes that Irish cuisine has changed over the years from the traditional fare due to the influence of immigrants into Ireland.

Just outside one of the pub's multiple entrances is a replica of a life-size bronze statue of celebrated poet Patrick Kavanagh seated on a bench. The original statue is situated along the banks of the Grand Canal in Dublin. In his much-loved poetry, Kavanagh depicted the canal as a place of solitude and contemplation. At his request, made shortly before his death in 1967, there is a place on the bench for passersby to sit and reflect with him.

"On Raglan Road" is a song based on a poem written by Kavanagh in 1946 about a love affair that began while he was taking a walk on Dublin's Raglan Road where he lived. Shortly prior to his death, while having a pint in the landmark Bailey pub in Dublin, he met Luke Kelly, lead singer of the well-known band The Dubliners, who suggested setting his poem to music. Using the melody of the 16th century marching song "The Dawning of the Day," The Dubliners recorded one of the best-

Disney culture, he notes. Customer feedback indicates that the pub is one of the most popular repeat visit destinations in the park for children of all ages.

Pub owners John Cooke and Paul Nolan are from Dublin. They opened Irish pubs in many countries when they worked for the Irish Pub Company, the largest designer and supplier of Irish pubs in the world. Sean worked with them on some of their projects.

known Irish songs of all time.

The interior of the pub consists of a large domed Grand Room that pays tribute to 18th century Dublin Georgian architecture. At one side is a stage for musical performances and in the middle of the room an ancient converted preacher's platform serves as a stage for one of the pub's regular dancers, all of whom are former River Dance or Lord of the Dance professionals. Substantial wood tables for four with solid slat-back chairs fill the floor. Opposite the stage runs a long mahogany and oak bar, one of several in the building. Running up the walls behind the bar are many small drawers from a nearly 200 year old apothecary shop in Dublin. This is historic preservation at its best, repurposing the old to create the new.

The Grand Room opens on to the much smaller Music Room where photographs of famous Irish musicians adorn the walls. The larger Raglan Room features 200 year-old paneling from a home on Raglan Road. On the far wall hangs a huge portrait of the meeting between Patrick Kavanagh and Luke Kelly at the Bailey pub, which dates to the 1850s and was for a long time a haunt for Dublin's literati. A large snug to one side of the room accommodates a dozen patrons and features photos and paintings of some of Ireland's most famous writers. Adjacent to the main building is Cooke's, the pub's restaurant specializing in fish and chips and other traditional dishes and its outside seating area, The Hole in the Wall.

Raglan Road delightfully and skillfully reproduces a traditional pub, only on a much larger scale.

ABOVE: Behind the Grand Room bar are drawers from a 200-year-old Dublin apothecary shop. The drawer pulls identify some esoteric substances used to create remedies for ills and for other purposes: digitalis, hordeum, prunus Virginia, maranta and potassium bitartrate, among others.

RIGHT: The handsome Georgian style Grand Room cannot fail to impress and provides ample space for diners, entertainment and for having a pint at the bar.

On Raglan Road

On Raglan Road is a poem by noted Irish poet Patrick Kavanagh. It was set to music by The Dubliners and is one of Ireland's most beloved poems. Here is the first verse.

On Raglan Road of an autumn day
I saw her first and knew
That her dark hair would weave a snare
That I might one day rue
I saw the danger and I passed
Along the enchanted way
And said let grief be a fallen leaf
At the dawning of the day

Rí Rá

ATLANTA, GEORGIA

A Real Irish Pub From Ireland

Alcohol is necessary for a man so that he can have a good opinion of himself, undisturbed by the facts.   -Finley Peter Dunne

Hubbub, commotion, noise— that's what its name means in Gaelic, and on a Friday or Saturday night, Rí Rá is all of that, especially when the World Cup is showing on its 15 foot screen. Step over the threshold, pass through a Victorian Dublin store front door with an impressive acid-etched glass panel and you immediately respond to the sheer size of the place. Rí Rá Atlanta is huge, more than 6000 square feet, and no wonder. It was built in 2009 in the heart of Midtown where several shops and a nightclub once stood on a sloping embankment. The resulting three rooms lined up in a row on different levels engulf the senses. Like every one of 12 Rí Rá pubs in the United States, the Atlanta pub is unique and devoted to bringing the authentic flavor of Ireland to the United States.

What better way to preserve a country's heritage than to find new economic uses for obsolete historic treasures that might otherwise be lost? Rí Rá works to safeguard valued assets from days gone by.

Victorian era snugs harmonize with the mid-19th century Titanic bar in the main room, so named because the room's parquet floor came from the Harland & Wolfe shipyard in Belfast where the Titanic was

Since opening in 2009, Rí Rá has become a very popular watering hole appealing to locals and out-of-towners alike.

fabricated. The enormous dry dock where the ship spent the eve of her first and last voyage and the adjacent pump house filled with engineering marvels of its time are still there for all to see.

The centerpiece of the middle room, or Library, is an antique Dublin storefront lovingly preserved, dating back to 1784. Pictures of famous Atlantans of Irish descent adorn the walls.

Go through antique doors from a long ago closed Dublin theater to the upper room, or Harbor Bar, and enjoy a pint at a bar that was originally in the small Northern Ireland seaport of Portstewart, a popular seaside holiday destination for Victorian era families.

The sense of authenticity extends to the staff. General Manager Dermot Lloyd comes from the parish of Killmallcok in County Limerick. Of considerable importance during the Middle Ages, the remains of the medieval wall that encircled the town are still evident. It was also the scene of fierce battles during the Irish Civil War in 1922. Assistant Manager Erick Tierney hails from Galway, nicknamed Ireland's Cultural Heart because of the town's many artistic events and festivals. His grandfather and granduncle owned pubs in Galway, so naturally Erick developed a knack for the publican's life. Rí Rá hosts a training program under the State Department's J-1 Visa Exchange Visitors Program which brings hospitality students from Ireland to work in the pub for extended periods.

Rí Rá also takes pride in its community involvement. Managers shave their heads to raise money for kids fighting cancer through the St. Baldrick's Foundation, with more

Teams of naval architects and draftsmen prepared the RMS Titanic's concept design and detailed construction drawings in the cathedral-like atmosphere of the Design House in Belfast. Rí Rá customers tread the same parquet floor that once graced the Design House. © National Museums Northern Ireland; Collection Harland & Wolff, Ulster Folk & Transport Museum

Workers are dwarfed by the RMS Titanic's giant propellers during construction in Belfast. The ill-fated ship is linked through time to the Rí Rá Irish pub in Atlanta. © National Museums Northern Ireland; Collection Harland & Wolff, Ulster Folk & Transport Museum

than $335,000 raised to date. An annual golf tournament supports children with disabilities. As sponsors of the Atlanta Clan nGael men's and ladies Gaelic football and hurling club, Renegades Rugby Football Club and the local Gaelic Athletic Association, Rí Rá helps people learn about Irish culture and heritage. On the lighter side, Rí Rá won the coveted 2012 Atlanta Perfect Pint Pouring Contest judged by senior Guinness officials, giving the pub serious bragging rights for years to come.

In spite of its success, as Erik Tierney points out, the Irish pub concept is changing. It is no longer "bicycles hanging from the ceiling. Craft beers, hand crafted cocktails and farm-to-table food are becoming more important in the business." As H. G. Wells said "Adapt or perish, now as ever, is nature's inexorable imperative."

According to the US Census Bureau, almost 12 percent of Americans claim Irish ancestry, or roughly six times the population of Ireland today. Atlanta has a similar percentage, which helps explain the popularity of all things Irish. Local pubs tap into that population by working with organizations such as the Hibernian Benevolent Society, Irish American Business Network, Irish Chamber of Commerce, Gaelic football and hurling teams and local Irish-American musicians. Although there are many Irish pubs in Atlanta competing for business, their continuing vigor and popularity is assured, because, after all, if you are not Irish yourself, you probably wish you were.

For the Love of Sport

The most popular sports in Ireland are Gaelic football and hurling.

Gaelic football is sometimes described as a cross between soccer and rugby, but it predates both of them. One of the few remaining truly amateur sports in the world, players and officials may not receive any compensation.

A Gaelic football playing field, or pitch, measures 130-145 meters long and 80-90 meters wide. There are 15 players on a side. The game consists of two 35-minute halves.

The game is played with a round leather ball similar to a volleyball. It may be kicked or hand passed by striking with the fist, never thrown. A point can be scored by either kicking the ball over the goal crossbar, or by fisting it over. A three point goal is scored when the ball is kicked below the crossbar into a net.

Gaelic football is similar in some respects to rugby, but there are differences. The Gaelic football is round whereas the Rugby ball is oval. A rugby player can run with the ball. In Gaelic Football the ball must be bounced or soloed (kicked from toe to hand) every four steps as the player runs. A player cannot touch the ball with his or her hand in soccer.

Gaelic football and Australian football are very similar, so much so that teams from both countries can play matches under a compromise system known as International Rules Football.

Hurling is an ancient stick and ball game native to Ireland played by men. It uses the same pitch, goals and scoring as Gaelic football and also has 15 players. A slightly different version called camogie is played by women.

Players use a broad bladed netless wooden stick, or hurley, to hit a small ball called a sliotar between the opponents' goalposts either over the crossbar for one point, or under the crossbar for three points. The sliotar can be caught in the hand and carried for up to four steps, or struck with the hurley in the air or on the ground. To carry the sliotar for more than four steps a player has to bounce it or balance it on the end of the hurley.

Hurling is perhaps the fastest of all team field sports. It is sometimes compared to field hockey or lacrosse.

The Irish Pub Concept and Its Evolution

My first experience of life in America was during the summer of 2001 at the Rí Rá pub in Burlington, Vermont. The state's green and undulating landscape reminded me of the West of Ireland and my hometown of Galway in the Province of Connacht.

What struck me first about Irish pubs in America was how contrived everything seemed compared to local pubs back home. While you find bric-a-brac, shelves adorned with books and the odd bike or horse saddle hanging from the ceiling back in Ireland, the décor and tone of some Irish pubs here seemed excessive to the point of being overbearing and intrusive; or to put it another way–they were simply trying too hard. That being said, it was evident that the locals couldn't get enough of it. Was this the future of things to come for the Irish pub in America? Fortunately as it turned out, the answer was no.

As the years passed and I kept returning to Rí Rá during my college vacations it became evident that a serious amount of time, effort & money–but most importantly passion and craftsmanship–was being injected into growing this particular Irish pub company. I found similar commitment and dedication evident in many Irish pubs across the United States.

I have watched as Irish pubs have spread out across the land bringing a taste of Ireland to millions of Americans. I am proud to have contributed to my company's progress from a cautious beginning to a pub concept that would easily give any of the big guns back home a run for their money.

-Erik Tierney
Rí Rá

OPPOSITE, TOP: The third level Harbor Bar features a tidy little bar from the scenic Northern Ireland seaport of Portstewart. It is used as a private events facility.

OPPOSITE, BOTTOM: Its singular three level design makes Rí Rá an architectural gem as well as an Atlanta favorite. This well designed pub is a pleasure to behold. The restored parquet floor consists of 10,000 pieces from the Harland and Wolfe Design House in Belfast where the Titanic was designed.

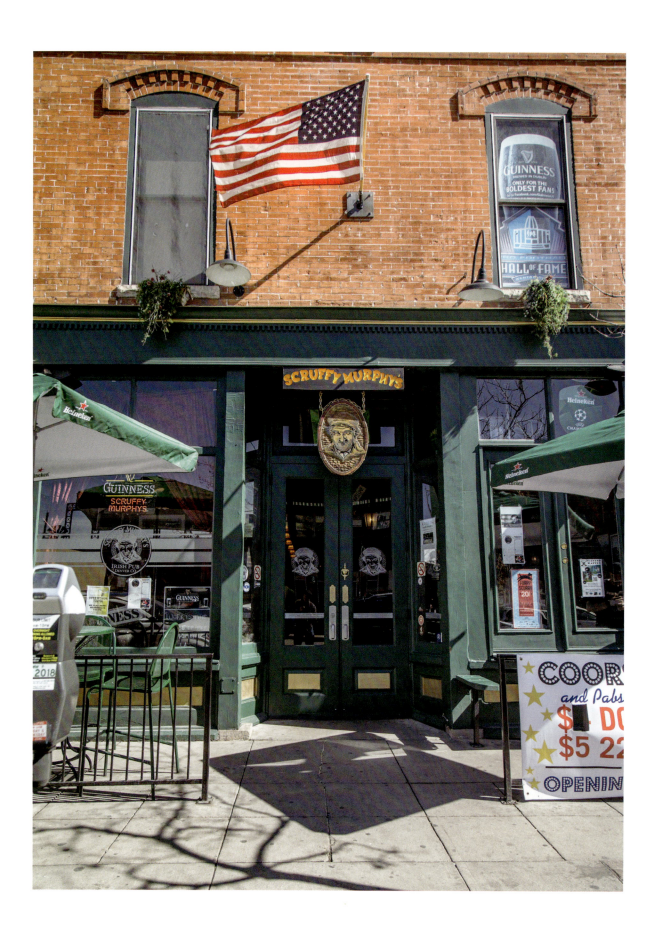

Scruffy Murphy's

DENVER, COLORADO

Everybody knows my name.

I never drink water; that is the stuff that rusts pipes.   -W. C. Fields

PEOPLE WHO KNOW IRISH PUBS know Scruffy Murphy's. It is one of the most common names around the world for many things Irish: pubs, restaurants, hotels, even bands. No one knows for certain why it is so popular or even who Scruffy Murphy was. Rumor has it, Scruffy was a coal miner way back when. He decided to open a pub, but sadly drank himself to death before the bar opened. Fortunately, the memory of his warmth and love of people live on through his name. So, whether you are in Ireland, England, Scotland, Norway, Singapore, Thailand, Australia or elsewhere, you are sure to find a warm Scruffy Murphy's welcome.

People of all age groups go to Scruffy's in Denver to have a good time in an old-world neighborhood pub open morning, noon and night. The atmosphere is relaxed during the day and effervescent at night. The name aptly describes the pub's mildly eccentric character, slightly worn and scruffy but always welcoming—like your Irish neighbor's living room. Scruffy's looks as if it has belonged in the same spot for eternity.

In reality, the pub dates back to 2004 when Andrew Toole, a commercial painting contractor, from the town of Ratoath in County Meath and a friend built it. The pub helped the neighborhood grow and transform from seedy to trendy. "People started to ask if I wanted to sell, and in 2010 I did," says Andrew, who still maintains a friendly relationship with the popular watering hole.

Today the pub is owned by Shannon Murray, her husband David Wisniewski (The Sarge) and Niall Byrne, an old friend, originally from County Wexford. Shannon says "the nice thing about owning an Irish pub is the opportunity it provides to fashion an environment where food, libation, furnishings and music combine to create a home away from home. Whether people stop by for a pint or a jar, they are taking a break from everyday life. There is a sense of

LEFT: Scruffy Murphy's occupies part of a historic building in Denver's famous Ballpark Neighborhood.

RIGHT: Slightly worn and scruffy, the pub feels very real.

timelessness in an Irish pub."

The brick building housing the pub is in the Ballpark Neighborhood, in the Larimer Street Historic District two blocks from Coors Field and close to Union Station for people taking the bus or monorail downtown. The building is more than 100 years old and shares the neighborhood's exuberant past, having been many things over the years including a flop house and a brothel. The local historical society stops by as part of its annual pub crawl.

Thanks in part to General Manager Steve Colligan, the pub is active with many local charities. These include fundraisers in memory of Steve's son Orion to support the Tennyson Center for Children which helps abused and neglected children, the annual motorcycle ride by police to assist families of fallen comrades, Hearts and Hand Center for at risk youth, the local cancer society and the pancreatic cancer society, the Wounded Warrior project and Denver Smile, which provides no-cost dental care to kids in need.

The thinner air at Denver's mile-high altitude affects the beer as well as the people who drink it, especially those visiting from lower altitudes. "Beer hits the brain a little quicker at high altitude," says long-time bartender Craig. Just as golf balls travel ten percent farther in Denver than at sea level and just as bakers have to take the altitude into account, so too do alcohol drinkers.

ABOVE: Flavored whiskeys are a Scruffy's trademark. New flavor concoctions are unveiled every few weeks.

OPPOSITE, TOP: Scruffy's no-frills décor is straight from the Emerald Isle. The back bar is lined with shelves burdened with bottles and dispensers of flavored whiskeys. At the end of the bar a snug with antique stained glass is popular with guests. Shelves around the room are heavy with a random collection of bric-à-brac.

OPPOSITE, BOTTOM: A favorite table by the window.

Tír na nÓg

NEW YORK, NEW YORK

The Land of Eternal Youth

When I read about the evils of drinking, I gave up reading. -Henny Youngman

In ancient Irish mythology, a paradise existed on islands far to the west where gods and ancestors never grew old and enjoyed unending happiness and perfect health forever. They called this Otherworld Tír na nÓg, The Land of Eternal Youth, where the goddess Niamh, the daughter of the god of the sea and queen of Tír na nÓg and her lover Oisin met their fate. The Tír na nÓg pub derives its name from this dramatic story of romance and adventure.

The Tír na nÓg occupies the ground floor of 5 Penn Plaza, a 24-floor landmark office building in the heart of midtown Manhattan, whose striking exterior delights the eye. Constructed in 1925, the building was initially known as the Printing Crafts Building and was home to many printing industry tenants. The space housing the pub was previously a delicatessen and a jewelry store. The pub demonstrates the symbiotic relationship that can exist between a large commercial building and a more intimate business that depends on the warmth of personal relationships to make people feel comfortable and at home. This is a place where the staff obviously enjoys their work. The pub draws its clientele from neighborhoods in close proximity, from commuters who stop by before

catching their trains at nearby Pennsylvania Station, attendees at Madison Square Garden events and evening celebrants drawn to the pub by its reputation.

Interior artifacts were brought from Ireland to create an elegant Irish parlor appearance. The bar framework is from a cathedral organ in Northern Ireland as are the high back cathedral pews that occupy one wall. The main room is large enough to allow dancing on the weekends to the sounds of live music. Although the pub can accommodate 150 people, the space is divided into comfortable areas where patrons can enjoy their pints in relative privacy.

Manager Helen Woods recalls that a long time local client recently celebrated his 85th birthday at the pub, clearly illustrating that even in a big city, the neighborhood still reigns supreme.

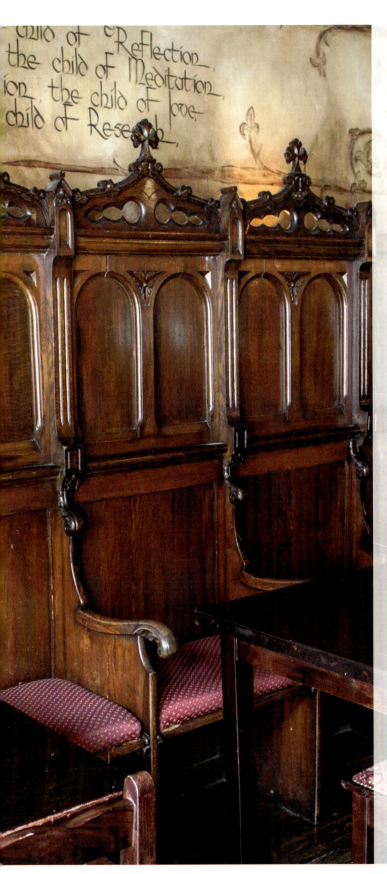

The Legend of Tír na nÓg

Tír na nÓg was a land far away over the western sea, beyond the edge of the map, where fairies lived in harmony, where no one ever grew old and time stood still, a place where everyone was beautiful and happy. One day, the lovely princess Niamh rode her great white horse across the waves to Conemarra where she met and fell in love with the handsome warrior Oisin. Together they returned to the blessed land of eternal youth on Niamh's magical horse to live happily ever after.

Eventually, however, Oisin became homesick for his native land. Niamh reluctantly agreed to allow him to return to visit his friends and family on her magical horse, but warned him that if his feet ever touched the ground, he could never return to Tír na nÓg. Upon reaching Conemarra, Oisin found his family's home was no longer there and discovered that they had been dead for hundreds of years, for you see, one year in Tír na nÓg was the same as a hundred years in Conemarra.

Discouraged but wiser, Oisin decided to ride his horse back across the waves to the land of eternal youth. On the way to the sea, he came across some hunters struggling to move a large boulder. He leaned from his saddle to help them and in the process fell from the horse. He aged in an instant and crumbled to the ground as dust. The frightened horse galloped across the ocean back to Tír na nÓg where princess Niamh tearfully realized that she would never see her beloved Oisin again.

Tom Bergin's Old Horseshoe Tavern

LOS ANGELES, CALIFORNIA

Phoenix Rising

For a quart of ale is a dish for a King.
   -William Shakespeare (A Winter's Tale)

WHEN WARNER EBBINK AND BRANDON Boudet closed Tom Bergin's Tavern in early 2012 for a nine-month restoration, longtime devotees of the establishment were apprehensive. They were most concerned about the fate of some 10,000 cardboard shamrocks cut out from beer cartons that ordinary folks as well as celebrities had signed and stapled to the ceiling throughout the previous sixty years.

The property had not been updated for more than a half century and was in need of a facelift. Whenever it rained, 15 buckets were set on the bar to catch the leaks.

While retaining the bar's classic dark wood personality, the partners gave the building a new roof, installed an up-to-date kitchen, expanded the parking lot, created a handicapped entrance and set up a modern beer tap system with insulated lines so the beer would maintain its ideal temperature from the head to the tap. They installed a copper top on the deteriorating wood bar to preserve the original. Boxes of memorabilia stashed in the attic for years were brought down and examined; the best items were affixed to the walls. It was like the rebirth of the phoenix rising from the ashes with renewed youth and vigor.

Aware of the historical and emotional significance of the cardboard shamrocks on the ceiling that memorialized the tavern's customers, the new owners carefully removed each one, dusted if off and put it back when the reparations were complete, much to the relief of the regulars.

Some old-timers did not appreciate the changes, and a few fell by the wayside. On the other hand, the pub's updated appearance recaptured some customers who had left years before, and attracted a new generation of fans interested in quality dining.

Nevertheless, the pub closed in July 2013, and as of this writing is scheduled to re-open under new management.

The pub was established in 1936 by attorney Tom Bergin as Tom Bergin's Old Horseshoe and Thoroughbred Club. Not much is known about his legal practice, but it brought him into contact with a bevy of Hollywood personalities. Bing Crosby was reportedly a friend and a regular at the pub. Tom collaborated with Bing and a group of his Hollywood pals to open the Turf Club at the Del Mar Race Track which became known as the playground of the stars. Bing's close friend Pat O'Brien was frequently at the pub, and for thirty years Cary Grant spent nearly every Sunday afternoon in his reserved booth.

The pub was always something of a media watering hole. Located near Hollywood and

Wilshire Boulevards, it is at the epicenter of the entertainment and publishing industries. Variety, The Hollywood Reporter, Los Angeles Magazine and Condé Nast are within a few blocks. A short distance away is the mammoth Los Angeles County Museum of Art, whose roots go back to 1910, and which attracts large numbers of attendees, many of whom managed to find their way to Tom Bergin's.

Like so many urban areas that suffered physical and population declines in the 1980s, this section of Los Angeles has experienced significant renewal. Nearby homes are valued in the million dollar plus range, and many young professionals have moved into the neighborhood's apartments and condominiums.

Since its earliest days, the bar has had a connection with horseracing. Champion jockey Bill Shoemaker was a loyal customer when he was not racing at nearby Hollywood Racetrack where he won six races in one day – twice. Gracing the walls in the pub's dining area with its warm fireplace and white tablecloths are several large paintings done by a customer in the 1940s in exchange for a bar tab of famous horses.

PREVIOUS SPREAD: A vintage Los Angeles haunt where old time movie greats used to hang out, famous for its Irish coffee and admirable menu.

ABOVE: The casual U-shaped bar gave the original Tom Bergin's Old Horseshoe Bar and Thoroughbred Club its name. The bar was moved to the pub's current location in 1949.

LEFT: The formal dining area featured white table clothes, a large fireplace and paintings of famous horses done by a customer in exchange for a bar tab.

Waxy O'Connor's

FORT LAUDERDALE, FLORIDA

Built in Ireland

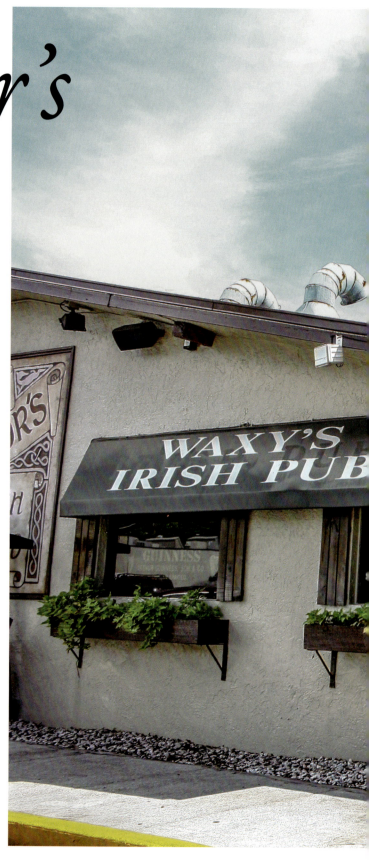

Without question, the greatest invention in the history of mankind is beer. Oh, I grant you that the wheel was also a fine invention, but the wheel does not go nearly as well with pizza.   -Dave Barry

LIFE GETS PRETTY HECTIC AT Waxy O'Connors in late October when the Fort Lauderdale International Boat Show comes to town. Known as the Yachting Capital of the World, the city has hosted the boat show for more than 50 years. Thousands of people and more than 1300 exhibitors attend the show from all over the world, many of whom are in the mood for a good pint at the end of each hectic day. The boat show kicks off a busy season of conventions, fishermen in quest of the magical tarpon and so-called snowbird visitors from cold northern climes. The frenzied season lasts until Memorial Day when the weather turns warm and the city calms down.

Waxy's has the look and feel of a true Irish pub because it is just that. It was built at the Truwood Joinery Shop in County Monaghan along with six other Waxy pubs and shipped to the US. Owners Mark Rohleder and his wife Noreen McCauley erected it on its present site with the help of Irish construction workers sent over from the Emerald Isle. County Monaghan proudly calls itself the furniture capital of the world with some 30 manufacturers, large and small.

Situated just a few feet from a busy highway, Waxy's exudes pure Irishness. It is clear that Mark and Noreen are passionate fans of the traditional Irish pub. Dimly lit and intimate, it is the kind of

place that makes you want to come back again and again to escape the hustle and bustle of the world outside. It is hard to explain why that is. Mark says "you can't create an atmosphere like that; it just happens."

Perhaps part of the explanation is that Waxy's works hard to attract patrons with regular whiskey tastings, boat show parties and other special events. The most popular whiskey is Jameson by far.

The pub's name originates from an old tale about a candle maker somewhere in Ireland whose nickname was Waxy for obvious reasons. Waxy O'Connor lived above his candle shop. One night, after he had a little too much to drink, his shop caught fire but miraculously Waxy escaped unscathed. Waxy became an instant celebrity known for his good luck. That is how waxy became a slang term for lucky.

Just as candle makers in Ireland were known as waxies, working-class women who toiled in linen mills were millies, explains Noreen. In Northern Ireland, linen manufacturing has been an important industry for more than 300 years, particularly in the 18th and 19th centuries, when nearly every town had a mill or factory. At one point, 70,000 women worked in the in Belfast mills under extremely difficult conditions. Today the industry is very much smaller, but Irish linen, spun from pure flax fiber, is still synonymous with high quality.

Mark got his start in the pub industry 20 years ago at O'Flanagan's Bar on the Upper East Side of New York City, which is where he met Noreen. They established Waxy's in 1997 and built a solid business over the years. Like so many other businesses, the recent recession affected business. Mark and Noreen kept doing what they do best; provide great atmosphere, food and drink. Their guests, better known as friends, still showed up at their home away from home and Waxy's weathered the storm.

ABOVE: A prized historical object in the pub is a century old iron milestone marker which stood at a crossroads in Ahoghill in the rural county of Antrim in Northern Ireland. Originally perched on a large stone, the marker is very heavy. Co-owner Noreen McCauley grew up in the village where the marker was located.

OPPOSITE, TOP: The well-stocked bar.

OPPOSITE, BOTTOM: A quiet corner.

PREVIOUS SPREAD: Waxy's has the look and feel of a down-to-earth Irish pub with little surprises at every glance.

Johnny Doherty

My husband, Mark, had a grand Uncle Johnny Doherty (God rest his soul) who was born in rural Donegal in 1900. He never married nor had any children. His great love was music, and he was reputed to be one of the best fiddle players in Ireland, if not the best.

All Johnny had were the clothes on his back and a fiddle (and sometimes not even that). He traveled from village to towns and played his music. In return, he got food and a bed for the night and maybe a pint or two. He liked to walk wherever he went and did not trust cars. He would only take a lift from the local priest Fr. Colm because no harm would come to him in the priest's presence.

Johnny came from a family of travelers and had it in his blood. His life was unconventional by any standard, free from the materialistic world we live in today. It would be difficult to mirror that kind of existence in modern Ireland, but what a life to play his music where and when he wanted and roam near and far at his whim. He had all the riches he ever needed. We should all be that lucky.

Noreen McCauley
Co-owner
Waxy O'Connor's Irish
Pub and Eatery

Wolfe Tone's Pub

at Blackthorne Inn

UPPERVILLE, VIRGINIA

For the Love of Dogs and Horses

This life is a shadowy thing, lad. We live in a crowded space of lights and shadows, and when left to ourselves, we all too often fail to see the brightest light of all.
 -James Michael Pratt, *The Lighthouse Keeper*

IN 2007 CHEF SHANE O'CONNOR fulfilled his dream when he purchased a historic Upperville inn.

Shane's father, like his grandfather and great-grandfather before him, was a lighthouse keeper in Ireland. It was a remarkable life's work, spending one month on and one month off a small rock miles into the Atlantic off the rugged Irish coast. Living among the lights and prisms, keepers kept busy maintaining daily logbooks, scrubbing, painting, cleaning lenses and in the early days, lugging oilcans for the light up flights of stairs to the lantern room. They also spent

---

LEFT: The Blackthorne Inn and Wolfe Tone Irish pub are popular with the local fox hunting community. Here professional huntsman Spencer Allen is shown in front of the historic inn, once owned by George Washington.

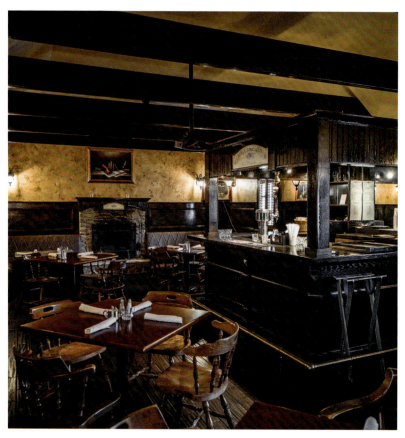

long hours in solitary pursuits. Shane's father was a wood carver. He devoted many hours creating walking sticks and shillelaghs out of blackthorn wood he carried by small boat to his remote postings.

The blackthorn is a thorny shrub with dark bark and heavy, dense wood. Carvings, typically smeared with butter and placed in a chimney to cure, attain a shiny, black appearance. Shillelaghs, named after a village in County Wicklow, are traditional Irish weapons used as clubs to bludgeon a foe.

Shane's dad retired when lighthouses were automated in the 1980s. Economic conditions were difficult in Ireland in those days, so he moved his entire family to Virginia, where he found employment on the famous Llangollen horse and cattle farm in Upperville. Shane was a teenager at the time and worked as a chef's assistant at the historic Windsor House Inn in nearby Middleburg, a quaint village of some 600 people and the site of numerous pre-Revolutionary War buildings. Shane later honed his culinary skills with his own catering company.

Shane called his new inn The Blackthorne Inn and Restaurant in honor of his father's extraordinary career. He immediately set about constructing an Irish pub adjacent to the inn which he named Wolfe Tone after a leading figure in the Irish Rebellion of 1798.

The inn is rich in historic lore. Nestled at the foot of the Blue Ridge Mountains, the building was originally known as the Greystone House. It was constructed in 1763, the same year that Wolfe Tone was born, on land sold to George Washington by his close friend Byron Fairfax, the Eighth Lord Fairfax. In response to the inevitable question, Shane says "no one knows if George Washington slept here," but since it was on a route he sometimes took from Mount Vernon, it is quite likely that he did indeed bed down in the inn.

The original two-story main building is

constructed of massive gray and brown field stones, common to the foothills area. Five fireplaces kept occupants warm in winter. Additionally, a basement kitchen with stone floor and log beamed ceiling has a large cooking fireplace. Original oak floors with foot-wide planks have weathered the footprints of centuries. The section Shane added to the building houses the cozy, totally-Irish pub on the main floor, an upstairs bar for special occasions and three small elegant dining rooms.

The emerald fields and endless stone walls of northern Virginia could be confused with the lush landscape of Ireland. Long a destination for Irish immigrants, the gently rolling Virginia hills are the nerve center of one of Ireland's most stirring exports to the United States, fox hunting.

Basically, in foxhunting a fox is pursued by riders on horseback accompanied by a pack of highly trained and well-loved hounds. Simple as it sounds, fox hunting is highly regulated, with rules covering every aspect of the complex sport. Local clubs, called hunts, are registered by the Masters of Foxhounds Association and given dominion over a defined geographic area. Virginia enjoys the distinction of having the largest number of registered hunts in the United States, followed by Pennsylvania. The oldest hunt in the country is Upperville's Piedmont Fox Hounds, formed in 1840. In addition to organizing hunts, the organization actively pursues conservation efforts. In North America, the goal of the hunt is to "account for" the fox, rather than to kill it, the chase being the focus of the sport, followed by a friendly pint at the local pub.

THIS PAGE: The pub is very much like a country pub in rural Ireland.

OPPOSITE PAGE, LEFT: Entrance to the pub

OPPOSITE, RIGHT: The upstairs bar provides a warm and intimate environment for special occasions.

FOXHUNTING: STEEPED IN TRADITION

Americans have been enjoying foxhunting since Colonial days. George Washington was an avid hunter, and his diaries and letters abound with references to the sport. He raised his own hounds and bred them carefully.

Traditional fox hunting is preserved by numerous dedicated clubs called "hunts." The Piedmont Hunt, founded in 1840 and headquartered in Upperville, is the oldest in the nation. People involved with the hunt fill specific roles. Masters are responsible for the overall management of the hunt and for maintaining good relations with local landowners. Professional salaried hunt servants support the hunt. The Huntsman is responsible for the care and training of the hounds and directs each day's hunting. The assistant to the Huntsman is known as the Whipper-in.

Proper attire is among the most recognized traditions. Masters and hunt servants, such as the Huntsman, wear red coats and light colored pants while members of the "field," the riders following the hounds, traditionally wear black coats

Specially bred foxhounds are trained to chase foxes based on their scent.

Spencer Allen, Piedmont's current huntsman, joined the hunt in 2006 as whipper-in following a tour of duty in Iraq as a US Marine and stints as a bronco rider and blacksmith. He says he has finally found his passion.

THIS PAGE: George Washington was a skilled horseman and an avid fox hunter as illustrated in this 1909 oil painting *The First Gentlemen of Virginia* by John Ward Dunsmore. Photo courtesy Fraunces Tavern Museum.

OPPOSITE, TOP: The emerald green fields and mile upon mile of hand-stacked stone walls, recall the beautiful Irish countryside. The similarity with Ireland drew Irish immigrants to this area like a magnet.

OPPOSITE, BOTTOM: Several elegant dining rooms with fireplaces provide a warm welcome to visitors.

Recipes

The recipes that follow were provided by the pubs featured in this book. Thus the recipes vary in length, and some include additional information about their origins. A number of the recipes were handed down from relatives in Ireland; others are signature recipes offered in the pubs. The authors greatly appreciate the pubs' contributions to this section and have not altered the language nor recipes except to standardize measurements. We hope you enjoy them.

The Incredible Lamb Burger	300	Batter For Fish And Chips	316
Shepherd's Pie	300	Irish Nachos	317
Corned Beef Parsnip Mash	301	Kieran's Curry Wings	317
With Mustard & Cider Sauce		Warm Corn Blinis	318
Sauteed Brussel Sprouts	301	With Smoked Salmon & Lemon Dill Cream	
With Irish Bacon & Caramelized Onions		Ale & Cheddar Dip	318
Scotch Eggs With Dijon Ale Sauce	302	New Orleans Irish Cabbage	319
Cottage Pie	302	Perfect Cabbage	319
Pork Pie With Carmelized Apples	303	Fire Cracker Salad	320
Open Faced Hot Turkey Sandwich	303	Crispy Irish Bacon Salad With Clonakility	320
Boxty	304	Black Pudding With A Poached Egg On Top	
Pork Sausage	304	Irish Soda Bread	321
With Leek And Parsnip Mash & Onion Gravy		Treacle Bread	321
Irish Corned Beef & Cabbage	305	Irish Brown Bread	322
With A Middle Eastern Twist		Hearty Irish Brown Bread	322
Chicken Shots	305	The Irish Inn Scones	323
Entrecote Jameson	306	Traditional Irish Soda Bread	323
Smoked Salmon	306	Jameson Pecan Pie Filling	324
Caramelized Peach Pork Chops	307	Bread Pudding	324
Shepherd's Pie	308	Brown Bread Ice Cream	325
Meatloaf	309	Whiskey Bread Pudding	325
Gaelic Steak	309	With Baileys Ice Cream And Guinness Caramel	
Crab Cakes	309	Trifle	326
Turkey Pot Pie	310	Molten Chocolate Lava Cake	326
Crab Cakes	310	Plum Pudding With Amber Sauce	327
With Chive Aioli And Napa Cabbage Slaw		Apple Cake	327
Corned Beef Reuben	311	Bailey's Cheesecake	328
With Warm Red Cabbage Slaw		Bread Pudding	328
Guinness Stout Onion Soup	312	Maggie May's Bread Pudding	329
Potato And Leek Soup	312	Dublin Mule	330
Fish Stew	313	Irish Apple	330
Guinness Beef Stew	314	Irish Coffee	330
Irish Potato Soup	314	McGuire's Irish Coffee	331
Bill's Bachelor Beef Stew	315	Great Grandmother Bridget Burke's Eggnog	331
Lamb Stew	315		
Black Pudding Pâté	316		
Smoked Salmon Spread	316		

The Incredible Lamb Burger (serves 1)

Bernie Reilly, Owner | The Perfect Pint | New York, New York

The name of this burger should be enough to describe this lunchtime favorite. Rarely do you see something like this in an Irish Pub, but because of our special Gaelic spin. It is something that everyone should try at least once, but in our experience, it is usually tried a few more times.

Chargrilled lamb burger and topped with pepper jack cheese dressed with sweet curry aioli and cool tzatziki sauce. Piled high on a brioche bun with lettuce, tomato and red onion.

- 8 oz. ground lamb meat laced with a combination of secret herbs and spices
- brioche bun
- pepper jack cheese
- tzatziki sauce
- curry aioli
- lettuce, tomato, red onion

Shepherd's Pie (serves 8)

Ross Vandiver, Chef | Irish Inn | Glen Echo, Maryland

The concept of this recipe is based on our general manager's (Barry Nolan) grandmother's recipe, which she used over the years. We refined it at Irish Inn 10 years ago for the restaurant while staying true to the roots of Irish farmhouse cooking.

Cook ground beef, remove from pan and drain off the excess fat. Sweat the onions, carrots, celery and mushrooms.

Add the whiskey, reduce slightly and then add the cooked ground beef.

Season with salt, pepper, and 1 tsp. fresh grated or ground nutmeg and 1 Tbsp. dry Italian herb mix or your favorite herb mix. Pour into casserole dish. Lightly cover with your favorite mashed potato recipe.

Bake in 350 degree F oven until potatoes are lightly browned.

- 3 lbs. lean ground beef
- 1-2 medium carrots, diced
- 2 stalks celery, medium diced
- ½ yellow onion, medium diced
- 6 oz. button mushrooms, medium diced
- 1 shot Irish whiskey or your favorite whiskey (optional)
- Salt, pepper, nutmeg, Italian herb mix
- 2 c. veal demi glace*

*2 Packets of brown gravy such as McCormick's or Knorr. Follow recipe on the package. You will need at least 2 cups prepared or you can use 2 cups of fairly thick veal stock.

Corned Beef Parsnip Mash With Mustard & Cider Sauce (serves 6)

Bernie Reilly, Owner | The Perfect Pint | New York, New York

- 4 lbs. Corned beef
- 1 carrot
- 2 stalks celery
- 1 leek
- 1 tsp. peppercorns

Parsnip Mash
- 1 lb. potatoes
- 1 lb. parsnips
- ½ c. cream
- 1 Tbsp. butter

Irish Mustard & Cider Sauce
- 1 tsp. butter
- 2/3 tsp. flour
- 1 Tbsp. mustard
- ½ c. cider
- ¼ c. cream
- 4 spring onions

The Irish love their corned beef and this recipe is exceptionally good.

Place beef in a large saucepan with all the vegetables, peppercorns and cider. Add enough water to cover the meat and bring to boil. Simmer for approximately 1.5 hours or until the beef is cooked. Leave in the liquid until ready to serve.

While meat is cooking place potatoes and parsnips in a pot, cover with water, season with salt and bring to a boil. Simmer until cooked (40 min). When cooked, drain well and prepare mash in the usual way. Add the cream and butter, spring onions and correct the seasoning, set aside.

To prepare the sauce, melt the butter in a pot then add in the flour, cook out for 3 minutes. Add the cider and bring to boil then add mustard. Add some cream and chopped spring onions and correct the seasoning with salt and pepper.

Sauteed Brussel Sprouts With Irish Bacon & Caramelized Onions (serves 2)

James Stephens, Owner | Black Sheep Irish Pub | Philadelphia, Pennsylvania

- 6 oz. Brussel sprouts, clipped and cut in half
- ¼ c milk
- 1 Tbsp. olive oil
- ¼ c. Irish bacon, diced
- ½ c. onions, sliced thin
- Salt and fresh ground black pepper

My Nana Rodgers first introduced me to this dish. She owned a butcher shop in the Sandy Row area of Belfast and would try to get meat into as many dishes as possible. This dish is delicious and was always a family favorite and a staple for our Christmas dinner.

Add milk to 3 cups of water in pot and bring to a boil. Cook the Brussel sprouts until tender then drain and rinse with cold water until cool.

In sauté pan, heat olive oil then add Irish bacon; cook over medium heat. When bacon is halfway cooked, add onions and black pepper. When onions are cooked through and Irish bacon begins to crisp, add Brussel sprouts and reduce heat. Continue to cook on low several minutes until Brussel sprouts are hot and add salt and more pepper. Serve immediately.

Scotch Eggs With Dijon Ale Sauce (serves 4)

Dan Vickers, Chef | Durty Nelly's | San Francisco, California

Scotch eggs are a real crowd pleaser, and the sauce is an added bonus.

Hard boil 8 eggs. In a large mixing bowl combine the ground pork, sage, rosemary, garlic, salt and pepper. Incorporate all spices throughout the ground pork. Once the eggs are done, peel them and wrap them in a layer of the pork mixture. Next beat the remaining eggs. Dip each pork covered egg in beaten raw egg and roll in sourdough crumbs until completely coated. Bake the scotch eggs at 375 degrees F for 20 minutes. Let cool and enjoy!!

Dijon Ale Sauce: Combine Dijon mustard and Smithwicks ale. Add salt and pepper to taste!

- 1 lb. ground pork
- 1 dozen eggs
- ½ tsp. ground sage
- ½ tsp. dried rosemary
- 1 tsp. fresh minced garlic
- Salt and pepper to taste
- 1 c. dry sourdough crumbs
- ¼ c. Smithwicks ale
- ¼ c. Dijon mustard

Cottage Pie (serves 4)

Larry Doyle, Chef | Johnny Foley's | San Francisco, California

This is one of Johnny Foley's most popular dishes and probably the most requested recipe.

Place potatoes in a pot and cover with cold water. Add a pinch of salt and bring to boil. Lower heat and simmer for about 15-20 minutes until potatoes are soft. Drain well. Return the potatoes to pot, add butter and cream and mash well. Season with salt and pepper and keep warm until needed.

Heat oven to 375 degrees F

Heat oil in a thick-bottomed pan and add the ground beef. Cook, stirring for about 5 minutes, until browned. Remove to a colander and set aside to allow the fat to drain. Meanwhile add onions, carrots, celery and garlic to the pan and cook, stirring until lightly browned. Stir in the flour and tomato paste and cook, stirring for 2 minutes. Add stock, chili flakes and thyme. Bring mixture to a gentle boil, stirring constantly. Return beef to the pan and stir well to incorporate fully. Reduce heat and simmer gently for 30 minutes until mixture is thickened. Transfer mixture to a 2 quart casserole dish, set aside and allow to cool. When mixture has cooled, carefully spread on the mashed potatoes, sealing all the way to the edges. Fluff the top with a fork. Bake for 30-45 minutes until mashed potatoes are golden brown. Remove from oven, sprinkle with chopped parsley and serve.

For the filling
- 1 lb. lean ground beef
- ½ c. olive oil
- 1 large white onion, peeled and cut into ½ inch dice
- 2 medium carrots, peeled and cut into ½ inch dice
- 2 stalks celery, washed and cut into ½ inch dice
- 2 cloves garlic, finely chopped
- ½ c. all-purpose flour
- ¼ c. tomato paste
- 2 c. beef stock or chicken stock
- 1 pinch chili flakes
- 1 Tbsp. chopped fresh thyme
- salt and ground black pepper to taste

Mashed Potatoes
- 2 large russet potatoes, peeled and quartered
- ¼ cup butter
- ½ c. heavy cream
- Salt and ground white pepper to taste

❧ Pork Pie With Carmelized Apples (serves 6-8)

Jim Gallagher, Barman | Molly's Shebeen | New York, New York

- Tbsp. butter, plus more for greasing
- 1 medium cooking apple, peeled, cored and sliced
- 2 Tbsp. each finely chopped shallot, garlic, celery and carrot
- 1 Tbsp. honey
- 1 lb. pork sausage meat, crumbled (I use Myers of Keswick in NYC)
- ½ lb. Irish bacon (from Tommy Moloney, Irish butcher, Maspeth, NY)
- sliced cured pork loin (from Tommy Moloney)
- mild cured back rashers, diced (from Tommy Moloney)
- Salt and pepper
- 3 Tbsp. of minced mixed herbs such as thyme, rosemary and sage
- ½ lb. puff pastry (homemade)
- 1 duck egg, beaten

St. Patrick declared that the three most unforgivable crimes imaginable were (i) the killing of trained oxen, (ii) the rustling of cattle, (iii) the burning of byres. He could have also added the destruction of our ancient Celtic cooking tradition by our various occupying invaders.

Irish cooking is originally organic rustic farm cooking. Travel Ireland and the echoes of the past can be seen in not only the castles and estates but also in the old abandoned peasant homes, some of which are a legacy from the famine. Irish cooking encompassed all these social needs.

Preheat oven to 325 degrees F. Add 1 Tbsp. of butter to a medium skillet over heat, add the apples and honey and cook for about 10 minutes to caramelize, stirring well.

Grease a small casserole dish and put about 1/3 of sausage meat on the bottom and top with about 1/3 of bacon, season with salt and pepper and sprinkle 1 Tbsp. of herbs on top. Cover with a layer of caramelized apples. Repeat the process twice to use up all the sausage meat, bacon and herbs. Roll out the pastry big enough to cover the surface of the pie, cover the pie with pastry and press down lightly, with a fork prick the pastry and then brush with the beaten duck egg. Bake for one hour or until the pastry is puffed up and turned a golden brown. Enjoy!

❧ Open Faced Hot Turkey Sandwich (serves 4)

Don Murphy, Owner | Murphy's Bar and Grill | Honolulu, Hawaii

- 1 turkey hind quarter
- cranberry sauce
- gravy
- sliced carrots, onions, and celery; one cup each
- mashed potatoes
- hearty bread slices

Fresh Cranberry Sauce
- 1 lb. fresh cranberries
- 1 c. water
- 1 c. sugar
- 1 Tbsp. sliced orange rind
- 1 cinnamon stick broken in half
- 2 oz. of orange juice

Turkey is usually reserved for special occasions but this is a special sandwich for all occasions.

Place turkey hindquarter on baking sheet over sliced carrots, onions and celery. Bake for 2 ½ hours at 300 degrees F or until done. Let stand.

For the cranberry sauce, bring all ingredients to boil, reduce to simmer, and cook for 5 minutes.

Meanwhile back at the turkey… strip the meat off of the leg and place on bread of your choice, top with gravy and fresh cranberry sauce, serve with mashed potatoes and vegetables.

Boxty (serves 6)

Myles O'Reilly, Owner | O'Reilly's | San Francisco, California

This is an excellent recipe (not for the weak of heart but for the Irish that's in us all). Boxty is based on songs and stories of renowned heroes, the tales of glory that revealed what we were made of. We are indeed much more than what we eat, but what we eat makes us much more than what we are.

Heat oven to 200 degrees F. Chop half the potatoes into large slices, place in a medium saucepan, salt generously and cover with cold water covering the spuds by one inch; bring to boil and reduce heat to low; simmer uncovered until they are tender (about 8 minutes).

Grate remaining potatoes on a grater using the rougher larger holes. Toss with ¼ tsp. salt and place in a fine mesh strainer set over a medium bowl; leave to one side.

When the boiled spuds are ready, drain and return to pot; add ¼ c. milk and mash until smooth. Squeeze the grated potatoes to get all excess water out of the strainer; add to the mashed potatoes (no need to stir).

Mix the egg, ½ c. milk, flour, pepper and 1 tsp. salt in a large bowl and whisk until the cows come home (ten seconds). Add the potatoes and stir like hell until all are evenly bonded.

Heat a large non-stick frying pan or you can griddle over medium heat (important). Add a knob of Irish butter (Kerry gold) to season the pan enough to cover the bottom; drop into the seasoned buttered pan a quarter cup of the ready to pour batter and spread each to about ¼ inch thick. Cook until the pancake bottom is golden brown (4-5 minutes) and flip to the other side and cook as same.

Place on a baking sheet and set in a warm oven to maintain temperature; continue with the remaining Boxty batter; serve with a knob of butter. This is a slice of heaven.

Add topping of choice. There are many to choose from.

- 2 lbs. (3-4) Yukon gold potatoes, peeled
- ¾ c. whole milk
- 1 ¼ tsp. fine salt, plus a pinch for seasoning before cooking
- 1 large egg
- 1/3 c. flour
- ¼ tsp. freshly ground black pepper
- 1-2 Tbsp. unsalted butter cut into small pieces

Pork Sausage With Leek And Parsnip Mash & Onion Gravy (serves 4)

Steve Duggan, Manager | Paddy Reilly's | New York, New York

Pork has always been important in Ireland and featured strongly in the cuisine.

Put the sausages into a roasting tray and add lemon juice and the red currant jelly. Cook for 35 minutes, turning them now and again.

Put leeks, parsnips, and garlic into a saucepan covered with water. Cook until parsnips are tender. Drain and allow them to dry out and then add milk (which is better heated a little) and put all mash ingredients into a blender.

Add two Tbsp. of oil to a heated frying pan and fry the red onion. Add the vinegar and soy sauce and cook till onions are really soft. Then plate up by putting the mash on and then the sausages and then pour on the onion gravy.

- 12 large pork sausages
- 2 Tbsp. red current jelly
- 1 tsp. lemon juice
- 2 Tbsp. olive oil
- 14 oz. red onions
- 2 Tbsp. red wine vinegar
- 2 Tbsp. brown sugar
- 1 Tbsp. soy sauce

For the mash
- 1 lb. leeks
- 1 lb. parsnips
- 1 garlic clove
- 3 fl. oz. milk
- 1 Tbsp. parsley
- 1 Tbsp. Parmesan cheese
- salt and pepper

Irish Corned Beef & Cabbage With A Middle Eastern Twist (serves 6)

Saeed Ghazi, Owner | The Little Shamrock | San Francisco, California

- 2 to 3 lbs. corned beef brisket
- ½ Tbsp. coarsely ground black pepper
- 2 tsp. salt
- 1 tsp. ground allspice
- 1-2 bay leaves, according to taste
- 1 tsp. sugar
- 2 Tbsp. cider vinegar
- 2 cloves garlic, minced
- 1-2 onions cut into wedges, according to taste
- ¾ lb. carrots, cut into chunks, (approx. 4)
- 1 lb. potatoes, peeled and cut into chunks (approx. 3-4)
- ¼ lb. celery, diced (approx. 2 stalks)
- 1 small head cabbage, cut into wedges (approx. 2 lbs.)
- dash of turmeric, cumin and saffron

This recipe is very simple. The difference is in the spices that we use in cooking, namely turmeric, cumin and saffron. The turmeric, cumin and saffron add to the flavor and aroma of the dish, which has been very popular at The Little Shamrock for many years.

Place corned beef and other ingredients into an 8-quart slow cooker with 3 quarts of water. Cover and bring to a boil. Decrease heat to low and simmer for 2 ½ hours, or until vegetables are tender. Remove the bay leaves before serving.

Chicken Shots (serves 5)

Jason Hicks, Chef | The Local | Minneapolis, Minnesota

Whiskey Honey Glaze
- 4 oz. apple cider vinegar
- 1 1/4 oz. Irish Mist Liqueur
- 1 oz. 2 Ginger's Irish Whiskey
- 1 ¼ oz. ketchup
- ½ oz. molasses
- 1 ¼ oz. honey
- ¼ c. brown sugar
- 1 tsp. kosher salt
- 1/3 c. hot sauce
- ¼ tsp. crushed red pepper
- ¼ tsp. black pepper, table grind

Chicken
- 2 lbs. fresh chicken breasts (boneless & skinless)
- 1 c. buttermilk
- 1 c. self rising all purpose flour
- 1 c. diced green onions (for garnish)

A little Irish whiskey makes everything taste a little better!!

Combine ingredients for Whiskey Honey Glaze in pot. Bring to a boil over high heat. Simmer until thickened (about 30 minutes).

Remove from heat and cool. Store covered at room temperature. Can be made in advance and held.

Dice chicken breast to 1" cubes. Season to taste with salt & pepper.

Mix chicken with buttermilk and let stand for 10 minutes.

Toss marinated chicken with flour and shake off any excess flour. Make sure chicken is completely coated in flour.

Put oil in fryer or a pot with deep sides and a candy thermometer and heat to 350 degrees F. Cook chicken until done, drain excess oil, lightly season with salt and pepper.

Toss cooked chicken with sauce and garnish with diced green onions.

❦ Entrecote Jameson (serves 2)

Hugo Malone, Chef | The Dubliner | Washington, D.C.

This is a classical preparation of a traditional Irish dish and a favorite at The Dubliner.

We use a 14 oz. certified Angus Strip Steak.

Preheat oven to 450 degrees F. Heat a heavy cast iron skillet to smoking point; salt and dredge strip steak in cracked peppercorns. Add 2 oz. oil to skillet, add steak to skillet and brown on all sides about five minutes each side. Transfer skillet to pre-heated 450 degrees oven and finish to desired doneness, 5-7 minutes. For rare, remove the steaks to a rack to rest.

For the sauce: Return the skillet to stovetop, add Jameson to pan carefully, stir and scrape pan to deglaze. Reduce Jameson by half, add veal stock and reduce until thick enough to coat the spoon. Whisk in cream, butter, tomato, salt and pepper to taste. Pour over steak and serve.

- 14 oz. New York strip steak
- olive oil
- 2 oz. fresh cracked peppercorns (crushed not ground)
- 2 oz. sweet butter
- 8 oz. strong dark veal stock
- 1 oz. diced tomato
- 2 oz. Jameson Irish whiskey
- 2 oz. heavy cream

❦ Smoked Salmon

Larry Doyle, Chef | Johnny Foley's | San Francisco, California

There is nothing more elegant that smoked salmon, and this recipe is at the top of the list.

Combine ingredients and thoroughly mix well to make sure there is an even distribution of both ingredients.

Trim belly section from salmon filets (pin bones removed) and discard or reserve for other uses.

Thoroughly rub salmon filets with cure mixture. Set salmon on a sheet pan and let sit in refrigerator for 24 hours. It is important that the salmon has enough time in the fridge with the cure so that enough moisture is removed from the fish.

The next day, rinse remaining cure from salmon thoroughly with running cold water.

Place soaked wood chips (can soak in whiskey or water) in smoke box and place inside alto sham. Place salmon inside smoker with a hotel pan filled with ice underneath. This is so the smoke stays cold and the fish isn't hot smoked.

Let fish sit in smoker for 90 minutes. Remove and place in refrigerator with plastic wrap until used.

- Salmon

Cure:

- 3 lbs. kosher salt
- 2 lbs. light brown sugar

Caramelized Peach Pork Chops (serves 4)

Jenna Shannon-Garvey, Owner | A Terrible Beauty | Seattle, Washington

- 4 10 oz. bone in pork chops
- Wine

Herb Brine
- ¼ c. sugar
- ¼ c. salt
- 4 c. water
- ¼ oz. rosemary sprigs
- ¼ oz. thyme
- 4 c. ice

Potato Cakes
- 1 lb. russet potatoes
- 2 Tbsp. garlic
- ¾ c. shredded hash browns
- 1 egg
- ¼ c. green onions
- 1 tsp. salt
- 1 tsp. black pepper
- Panko, as needed
- Cooking oil, as needed
- 4 oz. sour cream

Peach Chutney
- 1 ¼ tsp. olive oil
- 1 ½ Tbsp. onion
- ¾ tsp. garlic
- 1 Tbsp. cider vinegar
- 2/3 c. brown sugar
- 1 ½ Tbsp. white sugar
- ¼ tsp. black pepper
- 1 lb. peaches, sliced
- 1 ¼ tsp. tarragon

Cabbage & Mustard Butter
- 1 head cabbage
- ¼ c. unsalted butter
- ¼ c. stone ground mustard

Center cut pork chops glazed with peach chutney and served with Irish potato cakes and steamed cabbage. Food for the Gods.

Pork Chops (Herb Brine): Dissolve salt and sugar in hot water. Add herbs and let steep for 5 minutes. Add ice to cool mixture and cover the pork chops for 12 hours in refrigerator.

Potato Cakes: Boil potatoes till soft, cool completely then remove skin. Lightly sauté the garlic in a small amount of olive oil until aromatic. Mix potatoes, hash browns, chopped green onion, egg, salt and pepper together by hand until well incorporated. Measure out golf ball sized portions. Roll completely in Panko crumbs and flatten out with palm of hand to 2" cakes. In a thick bottomed pan heat ¼ c. cooking oil of your choice. Carefully place the potato cakes to cook over medium heat till crisp and golden brown on both sides.

Peach Chutney & Pork Chops: In medium sized sauce pot, caramelize onions in olive oil. Add garlic and sauté till aromatic; mix in the vinegar, sugars and black pepper. Add sliced peaches and simmer until golden brown. Fold in fresh tarragon. Season the chop with salt & pepper on both sides.

Heat a large sauté pan to smoke point and carefully add tsp. of oil and place the chop in pan. Once chop has a nice sear on first side, flip the chop and place in oven to finish Once chop has reached desired temp, remove from pan to let rest. In same sauté pan, deglaze with wine away from flame. Return to heat and add the chutney. Reduce and add herbs and cream in butter. Place cabbage in seasoned boiling water and cook until desired level of softness. Remove cabbage and toss with mustard butter.

Place cabbage wedge on plate and angle rested chop on cabbage with bone up. Scoop chutney from pan and lay over chop. Add 2 potato cakes to side. Finish with dollop of sour cream on top of potato cakes. Garnish with sprinkle of leftover green onions. Serve and enjoy!

Shepherd's Pie (serves 6)

Lucille McAleese, Co-owner | Kell's Irish Pub | Portland, Oregon

With this recipe, we give homage to humble yet delicious food—our version of "Irish soul food" with the ultimate comfort recipe.

If you are not a beef lover, ground turkey or chicken are also perfect substitutes in this recipe, as is lamb. And if you are a vegetarian, barley or lentils are lovely in place of the meat.

At Kells, we recommend that you enjoy this dish with your favorite pint or a glass of red wine. Cheers!

- 1 ½ lbs. ground free-range beef
- ½ c. sweet onions, diced
- ½ c. baby carrots, diced
- ¼ c. Cabernet wine
- 1-2 tsp. garlic, minced or pressed
- ¼ c. Guinness draught stout
- 7 oz. (3/4 c. plus 2 Tbsp.) beef broth
- 1 tsp. Worcestershire sauce
- ¼ tsp. fresh basil
- ¼ tsp. fresh oregano
- ¼ tsp. fresh sage
- ¼ tsp. fresh marjoram
- 1 c. peas (preferably fresh or frozen)
- 2 Tbsp. butter
- 2 Tbsp. flour
- ½ tsp. salt
- ¼ tsp. pepper

Ulster Champ Topping

- 1 ¼ lbs. russet potatoes, 4 medium
- ¼ c. milk
- ¼ c. fresh parsley, finely minced
- 4 tbs. butter
- 1 c. finely grated Irish white cheddar cheese
- 1/3 c. scallions or chives, chopped
- salt and white pepper to taste

Brown beef in a Dutch oven or other large heave saucepot over low to moderate heat. Allow to simmer until cooked throughout, about 5-10 minutes. Drain excess fat when cooked and add onion, carrots, garlic, stout, wine, broth, Worcestershire sauce, basil, oregano, sage and marjoram. Stir and bring to a simmer over low heat. Cook 15 minutes or until carrots are fork tender; add peas.

While meat is simmering, bring large pot of water to boil for potatoes.

Meanwhile, in a small saucepan, melt butter and stir in flour to make a roux (paste of equal parts butter and flour used to thicken liquids). Slowly incorporate roux into simmering beef mixture until desired thickness is achieved. (If mixture was simmered too long or cooked too high, less roux is needed,) Continue to cook for 5-10 minutes to allow roux and flavors to meld; season with salt and pepper.

Remove to a 9 ½ inch round casserole dish or deep pie dish. While meat is simmering, preheat oven to 350 degrees F and prepare Ulster Champ Topping.

Scrub and peel potatoes. Cut into large pieces. Simmer potatoes in large pot until fork tender. Drain well and return to pot on low heat to remove excess moisture. Stir in butter and cheese and whip gradually adding milk, parsley and scallions or chives; season with salt and pepper.

Spoon potato topping evenly over meat mixture, making irregular peaks with the back of a spoon. Alternatively, use a pastry bag and star tip to pipe potatoes over meat mixture.

Bake for 20-30 minutes or until potatoes are golden brown and crusty on edges and mixture is heated throughout.

If desired, place casserole under broiler for 1-2 minutes to crisp potato topping. Remove from oven, allow to cool slightly to set and serve immediately from casserole dish. Serve wit HP Sauce(Irish-English steak-style sauce), steak sauce or pan gravy, if desired.

Note: Can also be cooked in individual baking dishes and adjust final baking time as needed.

Meatloaf (yields five two-pound loaves)

Mary Ellen Mullins, Owner | McGillin's Olde Ale House | Philadelphia, Pennsylvania

- 10 lbs. ground beef
- 5 eggs
- 2 c. chopped carrots
- 2 c. chopped onions
- 2 c. chopped celery
- 3 chopped green peppers
- 1 Tbsp. dried thyme
- 1 Tbsp. dried basil
- 2 Tbsp. granulated garlic
- ¾ c. Worcestershire sauce
- 2 c. ketchup
- 3 c. shredded cheddar jack
- Salt and pepper
- 2 c. Parmesan cheese
- 2 bunches fresh chopped parsley
- 3 c. Italian style bread crumbs

A meatloaf by any other name can't top this juicy one topped with cheese.

Combine above wet and dry ingredients seperately and then together.

Divide mix into 5 loaf pans and cover with aluminum.

Bake at 425 degrees F for 1 hour.

Remove foil, top loaves with marinara/ketchup blend, and return to oven uncovered for 45 minutes. Top loaves with shredded cheddar jack cheese and parsley, return to oven for 15 minutes more.

Gaelic Steak

Don Murphy, Owner | Murphy's Bar and Grill | Honolulu, Hawaii

Sauce
- 2 c. heavy cream
- 1 c. Worcestershire sauce
- 1 oz. green peppercorns in brine

This tasty steak is sure to please family and friends.

Sauce: Reduce cream and Worcestershire by one third. Add one ounce green peppercorns in brine and simmer for 10 minutes

Grill New York steak to the temperature you desire. Top with Gaelic Steak Sauce (green peppercorn sauce).

Crab Cakes (yields about 30 cakes)

Mark Toombs, Chef; Steve Ciapciak, Chef | John D. McGurk's Irish Pub and Garden | St Louis, Missouri

- 1 ½ c. mayonnaise
- 1 ½ c. red onion, minced
- 12 egg yolks
- 12 Tbsp. fresh lemon juice
- 6 Tbsp. Dijon mustard
- 2 c. red pepper, minced
- 1 c. fresh basil, chopped
- 1 tsp. black pepper
- 6 lbs. crab meat
- 3 c. breadcrumbs
- 6 Tbsp. lemon zest

A pint of frosty ale would go well with these flavorful crab cakes. Add a green salad and you have dinner.

Place all ingredients in a large bowl and mix thoroughly. Portion the mixture to 3 oz. balls and coat with more breadcrumbs. Place the crab cakes in a pan, label and refrigerate until ready to use.

🌿 Turkey Pot Pie

Patrick McGovern's Irish Pub | St. Paul, Minnesota

Roux: 1 lb. butter and 3 cups flour. Cook until it smells like roasted nuts. Add one 2 lb. bag of peas and carrots, 1 ½ tsp. poultry seasoning and 2 cold diced baked potatoes.

Put a handful of white and dark cubed turkey meat on bottom of each potpie bowl. Pour the above mixture on top of meat, filling almost to the top. Cover the top of the bowl with a puff pastry shell, slightly crimping the edges.

Bake at 350 degrees F for 15 minutes in a convection oven.

- cubed turkey
- puff pastry
- 1½ gallons water
- 1 medium onion, chopped
- ½ stock chopped celery
- ¾ c. chicken base
- 1 tsp. yellow food coloring
- 1½ Tbsp. poultry seasoning

🌿 Crab Cakes With Chive Aioli And Napa Cabbage Slaw (yields 6 cakes)

Mitchell Roberts, Executive Chef | Nine Fine Irishmen Pub | Las Vegas, Nevada

This is a favorite appetizer of mine that's very delicious and has fresh flavors that really please the taste buds of seafood lovers.

Crab cakes: Mix all ingredients together. Folding the crab not kneading it. Portion in 6 equal size cakes. Place in fridge for later use.

Slaw: Mix all items except mustard, oil and vinegar

Aioli: In small food processor, blend mayonnaise and chives until smooth. Fold in Crème Fraiche and salt and pepper. Place in fridge.

Final preparation: Lightly flour crab cakes and pan sear in olive oil until golden brown. Place in preheated 425 degree F. oven for approximately 6 minutes.

Mix slaw with oil, vinegar and mustard.

Place a small dollop of chive Aioli on a small 6 inch round plate and spread evenly.

Place crab cake on top of Aioli

Place a mound of slaw on top of crab cake and serve!

Crab cakes
- 1 lb. lump crab
- 1 oz. Dijon mustard
- 2 Oz. mayonnaise
- 1 Tbsp. fresh snipped chives
- 1 tsp. fresh lemon juice
- 1 whole egg
- Kosher salt to taste
- fresh ground black pepper to taste
- ¼ c. Panko breadcrumbs

Napa cabbage slaw
- ¼ head Napa cabbage, fine julienne
- watermelon radish, fine julienne
- ½ large whole peeled carrot, fine julienne
- 2 shallots
- 1 Tbsp. olive oil
- Dijon mustard to taste
- Kosher salt to taste
- ½ Tbsp. apple cider vinegar

Chive aioli
- 1 pkg. fresh chives
- ¼ c. mayonnaise
- 1/8 c. Crème Fraiche
- Kosher salt to taste
- black pepper to taste

Corned Beef Reuben With Warm Red Cabbage Slaw (serves 1)

Valintinus Domingo, Executive Chef | Meehan's Public House, Vinings | Atlanta, Georgia

- 6 oz. house made corned beef
- 3 Tbsp. Russian or 1000 island dressing
- 2 oz. sauerkraut
- 2 slices Swiss cheese
- 2 slices marbled rye bread

Warm Red Cabbage Slaw

- 3 oz. shaved red cabbage
- 1 Tbsp. toasted walnuts
- 2 tsp. balsamic glaze
- 1 Tbsp. blue cheese crumbles
- 1 Tbsp. canola oil
- salt and pepper to taste

Every Irishman dreams of a Reuben as tasty as this one.

Heat griddle to medium high temperature. On one side of each marble rye bread, spread Russian dressing and add Swiss cheese. Toast the marble rye bread on the griddle, cheese side up. While bread is toasting, heat up corned beef and sauerkraut on a separate side of grill. Once heated through place the corned beef and sauerkraut on one side of the marble rye bread and top with the other half. Grill till golden brown on each side and serve with warm red cabbage slaw.

Heat a sauté pan with canola oil. Sweat the shaved red cabbage. Add walnuts and sauté for 2 minutes over medium high flame. Season with salt and pepper. Deglaze with balsamic glaze and add blue cheese crumbles. Stir and continue to cook for another 1-5 minutes or until cabbage is soft and blue cheese is melted. Taste and re-season with salt and pepper.

Guinness Stout Onion Soup (serves 6-8)

Geoff Kokoszka, General Manager | Olde Blind Dog Irish Pub | Brookhaven, Georgia

Versions of this soup abound but the basic tenets are simple: onions, stock, croutons and melted cheese. We may be biased, but the addition of Guinness to this classic dish is nothing short of delicious.

Soup: Melt butter in a large saucepan. Add onions, salt and pepper to butter and cook on low heat, stirring occasionally until onions begin to brown.

Add brown sugar and turn heat to high to remove the majority of the moisture from the onions. Continue stirring.

When most of the moisture from the onions has been cooked off, add Guinness, water, beef and chicken pastes, thyme and bay leaf.

Turn heat to low and simmer for 20 minutes, stirring occasionally. When finished, ladle soup into a cup or bowl, top with croutons and cheese and either bake or broil until cheese is bubbly.

Croutons: Mix all ingredients except croutons in a medium sized mixing bowl.

Add croutons and lightly toss to coat them in herb and spice mixture.

Spread evenly on a parchment lined baking sheet and bake 10-15 minutes at 350 degrees F or until golden brown.

- 2 large onions
- 2 oz. unsalted butter
- 2 oz. chicken base paste
- 1 oz. beef base paste
- 2 c. Guinness
- 5 c. water
- 4 sprigs minced thyme
- 1 bay leaf
- 2 tsp. black pepper
- 1 Tbsp. kosher salt
- 5 Tbsp. brown sugar
- sliced white Cheddar or Provolone cheese

Croutons:
- 2 Hoagie rolls ½ to ¾ inch cubed
- ½ tsp. kosher salt
- ½ tsp. garlic powder
- ½ Tbsp. black pepper
- ½ Tbsp. dry oregano
- 2 Tbsp. minced curley parsley
- 2 Tbsp. grated Parmesan cheese
- ¼ c. extra virgin olive oil

Potato And Leek Soup (serves 12-14)

James Stephens, Owner | Black Sheep Irish Pub | Philadelphia, Pennsylvania

- 2 ½ lbs. all purpose potatoes, roughly sliced
- 1 bunch leeks, washed and sliced thin
- 1 lg. onion, diced medium
- 1 gallon chicken stock
- 4 cloves garlic, minced
- 3-4 sprigs fresh thyme
- salt and fresh ground black pepper
- Vegetable oil
- ¼ c. fresh chives, sliced
- 1 qt. heavy cream
- baguette or French bread

This is one of my favorite soups from my grandmother, Nana Rodgers.

Coat bottom of large pot with vegetable oil and heat. When hot add onion and cook over medium heat for about 5 minutes or until very tender. Add garlic and cook 2-3 minutes, then add leeks, thyme and several turns of black pepper. When vegetables are cooked and tender add chicken broth and bring to a simmer for 45 minutes, add potatoes and cream and continue to simmer until potatoes are very tender. Remove thyme sprigs. Remove from stove and allow cooling.

In batches, blend soup in blender till very smooth, adjusting seasoning. Reheat on stove; serve in soup bowls and garnish with chives.

Fish Stew (serves 6-8)

Shane O'Connor, Chef/Owner | Wolfe Tone Pub | Upperville, Virginia

- 12 little neck clams in shell
- 24 mussels in shell
- 12 select oysters
- 12 large shrimp
- 6 jumbo scallops
- 6 oz. lump fresh crab
- 8 oz. Farrow Island Scottish salmon, 2-inch cubes
- 6 oz. salted mackerel, 1-inch cubes
- 24 periwinkles (sea snails)
- 8 oz. orzo pasta
- 8 oz. pee wee potatoes
- 12 oz. smoked Andouille sausage, sliced thin
- 4 oz. turnips
- 4 oz. English peas
- 2 oz. nettles
- 2 oz. fresh herbs (thyme, oregano, parsley)
- 2 oz. chopped garlic
- 8 oz. diced Cippolini onions
- 8 oz. diced crispy leeks
- 8 oz. diced celery
- 8 oz. whole butter
- 8 oz. Chablis wine
- 4 c. lobster stock
- Cajun spice
- 24 oz. oven roasted tomatoes
- 8 c. red curry broth
- salt and pepper to taste

This is an old family recipe from my grandfather, Michael O'Connor. While working on the lighthouses throughout Ireland, he spent a lot of his time cooking for himself and other lighthouse keepers. The abundance of fresh seafood was never an issue and during warmer seasons they grew their own vegetables. As a young man, I spent summers on the lighthouse with my father, John Brendan O'Connor. We would create this fabulous stew from our catch of the day.

Pan sear in olive oil: salmon, cod, mackerel, scallops, oysters and shrimp until lightly brown. (Do not overcook). Take out of pan and put aside.

In 8 quart pan, sauté on medium heat: olive oil, Cippolini onions, leeks, celery, turnips, potatoes, peas and Andouille sausage for about 10 minutes, stir, do not burn.

Add: oven roasted tomatoes, garlic, red curry broth and lobster stock. Bring to a boil and simmer, stirring occasionally for about 25 minutes.

In a separate pot, add mussels, clams, periwinkles, Chablis and butter. As soon as mussels open turn off heat, take out of pot and put aside (clams may not open but you will finish cooking later). Add the remaining juices from the shellfish pot to your tomato and curry pan.

While on simmer, add your Cajun spices, nettles, fresh herbs, lump crab-meat and clams that did not open. Finally, add all of our remaining seafood (do not stir, you don't want to break up the delicate fish).

Cover pot with lid and simmer for 5 minutes. Season to taste with salt and pepper.

Stew is ready to be served. Accompany with a grilled baguette and a pint of Guinness.

❦ Guinness Beef Stew (serves 6)

NOELLE SOMERS, GENERAL MANAGER | GREEN DRAGON | BOSTON, MASSACHUSETTS

This is a traditional beef stew recipe passed down from generation to generation from my father's grandmother, Josephine Somers from the small village of Finuge in Listowel, County Kerry. It has been a recipe that we all come back to on those cold humid winter nights. It soothes the soul and warms the heart!

Preheat oven to 275 degrees F.

Heat olive oil and bay leaves in 6-quart oven-proof pot over high heat. Sear beef in the hot oil until the meat has a browned crust, about 3 minutes per side. Cook and stir onions with beef until onions are translucent, 5 more minutes. Reduce heat to low.

Combine thyme and rosemary leaves and 2 Tbsp. flour; stir mixture into beef and onions until thoroughly combined. Pour beer and beef stock into mixture, stir to combine, and bring to a simmer. Cook, stirring often, until thickened, about 5 minutes. Mix potatoes carrots, celery and parsley into beef and sauce; cover pot.

Braise stew in the preheated oven until potatoes are cooked through and beef is tender, about 3 hours; stir occasionally. Season with salt and black pepper.

- 2 Tbsp. olive oil
- 3 bay leaves
- 2 lb. beef stew meat, cut into 1 ½ inch cubes
- 2 yellow onions
- 1 tsp. dried thyme
- 1 tsp. dried rosemary leaves
- 2 Tbsp. all-purpose flour
- 1 (15 oz.) can Guinness Irish stout beer
- 1 c. beef stock
- 2 large potatoes, cut into 1 ½ inch cubes
- ½ lb. carrots, peeled and thickly sliced
- ½ lb. celery, thickly sliced
- 2 Tbsp. chopped parsley
- salt and ground black pepper to taste

❦ Irish Potato Soup (serves 16)

VIC POWER, OWNER | KEVIN BARRY'S | SAVANNAH, GEORGIA

A great choice anytime, this Irish Potato Soup comforts the soul.

Melt butter in a saucepan. Add flour, stirring until smooth.

Add heated milk, mix well, then add the chicken base.

Combine all ingredients, and whip until thick.

- 5 lbs. potatoes, peeled, sliced, and cooked
- 1 can chicken broth
- 1 yellow onion, sauteed until soft
- 1 qt. milk
- ¼ lb. butter
- 1 c. all purpose flour
- 1 Tbsp. chicken base
- ¼ tsp. accent leeks, to taste

Bill's Bachelor Beef Stew (serves 10-12)

Bill Comerford, Owner | O'Toole's Irish Pub | Honolulu, Hawaii

- 4-5 lb. stew beef
- 8 potatoes
- 1-2 lb. carrots
- 3 onions
- 1 qt. water
- 3 beef bouillon cubes
- 1 tsp. dry mustard
- 1 Tbsp. salt
- 1 tsp. pepper
- 4 bay leaves
- 1 Tbsp. Worcestershire sauce
- 2 tsp. onion powder
- 1 tsp. celery salt
- 1 can or jar spaghetti sauce (meat or traditional sauce)

This recipe's main ingredient to flavor is spaghetti sauce. Living in college with 3 to 4 roommates meant there was always nothing in the cupboards or refrigerator, thus the need for another source of spices (spaghetti sauce). With just a few ingredients but some cooking patience it makes a great stew.

Use a large stew pot with a lid, 5 quarts or larger. Start with the quart of water, bring to a low boil with a lid on. Add all bouillon cubes, salt and pepper, bay leaves, dry mustard, Worcestershire sauce, onion powder and celery salt. Bring the water down to a slow boil, keeping the lid on. Trim your beef to half-inch cubes. Remove all fat and gristle and add it to the boiling water as you trim beef. When you have cut all the beef into cubes, you can remove all the beef parts, fat and gristle from the pot with a scooped spoon or strainer. When you have all the trimmings removed you can add the cubed beef. Bring it to a boil and then to medium heat with the lid on. Peel potatoes and carrots and cut in 1 inch cubes. Peel onions and cut into 8 parts. Add spaghetti sauce, stir and add vegetables. Bring to boil with lid on and cook for 15-20 minutes. Reduce heat and let stew for 3-4 hours while testing the beef and vegetables for tenderness. Turn off heat and let sit to room temperature then refrigerate. Reheat and serve.

Lamb Stew (serves 4-6)

John Nallen | Nallen's Irish Pub | Denver, Colorado

- ½ leg of lamb, cut in 1 inch pieces
- 2 Tbsp. butter
- 2 cloves of garlic, sliced
- 2 Tbsp. flour
- 1 tsp. salt
- ¾ tsp. pepper
- 1 c. white wine
- 3 c. broth
- ½ tsp. marjoram
- 1 bay leaf
- 4 large carrots, cut in 2 inch pieces
- 8 white onions, peeled
- 4 medium boiled potatoes
- 1.5 c. water

This Lamb Stew is a real crowd pleaser and makes a hearty dinner.

Brown meat in butter in a large heavy pan, add wine, garlic, marjoram, bay leaf, broth, and enough water to cover the meat. Cover and slow simmer for 1½ hours. Stir occasionally. Add carrots, onions and potatoes. Simmer for 30 more minutes.

Black Pudding Pâté (serves 8-10)

Pauline Patterson, Co-owner | Finn McCool's Irish Pub | New Orleans, Louisiana

This is my mother-in-law's black pudding pâté. I serve it with my Mum's toasted bread.

Put liver into blender and blend until very fine and place in large mixing dish. Put brandy, sherry, garlic, parsley, onion, and spices and blend, adding a cup full of liver at a time. When all mixed add black pudding and season with salt, pepper, Tabasco or cayenne. Mix well.

Line loaf pan with bacon and fill with mixture then cover top with remaining bacon strips. Place in larger dish and top larger dish with 2-3 inches of water. Bake uncovered in a moderate oven 350 degrees F for 1½ hours.

Remove pate and cover with wax paper and press down with heavy weight to firm up dish. Chill in fridge for several hours. Serve with your mum's brown bread.

- 1 lb. black pudding
- 1 lb. pig's liver
- 2 Tbsp. Hennessy brandy
- 1 Tbsp. sherry
- 1 clove garlic
- 2 Tbsp. diced parsley
- 1 small onion, diced
- ¼ tsp. powdered ginger
- 1/8 tsp. cinnamon, clove and nutmeg
- salt and black pepper to taste
- dash Tabasco or cayenne and enough streaky bacon

Smoked Salmon Spread (serves 6)

Randy Burns, chef | Four Green Fields | Tampa, Florida

Salmon paired with horseradish is an elegant but tasty appetizer.

Poach salmon filet in water and liquid smoke for 10 minutes until just done. Rinse and chill filet until cool. Crumble filet in a large mixing bowl and add grated Parmesan cheese, hot sauce, horseradish and salt. Mix thoroughly and finish with sour cream. Adjust salt and hot sauce to taste. Serve on oiled and seasoned French bread rounds, toasted lightly.

- 1 lb. fresh skinless salmon filet
- ½ c. liquid smoke
- 5 c. water
- 1/3 c. Parmesan (grated) cheese
- ¼ c. hot sauce
- ¼ c. prepared horseradish
- 1/ tsp. salt
- ½ c. sour cream

Batter For Fish And Chips (yields batter for 3-4 pounds of fish)

Ross Vandiver, Chef | Irish Inn | Glen Echo, Maryland

Guinness adds lots of flavor to any recipe. This batter is tasty and light while giving fish a richer flavor.

Combine dry ingredients thoroughly. Add wet ingredients and mix with whisk until batter is the proper consistency (should coat fish well).

- 2 c. whole meal flour
- 2 c. all purpose flour
- 1 c. cornstarch
- 2 Tbsp. salt
- 1 Tbsp. Cajun seasoning
- 2 Tbsp. baking powder
- 1 pint Guinness
- 3-4 pints club soda

Irish Nachos (serves 2)

Lucille McAleese, Co-owner | Kell's Irish Pub | Portland, Oregon

- unsaturated oil for frying
- 2 medium russet potatoes, thinly sliced*
- kosher salt
- 2 c. shredded Tillamook cheese
- ½ c. diced tomatoes
- ½ c. sliced green onions
- ½ c. sliced black olives
- ½ c. quality thick cut bacon

This recipe for nachos could substitute for the main meal instead of an appetizer.

In a large heavy saucepan or personal deep fat fryer, fill oil no more that halfway to top and heat to 350 degrees F. Add potato slices in batches. Fry until they are a light golden brown in color, about 3 minutes. Drain on paper towels, season with kosher salt.

On a large ovenproof plate, alternate layers of potato chips and shredded cheddar making sure to leave enough cheese to top the nachos. Place the nachos in a 350 degree F oven for 4-5 minutes or until cheese is melted.

Top the finished nachos with the sour cream, tomatoes, onions, olives and bacon.

*The best way to slice the potatoes thinly is with a mandolin.

Kieran's Curry Wings (serves 4)

James Kelly, chef | Kieran's Irish Pub | Minneapolis, Minnesota

- 2 lbs. fresh chicken wings
- 1 oz. honey
- ¾ c. tomato paste
- 4 oz. Guinness
- 1 tsp. each: granulated white sugar iodized salt
- curry powder
- paprika
- cumin
- coriander
- Optional: pinch of cayenne & cinnamon

You may want to double the recipe in case someone wants seconds or thirds.

Rinse and dry wings. Place in oven proof baking dish.

Combine honey, tomato paste and Guinness. Pour over chicken wings and toss to combine.

Bake wings at 350 degrees F uncovered for 1 hour or until cooked through and tender. Remove from oven and cool in liquid.

Drain wings from liquid and pat dry.

Combine all spices in a separate dish.

Cook in one of the two following ways:
- Toss wings with curry spice and bake at 350 degrees F for 15 minutes or until heated through and internal temperature of 165 degrees.
- Saute wings in oil over med-high heat turning until crispy on all sides, then toss curry spice over wings until covered on all sides and hot.

❧ Warm Corn Blinis With Smoked Salmon & Lemon Dill Cream (serves 8)

Helen Woods | Tir na nOg | New York, New York

This recipe is quite easy and worth every minute spent making it.

In a mixing bowl place cornmeal, flour, baking soda, sugar and salt, gently mix. In another mixing bowl mix egg, ½ tsp. butter and buttermilk. Whisk this into the dry ingredients until smooth.

Heat a little butter in a non-stick fry pan adding 2 Tbsp. of corn pancake mix to make a 2-3 inch pancake. When bubbles form on top and little browning on the edges occurs, gently flip and cook other side. Place on warm plate and continue to make approximately 24 pancakes.

For lemon dill cream: Combine lemon juice, zest and crème fraiche; mix with a whip.

Place crème fraiche on warm pancake; fold smoked salmon pieces on top. May add salmon caviar or trout roe and dill for garnish.

- ¾ lb. good quality cold smoked salmon
- 1 c. cornmeal
- 1/3 c. all purpose flour
- 1 ¼ tsp. baking soda
- ½ tsp. salt
- 1½ c. buttermilk
- 1 egg
- 2½ Tbsp. melted butter
- Salmon or trout roe for garnishing (optional)
- dill sprigs for garnish (optional)
- 1 Tbsp. sugar

Lemon Dill Cream

- juice and zest of 1 lemon
- 6 oz. crème fraiche or sour cream
- 2 Tbsp. chopped dill

❧ Ale & Cheddar Dip (serves 4)

Geoff Kokoszka, General Manager | Olde Blind Dog Irish Pub | Milton, Georgia

This dip can be served with crackers or raw vegetables, but for a special treat serve it with warm pretzel bread.

Heat olive oil in 4 qt. pot over medium heat.

Finely puree sweet onion and add to heated oil. Saute until soft.

Add cheeses and start to melt. Once Velveeta starts to melt add beer and heavy cream. Add horseradish and whole grain mustard and cook until cheeses are melted and dip starts to thicken. Season to taste with salt and pepper.

Serve with crusty French bread, pretzels bread, chips or veggies. Enjoy!

- 2 Tbsp. extra virgin olive oil
- ½ medium sweet yellow onion, pureed
- 10 oz. Velveeta cheese
- 10 oz. Kerrygold Dubliner Irish cheddar
- 12 oz. brown ale
- ¼ c. heavy cream
- 1 Tbsp. horseradish
- 1 Tbsp. whole grain mustard
- kosher salt/black pepper to taste

New Orleans Irish Cabbage (serves 8)

Doris Bastiansen | The Kerry Irish Pub | New Orleans, Louisiana

- 2 medium head of cabbage, quartered
- 6-8 medium red potatoes, peeled and quartered
- 2 medium yellow onions, peeled and quartered
- 1 tsp. fresh minced garlic
- 4 shakes of Louisiana hot sauce of Tabasco
- 1 ½ lbs. pickled pork or pieces from butt of ham

My New Orleans Irish grandmother was always fond of reminding us that corned beef and cabbage was actually an Irish American concoction popularized on the East Coast in exotic places like New York and Boston.

Boiled cabbage in Ireland was prepared with ham and other pork meat, if they were lucky enough to afford it. Here is her recipe:

In a large pot combine cabbage, potatoes, onions, garlic, hot sauce and pickled pork or ham pieces.

Fill pot with enough water to cover ingredients.

Boil for 20 minutes and then lower the heat and continue to cook covered for 30-40 minutes or until the vegetables and meat are fork tender. Add salt and pepper to taste.

Perfect Cabbage (serves 4)

Myles O'Reilly, Owner | O'Reilly's Irish Pub | San Francisco, California

Here's the secret for preparing perfect cabbage.

Remove stump and outer withered leaves, cut the head in quarters and remove center stalk; wash cabbage well in plenty of cold water.

To conserve Vitamin C, it is important to cook in a small amount of fast boiling salted water until tender with the lid on, about 15 minutes. I always use a pinch of bread (baking) soda in the water. If preparing over night leave the cabbage in the soda water as the soda softens the leaves.

Use ¼ pint of water to 2 lbs. of green cabbage. Very green cabbage, I believe, is the only way to go to make an authentic presentation. Drain very well in a colander, pressing out all the water. Chop finely.

Melt a little butter or margarine in a saucepan; put in the cabbage, salt and pepper and reheat. Serve hot in a vegetable dish.

The same rules apply to curly kale and other leafy vegetables. For Brussels sprouts cook in salted boiling water for 15 minutes and serve the same way as the cabbage.

My mother always told me that all vegetables grown in the ground were to be brought to a boil starting with cold water and that vegetables grown above ground are to be cook in boiling water.

Me mother never ever lied.

Fire Cracker Salad (serves 1)

BERNIE REILLY, OWNER | THE PERFECT PINT | NEW YORK, NEW YORK

This delicious salad is among many of our healthy options whether you want to enjoy the warm chicken on a cold December day or feel refreshed by the light sesame ginger dressing in July. It is a rather large salad with the capability of splitting for 2, but typically it is the perfect amount for one.

Mix sesame-ginger vinaigrette with red food coloring, salt and pepper and marinate over night in refrigerator.

Preheat grill and chargrill until tender and done

Mix lettuce with red onion, tomato, cucumber, pepper and crispy wonton strips. Pour sesame-ginger vinaigrette dressing over salad.

Top with sliced chicken breast and garnish with toasted sesame seeds and thin bread sticks.

- sesame-ginger vinaigrette (for marinate and to dressed salad)
- Tbsp. of red food coloring
- 6 oz. chicken breast
- 5 oz. baby mixed greens
- chopped red onion
- chopped tomato
- chopped cucumber
- crispy wonton strips
- fresh pepper
- pinch toasted sesame seeds
- pinch of salt and pepper
- thin bread sticks (to mimic chop sticks)

Crispy Irish Bacon Salad With Clonakility Black Pudding With A Poached Egg On Top (serves 4)

STEVE DUGGAN, MANAGER | PADDY REILLY'S | NEW YORK, NEW YORK

This would be perfect for a weekend brunch—and a doodle to prepare!

Make the poached eggs as normal. Meanwhile heat a frying pan and pour in the olive oil and cook the black pudding for about a minute each side. Drain on paper towel and keep warm. Cook the rashers in a tsp of olive oil. Add the vinegar to the pan until it has been nearly boiled off and add the mustard and honey to the pan. After 1 minute put the contents of pan into a bowl and whisk in the rest of the olive oil .

It makes a nice thick dressing.

Put the salad leaves in middle of plate, break the black pudding into bits and scatter over the salad along with cut up rashers of bacon. Drizzle the dressing on and top with the poached egg.

Serve with crusty bread.

- 4 eggs
- 2 Tbsp. white wine vinegar
- 4 Tbsp. extra virgin olive oil
- 6 oz. Clonakility black pudding cut into half inch slices
- 4 rashers of bacon
- 6 oz. salad leaves
- 1 tsp. wholegrain mustard
- ½ tsp. Clear honey
- salt and pepper
- crusty bread, to serve

❦ Irish Soda Bread (serves 16)
Chris Clyde, General Manager | Emmit's Irish Pub | Chicago, Illinois

- 5 c. flour
- ½ c. margarine or butter
- 1 c. sugar
- 1 tsp. baking soda
- 2 eggs
- 2 tsp. baking powder
- 1 tsp. salt
- 2 c. buttermilk
- 1 package raisins

Here is an old recipe from Kathleen (Doherty) Clyde from my Mother's side of the family.

Mix flour and dry ingredients; mix raisins in dry ingredients.
Mix butter, sugar and eggs in separate bowl and add to dry ingredients.
Add 2 cups of buttermilk—mix all together until all is incorporated.
Grease and flour 2 bread pans or use an angel food pan.
Bake for 1 hour 20 minutes at 325 degrees F.
Makes 2 loaves of bread or one round angel cake pan.

❦ Treacle Bread (serves 12-14)
Peter Friel, Co-Owner | The Irish Bank | San Francisco, California

- 1 lb. flour, plain or self-rising
- 2 oz. sugar
- pinch of salt
- ½ tsp. baking powder
- ½ tsp. baking soda
- 1 ½ tsp. powdered ginger
- 1 beaten egg
- 1 c. buttermilk
- treacle

The food was really simple when I grew up in Ireland—not a whole pile of recipes memorable enough to pass on. However, I remember this particular item because of its personal significance. It was very remote and rural—Kerrykeel, a small village near Letterkenny, County Donegal. Many days on returning from school the clouds would be dark and turbulent, we knew the rain would hit. We would race home knowing the hot treacle bread with slappings of butter would be waiting!!

Mix together dry ingredients.

Using a dessert spoon dipped in hot water, scoop out treacle. Add beaten egg, milk and treacle to dry ingredients.

When mixed, turn out onto floured board. Knead in ¼ turns in center. Take care not to over knead!! Place in a 2 pound loaf tin and bake at 350 degrees F for 40 minutes. Test with a skewer or knitting needle. Tap hollow. Wrap in a tea towel to cool. This ensures a softer crust. Place on a cooling rack. Enjoy with butter and homemade jam!

❦ Irish Brown Bread (yields 12 slices)

Kevin Dundon, Executive Chef | Raglan Road Irish Pub & Restaurant | Orlando, Florida

This was my grandmother's recipe. I am very particular that the recipe is not altered in any way and is served at Raglan Road just as she would have made it.

Preheat oven to 350 degrees F.

Place all dry ingredients in a large bowl. Combine all wet ingredients in a separate bowl. Add the wet to the dry in three batches as you mix and fold by hand lightly; the mixture should be quite sticky.

Portion in the greased or buttered muffin or loaf pan. Sprinkle lightly with oats. Bake in oven until golden brown and it makes a hollow sound when tapped on the bottom, about 20-30 minutes. Remove from pan and cool slightly.

Enjoy with Kerry gold butter or Guinness reduction and olive oil.

Guinness Reduction: Combine Guinness and sugar in large stockpot. Bring to boil and reduce to simmer until reduced by half (about 1 hour). Remove from heat and allow to cool at room temperature. Refrigerate.

Place 2 oz. of olive oil in a saucer/small plate, drizzle 2 oz. of Guinness Reduction at room temperature. Serve as dip

- ½ c. Guinness
- ¾ lb. whole meal flour (whole wheat)
- 4 lb. all purpose flour
- 1 Tbsp. salt
- 1 Tbsp. baking soda
- 4 c. rolled oats
- 4 oz. molasses
- 2 qt. buttermilk

Guinness Reduction

- 1 pint Guinness
- 1 pint sugar

....

❦ Hearty Irish Brown Bread

Mikey Crawford, Owner | The Druid | Boston, Massachusetts

My mother makes a traditional Irish brown bread that is legendary in Ennistymon, County Claire. The recipe was handed down to her by my grandmother, Mary Crawford. It is earthy, dense, everyday bread, crusty on the outside and tender on the inside, with a hint of soda. Hearty brown bread is a staple in homes throughout Ireland. The recipe evokes childhood memories for me everyday when we serve it in The Druid.

Put the wheaten flour into a bowl. Rub in margarine or butter. Sift in flour, salt and soda and pour in the milk. Mix well with a spoon until loose dough is reached, adding more milk if needed. Turn out onto a floured board. Knead lightly until the bottom of the dough is smooth. Lay in a floured tin. Cut a cross on top with a knife.

Bake at 350 degrees F for 40-45 minutes. Insert a skewer. If it comes out clean, the bread is cooked.

- 8 oz. plain flour
- 1 oz. butter or margarine
- ½ tsp. salt
- 8 oz. wheaten flour
- ½ tsp. bread soda (baking soda)
- ½ pint sour milk or buttermilk

❦ The Irish Inn Scones (yields 20 scones)

Ross Vandiver, Chef | Irish Inn | Glen Echo, Maryland

- 4 cups all-purpose flour
- 1 c. sugar
- 2 oz. unsalted butter, cold
- 1 large egg
- 1 tsp. baking soda
- 1 tsp. kosher salt
- 3 oz. dark raisins, soaked in hot water
- 11 oz. buttermilk

These scones are a staple of the restaurant and are baked fresh and served every day for lunch. We get many requests for this recipe.

Combine all the dry ingredients and butter in bowl of a stand mixer. Mix thoroughly until butter is combined. Add egg and mix until combined. Add buttermilk and mix just until combined. Drain excess water from raisins and add to batter and briefly mix to combine.

It is important not to mix too much once the wet ingredients are incorporated or the scones will be tough.

Use a small ice cream scoop to portion them onto a cookie sheet and bake at 325 degrees F for approximately 12-15 minutes or until lightly golden brown.

❦ Traditional Irish Soda Bread (serves 6-8)

Deirdre Tierney, Bartender and Assistant Manager | The Field Irish Pub and Eatery | Dania Beach, Florida

- 1 lb. whole wheat flour
- 2 c. buttermilk
- 2 Tbsp. wheat germ
- 1 egg
- ½ c. Irish steel-cut oatmeal
- 1 oz. Kerrygold Irish butter
- 1 Tbsp. brown sugar
- 1 tsp. baking powder
- 1 tsp. baking soda
- ½ tsp. salt

This is my grandmother's traditional recipe for Irish soda bread. "Granny Tierney" has been making this generations-old recipe every day for as long as her family can remember. Like Granny, I am from County Cavan, and I continue our family baking tradition in South Florida where freshly baked artisan breads of such high quality are very hard to find. Irish soda bread in fact, is impossible to find. Irish soda bread is quick to make and uses baking soda instead of yeast which reacts with the buttermilk forming bubbles of carbon dioxide to make the bread rise.

Preheat oven to 325 degrees F. Mix all dry ingredients together. Combine butter into the mixture. Lightly beat the egg and add to buttermilk. Add to dry ingredients. Grease a one pound loaf baking pan. Pour in mixture and bake for 45-60 minutes.

Tip: To ensure bread is fully cooked, test by inserting knife into it. When ready the knife will come out clean.

Breakfast: Lightly toast and top with Kerrygold Irish butter and/or your favorite preserve or marmalade.
Lunch: Top with smoked salmon, capers, red onion, crème fraiche or sour cream with lemon.
Dinner: Serve with beef or lamb stew or a bowl of hearty soup.

Jameson Pecan Pie Filling (yields 6 12-inch pies)

Jeff Marino, Director of Restaurant Operations | Casey's | Los Angeles, California

This is hardly your "run of the mill" pecan pie. Jameson's makes everything taste a bit better.

Place brown sugar, cinnamon, salt and eggs in mixer and mix until combined. Make sure to scrape the bowl through out the mixing to ensure that the sugar in the bottom of the bowl is incorporated.

With mixer on, add the butter in a steady stream and mix until combined. Add the whiskey and mix well.

Add pecans and mix until combined.

Filling may be made in advance and chilled until ready to use. Make sure to mix well as the pecans will rise to the top during storage.

Fill baked pie shell with pie filling. Approx. 5-6 cups of filling. Return to oven and bake until set. Top shelf 15-30 minutes (rotate). Move to middle and bake another 7-10 minutes until center barely jiggles.

Makes 6 -12 inch pies
- 18 c. golden brown sugar
- 6 Tbsp. ground cinnamon
- 3 Tbsp. salt
- 36 eggs
- 18 oz. butter, melted and cooled
- 3 c. Jameson's Irish whiskey
- 18 c. pecan halves
- 6 Tbsp. vanilla extract

Makes 1-12 inch pie
- 3 c. golden brown sugar
- 1 Tbsp. ground cinnamon
- ½ Tbsp. salt
- 6 eggs
- 3 oz. butter
- ½ c. Jameson's Irish whiskey
- 3 c. pecan halves
- 1 Tbsp. vanilla extract

Bread Pudding (yields 36 servings)

Mark Toombs, Chef & Steve Ciapciak, Chef | John D. McGurk's Irish Pub and Garden | St. Louis, Missouri

Bread pudding has been enjoyed in Ireland for centuries. The added flavor of the whiskey butter is an added attraction.

Place the cubed bread in a 5 gallon bucket and drizzle with melted butter. In a separate bowl, combine the next 7 ingredients. Pour the mixture over the bread and butter, let sit for several minutes. Spray 2- two inch hotel pans with pan release; fill 2 four inch hotel pans ½ way with hot water. With potato masher, mash the bread and milk mixtures till thoroughly incorporated. Evenly pour this mixture into the 2 two inch hotel pans. Cover with foil and place in the 2 four inch hotel pans. Bake at 350 degrees F for 45 minutes. Remove water pans and foil. Bake for an additional 15 minutes. Let chill overnight. Cut each pan into 18 pieces. Individually wrap with plastic wrap, label and store in refrigerator.

- 6 lb. sourdough bread cubed
- 1 lb. butter, melted
- 1 gallon whole milk
- 24 eggs
- 12 egg yolks
- 6 c. sugar
- 2 Tbsp. vanilla
- 2 Tbsp. ground cinnamon
- 2 Tbsp. ground nutmeg

Whiskey Butter
- 4 lbs. butter, softened
- ½ bottle bourbon or whiskey
- 2 lbs. powdered sugar

Brown Bread Ice Cream (serves 4)

Kate Hickey, General Manager | Johnny Foley's | San Francisco, California

- 4 oz. brown sugar
- 5 oz. brown bread crumbs
- 4 eggs, separated
- 4 oz. icing sugar
- 10 oz. cream (½ pint)

I grew up in the Irish section of London. My mother made this ice cream when we had a surplus of cream left over from our 1 milking cow and leftover stale brown bread—we were never so happy to eat stale bread!

Scatter the brown sugar over the breadcrumbs and caramelize under a hot grill—watch carefully or they may burn. Cool and crush (blender easiest). Whisk the egg whites until stiff, then whisk in icing sugar one Tbsp at a time. Beat the egg yolks and whisk into meringue mixture. Whisk the cream until thick enough to hang on the whisk. Fold into meringue together with the cooled crushed breadcrumbs. If liked, a Tbsp. of Irish whiskey may be added at this stage. Put in a lidded container and freeze. It can be served straight from the freezer.

Whiskey Bread Pudding With Baileys Ice Cream And Guinness Caramel (serves 8)

Kyle Sailor, Chef | MacMcGee's | Decatur, Georgia

Whiskey Bread Pudding
- 3 Tbsp. butter
- 7 burger buns
- 3 c. whole milk
- 3 c. heavy whipping cream
- 2 c. white sugar
- 1 vanilla bean
- 2 shots of your favorite whiskey
- 5 whole eggs

Bailey's Ice Cream
- 1 c. heavy cream
- 1 c. whole milk
- ½ c. white sugar
- 10 egg yolks
- 3 Tbsp. Bailys Irish Cream
- 1 vanilla bean

Guinness Caramel
- 2 pints Guinness draught
- ½ c. brown sugar

What could be better, a little whiskey, a little Baileys and a little Guinness!! An over the top dessert!

Whiskey Bread Pudding: Preheat oven to 300 degrees F. Toast bread until golden brown. In saucepot, heat milk, cream, ½ sugar and vanilla bean and bring to a simmer and remove from heat. With the whisk, mix eggs, the other ½ of the sugar and whiskey in the mixing bowl. Slowly temper ½ of the diary mixture into the egg mixture and return to the remaining dairy. Use the butter to coat the lining of the 9 x 9 casserole dish. Place the toasted bread into the casserole dish and pour the custard mixture over the bread. Press the bread with your hands so that the bread becomes fully saturated with the custard base. Bake in oven for 3 hours.

Bailey's Ice Cream: Freeze the ice cream machine core the day before. Heat the dairy with ½ of the sugar and vanilla bean over medium heat to a simmer; remove from heat. With the whisk, mix the egg yolks, the other ½ of sugar and vanilla bean in mixing bowl. Temper ½ of the hot diary into the egg yolk mixture. Add dairy and yolk mixture back in other ½ of dairy. Add the custard to the core and spin the ice cream machine for 45 minutes. Place the mixture in a container, cover and freeze overnight.

Guinness Caramel: In a saucepot, add beer and sugar and thoroughly mix with a whisk. On the lowest heat possible, reduce liquid until syrupy (3hours).

Scoop bread pudding into a plate. Place ice cream over the top and lightly drizzle caramel over the entire ice cream.

Trifle (serves 6)

Jack Geary, Co-owner | Owl N' Thistle | Seattle, Washington

Here's a dessert recipe we used to make as kids growing up in Galway. Very easy to make and is light and refreshing, especially after a big dinner.

Mix the Jell-O in a large bowl with boiling water, a la the directions. Chop the sponge cake, the pears and banana into small slices. Add the sliced sponge cake, pears, banana and tin of mixed fruit into the Jell-O and gently fold. The sponge cake will float to the top with the banana, while the other fruit will layer underneath. Let cool and refrigerate overnight.

The following day mix the Birds custard per package directions and let cool or use whipped cream, whichever you are using and chill for an hour. Serve a scoop of trifle with a scoop of custard on top. We used to add a Tbsp of brandy or sherry around Christmas time as a special treat. Don't tell anybody. It sure didn't do us no harm.

- Packet of Jell-O
- 1 sponge cake (or pound cake)
- banana
- 1 can mixed fruit, drained
- 1 can pears (optional)
- packet of Birds custard or whipped cream

Molten Chocolate Lava Cake (serves 4)

Bernie Reilly, Owner | The Perfect Pint | New York, New York

We cannot say that this rich dessert has no calories, but if you are willing to live a little this is the dessert for you. This is a Perfect Pint original and has been suited as the perfect ending for a dinner of two. It is a must-have when dining at the Perfect Pint.

Generously butter the inside of 4 (5 1/2 oz.) ramekins. Place in large hotel pan. Whisk together egg yolks, eggs and sugar in a bowl until light, foamy. Melt chocolate and butter in a double boiler. Stir melted chocolate mixture into egg and sugar mixture until combined.

Sift cocoa powder into mixture; stir to combine. Sift flour and salt into the mixture; stir to combine into a batter. Stir in vanilla extract.

Using a pastry bag, divide batter evenly between the prepared ramekins: tap gently to remove any air bubbles.

Refrigerate for 45 minutes. Preheat oven to 425 degrees F.

Arrange ramekins in pan and pour enough hot tap water into the pan to reach halfway up the sides of the ramekins.

Bake in preheated oven for 15-18 minutes. Set aside to cool for 15 minutes. Loosen edges from ramekins with knife. Invert each cake onto a plate and dust with powdered sugar. Serve with vanilla ice cream and fresh whipped cream.

- butter as needed
- 2 egg yolks
- 2 eggs
- 3 Tbsp. white sugar
- 3½ oz. chopped dark chocolate
- 5 Tbsp. butter
- 4 tsp. unsweetened cocoa powder
- 3 Tbsp. flour
- 1 pinch salt
- 1/8 tsp. vanilla

Plum Pudding With Amber Sauce (serves 6-8)

Adrian Nugent, Manager, Coleman's Irish Ambassador | Coleman's Authentic Irish Pub | Syracuse, New York

- 1 c. milk
- 3 c. soft breadcrumbs (5 slices)
- ½ c. melted shortening
- ½ c. molasses
- ½ c. raisins
- ½ c. currants
- ½ c. finely chopped candied citron
- 2 tsp. cinnamon
- 1 tsp. baking soda
- ½ tsp. salt
- ¼ tsp. allspice
- ¼ tsp. cloves
- 1 c. flour

Amber Sauce

- ¼ c. butter
- ½ c. half and half
- ½ c. light corn syrup
- 1 c. packed light brown sugar

Michele McGealy, my sister in Ireland, provided this recipe. It was given to my mother, Genevieve Nugent, by her mother, Sara Pallis and has been in the family for about 100 years. It is very traditional to have plum pudding during the Christmas season in Ireland, and we use the same recipe at Coleman's between Thanksgiving and New Year's Day. I have been at Coleman's since 1986 and my mother used to make the plum pudding and send one over from her home in Donabate, a small town just north of Dublin, every Christmas. I would wait anxiously to savor it every year until she passed away in 1993. Then my sister took over and she make it to perfection. The sauce is delicious. Some people use brandy sauce or butter cream for the topping but you could just as easily use nothing or whipped cream or even ice cream.

Generously grease bottom and sides of 4 c. heatproof mold. In large bowl pour milk over breadcrumbs. Stir in shortening and molasses. Stir in remaining ingredients. Pour into mold and cover with foil.

Place mold on rack in Dutch oven; pour in boiling water up to level of rack. Cover and heat to boiling. Keep water boiling over low heat 3 hours or until toothpick inserted in center comes out clean.

Garnish with fresh berries and orange peel.

Amber sauce: In saucepan, mix all ingredients and cook over low heat 5 minutes, stirring occasionally. Unmold pudding, cut into slices and serve warm with fresh berries and orange peel.

Apple Cake (serves 6)

James Moore, Director of Project & Food Development | Fado Irish Pub | Atlanta, Georgia

- 1 tsp. cinnamon
- 1 ½ c. flour, selfrising
- ¾ c. butter
- ¾ c superfine sugar
- 3 eggs
- 2 Tbsp. milk
- 3 eating apples, green, semisweet peeled and sliced

Homemade apple cakes are one of the more popular desserts made in rural Ireland, and apples on the whole are the base of many traditional and contemporary Irish desserts. Apple cakes, like the one in this recipe, are very traditional. The recipe may vary from home to home and in many cases the individual techniques have been passed for generations. It would originally have been baked in a Bastible (Dutch oven) or pot beside an open fire and later in the oven or stove on tin or enamel plates.

Sift cinnamon and flour into a bowl. Cream the butter and sugar until light and soft. Slowly beat in 1 egg then 2 Tbsp. flour – repeat this with the remaining egg. Fold in two thirds of the remaining flour. Stir in the milk then fold in the last of the flour.

Grease the sides and bottom of a cake pan. Pour half the batter mix into the bottom of the pan then layer with the sliced apples. Cover with the remaining batter.

Bake in a 350 degree F oven for 15 minutes then reduce the heat to 325 degrees F and bake another 30 minutes until golden brown and firm to the touch.

❦ Bailey's Cheesecake (yields 4 cakes)

Mark Toombs, Chef & Steve Ciapciak, Chef | John D. McGurk's Irish Pub and Garden | St. Louis, Missouri

This is a great finale for that very special dinner party.

Wrap 4 spring form pans with 2 layers of foil; spray with pan release. Mix all of ingredients together for the crust and place 7 oz. in each pan. Press mixture firmly to the bottom of the pan and bake at 350 degrees F for 5-7 minutes. Let the pans cool to room temperature.

In the mixer, cream the sugar and cream cheese together until smooth. Add the sour cream and Bailey's and continue to mix. Slowly add the eggs, one at a time, just until incorporated. Pour into spring form pans.

Bake the cheesecakes in a water bath at 300 degrees F for an hour. Remove from the water and cool to room temperature. Chill in refrigerator overnight and wrap in plastic wrap. Label and freeze if desired. They need a day in refrigerator to properly thaw.

- 6 lbs. cream cheese, room temperature
- 6 c. sugar
- 16 eggs
- 1 c. sour cream
- 2½ c. Bailey's Irish cream

Graham Cracker Crust

- 5 lbs. graham cracker crumbs
- 1 lb. sugar
- 1 lb. butter, melted
- 4 oz. egg whites

❦ Bread Pudding (serves 8-10)

Shelly Freitag, General Manager | O'Rouke's Public House | South Bend, Indiana

Cut the bread in 1" x 1" cubes and let dry out for 1 day.

Mix cream, milk, eggs, sugar, cinnamon and vanilla in a large bowl.
Soak craisins in Jameson's for at least 24 hours.
Drain craisins, saving the whiskey.
Add bread and drained craisins into the wet mixture.
Butter sides and bottom of a 2 ½" hotel pan.
Place bread mixture in buttered pan and bake at 350 degrees F for 20 minutes.

- 2 loaves Sourdough bread
- 4 c. heavy whipping cream
- 4 c. milk
- 6 eggs
- 4 c. granulated sugar
- 1 1/2 c. craisins
- 1 Tbsp. cinnamon
- 1 Tbsp. vanilla
- 1 1/2 c. Jameson's Irish whiskey
- zest of 2 oranges

Maggie May's Bread Pudding (serves 10-12)

Heather Byrne | Scruffy Murphy's Irish Pub | Denver, Colorado

- 4 c. or simply half loaf of stale bread torn in pieces (The better quality bread the better quality the pudding)
- 3 large farm eggs
- 3 c. milk
- 2 tsp. vanilla
- 1 ½ c. sugar
- ½ c. raisins (optional)
- 1 ½ stick of butter, melted
- A good strong pinch of cinnamon (ground, if possible)

Maggie May's bread pudding is our family's spin on two different versions handed down from my German mother and my husband's grandmother who hailed from Dublin. Both ladies were handy around the kitchen and both loved bread pudding, especially around the holidays. A perfectly good loaf of stale white bread never goes to waste when it can be made into this delicious dessert.

Preheat oven to 350 degrees F.

Lightly butter a 12 x 8 baking dish or pan.

Mix up the already stale bread and milk into a large bowl. Once mixed well, let stand for 5 minutes.

In a separate dish, mix eggs, vanilla, sugar and cinnamon. Gradually stir in the melted butter.

Now pour the contents of both bowls into the already prepared 12 x 8 dish, stirring them as you go.

Bake for approximately 40 minutes or until golden brown.

Let cool for 5 to 10 minutes and serve with some freshly whipped cream.

Dublin Mule
John Nallen | Nallen's Irish Pub | Denver, Colorado

This drink is a real kicker!
Fill copper mug with ice. Add Jameson and ginger beer. Squeeze with the lime wedge.

- 1 shot Jameson Irish whiskey
- ½ can ginger beer
- ¼ lime
- ice

Irish Apple
Steven Colligan, Manager | Scruffy Murphy's Irish Pub | Denver, Colorado

Add all ingredients in a cocktail shaker.
Shake vigorously for 30 seconds.
Strain into a chilled martini glass.
Garnish with an apple slice, if desired.

- 3 parts Jameson's Irish whiskey
- 1 part peach Schnapps
- splash of cranberry juice

Irish Coffee (serves 8)
Bobby McGuire, Owner | Butch McGuire's Irish Pub | Chicago, Illinois

Could be the best Irish coffee I have ever had!
Chill a deep bowl and the mixer beaters for 20 minutes.
Add 1 ½ c. heavy cream, chilled, 1 ½ tsp. sugar and ½ tsp. vanilla. Beat on low for 30 seconds or until small bubbles form. Increase speed to medium for another 30 seconds (beater should leave a trail). Increase speed to high for about 20 seconds. Should be smooth and thick, volume should double. Use immediately or refrigerate for up to 8 hours.
Drop a sugar cube or two into the bottom of a mug.
Pour 1 ½ oz. or two Tullamore Dew over the top of the sugar
Pour in coffee stopping 1 inch from top of mug.
Spoon a generous serving of whipped cream on top
Sit back and enjoy.

- bottle of Tullamore Dew (or Irish whiskey of your choosing). We prefer the Dew as it is slightly sweeter.
- sugar cubes
- whipped cream
- 1 ½ c. heavy cream, preferably pasteurized or organic
- 1 ½ tsp. granulated sugar
- ½ tsp. vanilla (buy a good one as it makes a difference)

McGuire's Irish Coffee

McGuire Martin, Owner | McGuire's Irish Pub | Pensacola, Florida

- 1½ Tbsp. Irish whiskey
- 1 ½ Tbsp. Kahlua coffee-flavored liqueur
- 1 c. freshly brewed hot coffee
- 1 Tbsp. whipped cream
- Crème de menthe for garnish

Although some insist that Irish coffee was first created in San Francisco, this old recipe may be proof that it's really from some authentic pub on the "old sod."

Combine the whiskey and Kahlua in a large (10 oz.) coffee mug or heat-proof Irish coffee glass. Slowly stir in the coffee. Mound the whipped cream on top and drizzle with crème de menthe. Don't stir or you'll miss the delightful sensation of drinking the hot coffee and Irish whiskey through the coolness of the whipped cream.

Great Grandmother Bridget Burke's Eggnog (serves 12-14)

Tom Mooney, Owner | Murphy's | Alexandria, Virginia

- 12 egg yolks
- 1 lb. confectioners' sugar (powdered)
- ½ jigger rum
- 1/8 tsp. cloves
- 1/8 tsp. allspice
- 1/8 tsp. cinnamon
- ½ tsp. nutmeg
- 1/8 tsp. cream of tartar

Bridget Burke came to America in 1883 with her 13 year old son, Patrick, who was my grandfather.

Beat egg yolks separately and thoroughly. Add the 1 lb. powdered sugar as needed. Add the spices. Beat the egg whites stiff then fold into the other ingredients.

Batter is thick.

Warm mug. Add 2 Tbsp. batter. ½ jigger brandy, and ½ jigger rum. Fill with hot milk and sprinkle with nutmeg

Meet the Authors

Robert Meyers

Bob Meyers' career was split evenly between the U.S. Foreign Service and the private sector. As a diplomat, he was responsible for media relations is several European and Latin American countries and served as a negotiator and U.S. Spokesman at the Tokyo Round of Multilateral Trade Negotiations in Geneva, Switzerland. He served as Director of the U.S. Government's Foreign Press Centers in Washington, DC and New York City. At one point in his career, he was a Special Assistant to the White House Staff Director.

In the private sector, Meyers was responsible for global employee communications for AlliedSignal (now Honeywell) a Fortune 100 company. He later served as Vice President of Corporate Communications and Investor Relations for Scientific-Atlanta (now Cisco), a Fortune 500 company.

He is the author of the award-winning coffee-table book *Bygone Treasures and Timeless Beauties: Barns of Old Milton County*. The first edition sold out in one month in 2011/12.

He and his wife Linda have lived in Georgia for 25 years. They have two daughters and three grandchildren.

Ron Wallace

Prior to retiring, Ron was President of UPS International where he was responsible for UPS in more than 200 countries and territories with more than 60,000 people under his direction. He also served on the corporate management committee that oversaw the day-to-day operations of UPS and its 400,000 employees. He was chairman or co-chairman of 33 boards of directors of highly successful companies.

In his earlier days he was a professional race car driver and played semi-pro football in Europe.

He serves on numerous boards and foundations, two of which he was a founding member. Shortly after retiring he was named as the Chairman of the Governors commission and charged with forming the City of Milton, Georgia.

Wallace, a campaign consultant, wrote the book *Power of the Campaign Pyramid* and has completed a leadership book titled *What Brown Did For Me*.

Ron and his wife, Kate, co-founded Olde Blind Dog Irish Pub, with two locations north of Atlanta. They have a daughter, and two grandchildren.

Acknowledgments

To CHRONICLE THE HISTORIES, LORE and recipes of more than 50 Irish pubs, more than 200 publicans and employees were interviewed. It was often a challenging task to track down just the right people at the right time. Extensive research and travel from one end of the country to the other were required. Our quest for truly outstanding Irish pubs would not have been possible without the help of many people.

First and foremost, we are indebted to our wives for their constant support. We worked closely with Bob, Jan, Mark Babcock and Matt King of Deeds Publishing, a great team. Among those to whom we are particularly indebted, whose names do not appear in the text, are Adrienne Smith, Frank Schwiep, Fred Shirley, Janet Sweet, Adrienne Noyes, Matt Kunz, Bill Lusk, Lee Waldon, Nathanial Parks, Rob and Melanie Limacher, Ron Weeden, John Breyer, Jennifer Dickson, Leslie and Jeff Watson, Craig Horvath, Dan Ward, Jan Crawford, Sharon Holt, and David Penman. Try as we might it would not be possible to acknowledge everyone who helped, and any omissions are entirely our fault.

Every effort was made to achieve accuracy, and we regret any factual errors that may exist. Please feel free to contact us with any corrections or suggestions for a second edition.

Bob Meyers
Ron Wallace